THE GREAT PEARL HEIST

The

GREAT PEARL
HEIST

London's Greatest Thief
and Scotland Yard's Hunt
for the World's Most Valuable Necklace

MOLLY CALDWELL CROSBY

BERKLEY BOOKS, NEW YORK

BERKLEY BOOKS
Published by the Penguin Group
Penguin Group (USA) Inc.
375 Hudson Street, New York, New York 10014, USA
Penguin Group (Canada), 90 Eglinton Avenue East, Suite 700, Toronto, Ontario M4P 2Y3, Canada
(a division of Pearson Penguin Canada Inc.) • Penguin Books Ltd., 80 Strand, London WC2R 0RL,
England • Penguin Group Ireland, 25 St. Stephen's Green, Dublin 2, Ireland (a division of Penguin
Books Ltd.) • Penguin Group (Australia), 250 Camberwell Road, Camberwell, Victoria 3124, Australia
(a division of Pearson Australia Group Pty. Ltd.) • Penguin Books India Pvt. Ltd., 11 Community
Centre, Panchsheel Park, New Delhi—110 017, India • Penguin Group (NZ), 67 Apollo Drive,
Rosedale, Auckland 0632, New Zealand (a division of Pearson New Zealand Ltd.) • Penguin Books
(South Africa) (Pty.) Ltd., 24 Sturdee Avenue, Rosebank, Johannesburg 2196, South Africa

Penguin Books Ltd., Registered Offices: 80 Strand, London WC2R 0RL, England

The publisher does not have any control over and does not assume any responsibility for
author or third-party websites or their content.

First Edition: December 2012

Library of Congress Cataloging-in-Publication Data

Crosby, Molly Caldwell.
The great pearl heist : London's greatest thief and Scotland Yard's hunt for
the world's most valuable necklace / by Molly Caldwell Crosby.
p.   cm.
Includes bibliographical references and index.
ISBN 978-0-425-25280-2 (alk. paper)
1. Jewelry theft—England—London—Case studies.   2. Receiving stolen goods—England—
London—Case studies. 3. Burglary investigation—England—London—Case studies.
4. Robbery investigation—England—London—Case studies.   I. Title.
HV6665.G7C76 2012
364.16'2873927—dc23
2012008261

PRINTED IN THE UNITED STATES OF AMERICA

10 9 8 7 6 5 4 3 2

For my parents,
Tom and Mary Elizabeth Caldwell,
Anglophiles, misplaced in Texas

CONTENTS

Contents

THE GRIZZARD GANG

JOSEPH GRIZZARD, aka Kemmy, Cammi, or Joseph Goldsmith: Greatest receiver, fence, and putter-up of his time.

JAMES LOCKETT, aka "The Prince of Thieves," Lockett-the-Lion-hearted, Fitzpatrick, William Preston, Harry Graham, and James Howard: One of London's greatest burglars and screwsmen, second in command to Grizzard.

SIMON SILVERMAN: Associate of Grizzard and Lockett. He worked as a legitimate and illegitimate jeweler operating out of an office in Hatton Garden.

LESIR GUTWIRTH: A Hatton Garden trader, not highly regarded by jewelers or thieves.

DANIEL McCARTHY: At the time of the pearl heist, McCarthy was eighty-two years old with a long and successful career as a thief.

SCOTLAND YARD DETECTIVES

ALFRED WARD: Chief inspector; one of Scotland Yard's original and most talented detectives. He was lead detective in the pearl necklace case.

ALFRED LEACH: A former superintendent. He shadowed and investigated Joseph Grizzard until retiring. Worked as a consultant during the pearl heist case.

FRANK FROEST: Superintendent from 1906 to 1913, overseeing what was considered the most talented group of detectives in Scotland Yard's history.

BASIL THOMPSON: Superintendent at the time of the heist.

SERGEANT CORNISH: Ward's second in command.

OTHER YARDMEN ON THE CASE: Sergeants Cooper, Fondville, Haymann, Gamblett, Soden, Booth, Coles, Moorman, Goodwillie, and Prosser.

OTHER PRINCIPAL PLAYERS

MAX MAYER: One of Hatton Garden's most refined jewelers. He specialized in pearls.

HENRI SOLOMANS: An associate of Mayer's who worked in the jewel district of Paris.

FRANK BEAUMONT PRICE: The underwriter who insured the necklace for Lloyd's of London.

SAMUEL BRANDSTATTER: A distant cousin of Lesir Gutwirth's whose interest in the pearl necklace was piqued by a reward offered for its return. He lived in Paris.

MYER QUADRATSTEIN: A cousin of Brandstatter's who had far more experience and worldly understanding. He also lived in Paris.

MAX SPANIER: The self-described "expert" from Paris who played the part of French receiver.

SIR RICHARD MUIR: A talented barrister, he served as lead prosecutor for the Crown.

THE NECKLACE

There are many ways to calculate the value of the pearl necklace. In 1913, the necklace was insured with Lloyd's of London for £135,000. The exchange rate at that time was about $4.87 for £1, placing the value of the necklace anywhere from $650,000 to $750,000 USD. Today, in simplest terms, the purchasing power of that amount would be close to £10 million or $18 million, which puts this necklace among the most expensive jewels sold in recent years. To understand the real value of the necklace, however, you have to consider the GDP—gross domestic product—as well. And the GDP share of that amount would be around £81 million or over $121 million in today's dollar. In other words, when you take the value of the necklace in 1913 and put it in perspective with the overall economy of Britain during the same time period, the pearls become even more valuable. To gather these numbers, I used historic purchasing-power calculators from the Economic History Association in the United Kingdom at measuring worth.com. Regardless of how you calculate the relative value, during its time, this strand of pearls was considered the most valuable necklace in the world, worth twice the price of the Hope Diamond.

VERNACULAR

Burglary—Breaking into and entering a structure in order to take valuables. Burglars were also referred to as *screwsmen*.

Confederate—A trusted member of a gang or group of thieves.

Confidence trickster—A con man or con artist. Someone who gains the confidence of others to trick or defraud them.

Crusher—Policeman on the beat.

Fence—Someone who knowingly buys stolen goods for resale. Also known as a *receiver*. A fence often organized and funded large-scale burglaries and heists.

Grass—Criminals who work with the police as informers. *Shopping* was another term for informing on others.

Larceny—Legal term for *theft*. Unlike burglary or robbery, larceny does not involve violence but rather the taking of personal property.

Penal servitude—A typical sentence in Victorian and Edwardian England for petty theft, burglary, fencing, or larceny, as well as more serious crimes against man. Sentence could last from months to years and usually involved physical labor.

Putter-up—The mastermind who arranges and *puts up* the money for elaborately planned thefts. At the turn of the twentieth century, a putter-up traveled around obtaining information that would be useful to professional burglars and thieves.

Receiver—One who receives stolen goods for resale. Receiving is among the crimes of dishonesty in English criminal law and is related to larceny.

Robbery—Taking something from someone forcibly.

Scotland Yard—Term most often applied to London's Metropolitan Police, derived from the department's original location near

Whitehall and Great Scotland Yard. Its current location is referred to as New Scotland Yard.

Screwsman—A burglar who also copies keys to gain entry to a residence or safe.

Sting operation—A deceptive plan used by law enforcement, designed to catch an individual in the process of committing a crime.

Thief—Someone who commits larceny. Unlike a burglar or robber, a thief remains more secretive and often unknown.

In this Gulf of uncertain light there were more illusions than realities.

—JOHN STEINBECK, *THE PEARL*

Holborn district in London at the turn of the twentieth century.

Empire of Thieves and Shadows

THE GETAWAY CAR SAT IDLING ON SHAFTESBURY AVENUE. "BLONDE Alice Smith" pulled the wide brim of her hat forward, angling her face into ecliptic shadow. Edgar Allan Poe once said that "The best place to hide anything is in plain view." Nothing would camouflage a thief's waiting auto better than the swarm of pedestrians, glaring electric lights, and miasmic fumes of London's Piccadilly Circus.

Café Monico was within view, its even archways and grid of windows a showcase of Edwardian architecture, its voluptuous salons and opulent interior the offspring of Victorian excess. It was half-past one, on the afternoon of July 1, 1909.

Inside the café, a jeweler named Frederick Goldschmidt sat dining beneath gilt moldings, mirrors, and chandeliers. To offset the shrill splendor, the floors were covered with large Persian rugs, and palm fronds fanned from marble pedestals. His table was draped in white cloth, and on it was a leather valise filled with £160,000 worth of jewels—which would be worth over £12 million (or $18 million) today.

Goldschmidt owned a jewelry store on Rue Lafayette, the gem district of Paris. He was a cautious man who constantly kept his leather case in his lap or tight within his grasp. Still, for all his vigilance, and in spite of the incredible valuables at his fingertips, he had apparently not noticed the gang of thieves shadowing his every move for the last several months—first in Paris, then in London.

This was no ordinary gang; it was a multifarious network of criminals. Unlike their counterparts in Chicago or New York, these gang members were nonviolent and they were not part of a single ethnicity or background. They were more akin to businessmen than brutes, each with his or her own talents, contributing to a corporation of crime. And that corporation's specialty was the international jewel trade.

At the head of this great conglomerate was the fence and putter-up—a gentleman named Joseph Grizzard. Though he had very humble beginnings in London's infamous Whitechapel neighborhood, Grizzard, known as "Cammi" or "Kemmy" on the streets, had worked his way to the top of the city's crime syndicate. In fact, his reputation as a mastermind criminal, quietly in the background, would become so well known that London's greatest prosecutor of the time compared Grizzard to Professor Moriarty, the nemesis of Sir Arthur Conan Doyle's Sherlock Holmes—the brilliant, obscure, dark figure so often controlling everyone from the shadows.

To the Metropolitan Police, Grizzard defied logic. He was finely dressed, extremely intelligent, and affluent, with a family and nice home. He could easily retire to live a life of leisure—a remarkable achievement for someone raised on the streets of London's East End.

For most criminals, crime was a way to live, a necessity. But for Grizzard, it was a sport. He was the type of thief who bought rounds of drinks at the local public houses for the plainclothes detectives shadowing him.

Grizzard, however, was also calculating and methodical. He visited Paris often and always stayed on Rue Lafayette in the thick of the jewel district. Though he claimed to be a gem dealer, more often than not he went to Paris to case the jewelers who frequently traveled between the Continent and England on business. Thieving had made Grizzard a very wealthy man, and a sharp mind made him patient. He could afford to spend weeks simply watching and waiting.

Through his own reconnaissance, Grizzard had chosen Goldschmidt as his next mark—the jeweler, like many of his colleagues, traveled to London often to sell and buy gems. Grizzard, who both organized the heist and funded it with his own money, had then selected three talented thieves for the job: Blonde Alice Smith, John Higgins, and Harry Grimshaw. The thieves drew cards to see who would play which role. Smith drew the high card, followed by Higgins, and finally Grimshaw had drawn the two of spades.

Blonde Alice Smith, or "Diamond Dolly," waited patiently, gloved hands on the steering wheel, her eyes steeled on the door to the café. Smith, an American, had come to England from Manhattan by way of elopement. The marriage collapsed when she learned of her husband's numerous affairs, and Smith left to look for work in London. She ended up in the home of confidence tricksters, a husband-and-wife team, who taught her how to make money on the streets. Soon thereafter, she was recruited by Grizzard to work as a message taker and "passer-in of tools." Smith proved especially adept at blending in, so she was often instructed to walk by a theft in progress, pocket the stolen jewels, and disappear into the crowd again, leaving gang members free of evidence should they be caught or arrested.

John Higgins was a cheesemonger in a shop near Hatton Garden, London's jewel district. He and Smith had worked together for years, and they had both been put away in 1892 for larceny—though prison did little to deter them from a life of crime.

Harry Grimshaw, the third player in the heist, had retired in 1904 from a successful run as a lightweight jockey. Since retirement, he had worked in his father's shop before joining Grizzard's gang of thieves.

On April 12, 1909, Grimshaw and Smith rented a room near De Keyser's Royal Hotel, the lodgings Goldschmidt usually preferred. De Keyser's, looming over the Victoria Embankment, was a colossal Victorian hotel that catered to international businessmen with its assortment of services—a telephone in every room, hairdressing salon, typewriting office, lounge, reading room, and of course, billiards.

Under the names "Mr. and Mrs. White," Smith and Grimshaw continued to live nearby, off and on, for the next three months. "Mr. White," described as a small man with a mustache, was often seen in the hotel lounge playing billiards or sitting in the smoking room.

Through "White's" observation, Grizzard learned everything he needed to know about Goldschmidt's habits. Although his moves were very predictable and he spent nearly all of his time in his hotel, meeting with Hatton Garden jewelers, or at his favorite café, there was one problem—he never set his leather case down, let alone left it unattended. So, the thieves thought of a way around that particular obstacle. At what time would a gentleman be forced to set down a bag he carried?

Goldschmidt rested the demitasse coffee on its saucer and stood from his table at Café Monico. Leaving his cloth napkin curled beside the plate, he picked up his leather case and made his way through the striated palm leaves to the lavatory. The facilities appeared empty at the time, except for one attendant named Batty. Just as Goldschmidt stood at the sink to wash his hands, he set his bag down long enough to pick up the bar of soap. He heard a noise and turned to look around, but noticed no one. With his hands still under the water, Goldschmidt saw another hand reach below and grab the leather valise.

Goldschmidt yelled, "Stop, thief! He's got my bag!" He managed to grasp the back of the thief's overcoat, but Harry Grimshaw pulled free and fled the lavatory. As the attendant and Goldschmidt ran toward the door to chase him down, a second, taller man stepped in to help, shouting "Stop, thief!" Just then the tall man tripped and fell, blocking the way entirely for Goldschmidt and Batty.

Grimshaw slowed to a brisk clip, tipped his bowler hat forward, walked out the glass doors of the café, and climbed into Alice Smith's getaway car. The two sped off into Piccadilly Circus. The tall gentleman, John Higgins, then stood and brushed himself off before leaving the café and walking swiftly in the other direction.

The three thieves reconvened at 2:20 P.M. at the apartment rented under the names Mr. and Mrs. White. They had the brown leather bag with them. As it turns out, Goldschmidt had already sold some of his jewelry, so the leather case contained pearls, gemstones, and a diamond necklace all valued around £60,000, significantly less than the original amount, but still a hefty profit worth roughly £5 million (over $7 million) in today's dollar.

As most thieves knew, the longer they held the jewels, the greater the chance of getting caught. So that very evening, Joseph Grizzard held a dinner party at his home for prospective buyers. Many fences in years to come would restrict their business dealings to public places, rarely meeting face-to-face. Grizzard not only met with his thieves in person, but also welcomed them and his clients into his own home.

That evening, Grizzard and his guests sat around the dining table in front of a bay window lacquered with candlelight. On a linen tablecloth, among the candlesticks, stood vases of summer flowers— snapdragons, lisianthus, delphinium—along with porcelain china and a legion of glinting silverware. An Edwardian dinner party had no shortage of formal details.

Still on the first course, Grizzard heard the front bell ring and a maid answer the door. In walked one of Scotland Yard's best-known detectives, Chief Inspector Alfred Ward, and several of his officers. Ward politely apologized to Grizzard for interrupting the dinner party and announced he carried a warrant to search the home for a missing diamond necklace from the heist at Café Monico. Calmly and courteously, Grizzard welcomed them into his home and told them they were free to search the premises. He leaned back in his chair and puffed on a cigar as he waited.

An hour later, the police had found nothing. Ward graciously apologized, and Grizzard just as graciously accepted. The housemaid walked the detectives through the passage and out the front gate as Grizzard listened for the door to shut and the latch to secure it. Then Grizzard and his guests continued with dinner. Although the candles were now down to the wick and the first course had grown cold, Grizzard picked up his soupspoon, finished eating his tepid pea soup—and pulled a long string of diamonds from the bottom of the bowl. He cleaned them off and sold them as planned.

The next day, the dailies and weeklies followed the story of the heist with gusto. Still, the thieves remained at large for several weeks until one September afternoon, a detective working off a tip, picked up John Higgins for questioning in connection with the Monico heist.

"That's a shame," Higgins said, unruffled. "I was having a drink with Sergeant Stephens in Leather Lane at half-past one that day, and the job happened at the Monico at twenty minutes to two." Unfortunately for Higgins, the sergeant denied it, and the thief was arrested on the spot.

Next, the detectives arrested Harry Grimshaw and took him to the Bow Street police station. Both Higgins and Grimshaw claimed they did not know the other and had nothing to do with the heist, but the two thieves had been dealt a blow of bad luck.

By chance, detectives had been watching De Keyser's Royal Hotel for some time, on the lookout for a notorious thief named Eddie Guerin who had escaped from Devil's Island, a French penal colony off South America. Aboard a makeshift raft, in shark-infested waters, all of the other escapees died of starvation. Only

Guerin survived. Fresh off his escape and lengthy stay aboard the raft, the "Man from Devil's Island" had made his way back to England and into the lobby of De Keyser's Hotel, where he was seen fraternizing with thieves, among them John Higgins and Harry Grimshaw.

Suspicious, the detectives had taken several of the men into custody and run them through identity parades. Goldschmidt, the barmaid, and the lavatory attendant from Café Monico had recognized Higgins and Grimshaw.

The Monico heist trial began in November of that year, and the prosecutor in the case was up-and-coming Richard Muir, later to become *Sir* Richard Muir thanks to a long and distinguished career. Goldschmidt, the lavatory attendant, detectives, barmaids, and eyewitnesses all testified on behalf of the prosecution.

The defense had a long list of jewel traders to act as character witnesses, though the star witness had yet to be called. Higgins took the stand in his own defense and faced off against Muir, who was known to be relentless on cross-examinations. In particular, Muir took issue with the motley collection of character witnesses, most of which had criminal records.

The star on the defense's witness list was a man named Goldsmith, who was described as a respectable gentleman and character witness. He was a local jewel dealer and trader, and he arrived at court in a fine suit with diamond-stud cuff links to speak on behalf of Higgins and Grimshaw. Muir saw the gentleman seated in the back of the courtroom and recognized "Mr. Goldsmith"—if not by appearance, then by reputation. Muir approached the witness box and looked directly at Higgins.

"The defense is going to call a witness named Goldsmith and describe him as a perfectly respectable person," began Muir. "Is he?"

"So far as I know," answered Higgins.

"What other names do you know him by?"

Higgins paused for a moment and said, "Cammi, a nickname."

Muir went on, lobbing questions at Higgins, eventually establishing that Goldsmith was in fact Grizzard, and that every character witness on the list worked for or with him in some capacity. Defeated, the defense asked to have Goldsmith/Grizzard removed from the witness list. Grizzard stood from his seat, resting his hat back on his head, tipping it toward Higgins, and smiled as he strode out of the courtroom. He had most likely operated under the alias Goldsmith before, but it would also be like Grizzard to choose that name just to irk his counterpart Goldschmidt.

Although Muir suspected Grizzard of being the mastermind behind the entire heist—and continued to be irritated that he had the gall to appear in court as a character witness—there was no evidence with which to charge him. The prosecution reported that, in all, they believed six men were involved, including "some of the most daring criminals in Europe who shadowed [Goldschmidt] down to the time of the thefts."

Higgins and Grimshaw refused to give statements that would implicate Grizzard in any way. Both of the men were found guilty—Grimshaw received three years penal servitude, and Higgins received fifteen months. The jewels were never recovered, and undoubtedly Grimshaw and Higgins served their terms and came out of prison with a hefty sum of money waiting for them. Blonde Alice Smith had wisely returned to the United States for an extended length of time.

⁓

The Café Monico heist served as something of a prelude. The lives of these three men—Joseph Grizzard, Chief Inspector Alfred Ward, and Sir Richard Muir—would be hemmed together in the years to come. Muir would face Grizzard several more times during his career as a barrister, and those were among the few cases he ever lost. Likewise, the Café Monico heist introduced Grizzard to Ward, and the two would become well acquainted with each other. You can't help but wonder if Grizzard and Ward recognized at that first meeting the talented adversary each had in the other—the jewel thief believed that he was far too clever ever to be trapped by Scotland Yard; the detective believed that with enough patience and persistence any criminal could be caught.

Another jewel heist would afford both the opportunity to find out.

In the fall of 1912, a pearl necklace worth more than the Hope Diamond was purchased by a London jeweler. By the following spring, the pearls had vanished in what was called the heist of the new century, and police on three continents were searching for the famed necklace and the thieves responsible for its disappearance. And by autumn of 1914, the stunning heist, its remarkable participants, and the exquisite pearls were all but lost to history as the world went to war.

This is the true story of those weeks in 1913, in a city scudding ahead of a world war on the horizon, when two brilliant minds—one a criminal, one a detective—matched wits over the most valuable necklace in the world.

PART ONE

THE HEIST

ONE

Queen of Gems

SUNLIGHT SKIMMED THE SURFACE, DRAPING A VEIL OF GOLD across the water. Waves washed against the side of the boat, creating salt-caked streams on the beaten wood. He pushed pieces of beeswax into each of his ears and pinned a forked bone across his nose to hold it closed. Then, tying a heavy stone to his feet, he threw the rock overboard, breaking the surface, and let it pull him, sinking, to the ocean's darker floor. Landing with bare feet was rough, for the ocean bottom was not made of smooth, soft sand, but hard, ragged shells and coral beds. They were a dead gray in color. Some shells were broken apart, their bivalves like open hands; most were still closed.

The pearl diver collected as many shells as he could in one breath, tossing them into a rope basket. Divers could stay underwater more than a minute, sometimes at depths well over a hundred feet. At times, after they cut free of the stone and surfaced too quickly, bubbles would arise in the bloodstream, and many pearl divers were lost to "diver's disease." Others died from drowning. Still others fell victim to sharks.

Pearling was a dangerous but lucrative industry, and pearl divers relied on superstitions, fortune-tellers, anything they could in order to foresee tragedy. Some carried a tiger's claw or a porcupine's quills. They took birds along with them in the boats, and if a rooster crowed just before a dive, the pearlers would stop and pray with rosary beads before continuing. Most would not dive if a shoal of zebra fish, swordfish, or devilfish passed—a superstition ensconced in logic since the shoals were often fleeing a predator. Christians abstained from diving if two shadows formed a cross in the water. Muslims believed pearls to be the breath of Allah, and therefore only the faithful could find them. To some, pearls were the milky tears of mermaids; for others, they were believed to bring tears to those who found them. For centuries, countries like Bahrain, India, Japan, Australia, and many others along the Persian Gulf, Indian Ocean, or the Pacific amassed most of their wealth during the four pearling months. Bahrain could produce as much as $5 million worth of pearls in one season.

Once the diver had enough baskets of oyster shells, and the ocean surface rusted from gold to red, he returned to shore, where the seabirds started circling. There, along the beach, brokers emerged at twilight from wooden shacks fronting the shoreline and bought the shells. It was a gamble—there was no way to tell from outward appearance whether or not a craggy mollusk might have a pearl grasped within its bivalve. Prying shells open with a broad knife, the shellers began pulling out oyster meat and hunting for the pearls. One among hundreds might be hiding nature's most perfect jewel.

Part of what made pearls, the "Queen of Gems," so valuable was their elusive nature. The only gemstones to come from a living being, pearls are also the only gems that require neither cutting nor polishing. What begins as an irritation—a piece of sand or microscopic parasite caught within the bivalves of a mollusk—becomes layer upon layer of iridescent flame as the light breaks between each mantle. It is not the mineral surface that creates the color, but the refracted light moving through and illuminating each porcelain layer. Depending on tissue within the mollusk, the complexion of a pearl takes on the color of the shell's flesh, whether ghostly white, tinged with gold, or a pink blush. And so what begins as something as simple as a grain of sand can evolve into one of the world's most coveted gemstones.

From the dangerous deepwater dives, to sifting through thousands of shells, to trades on the shore, the pearls made their way to traders in Bombay or along the Persian Gulf. The brokers learned the different customs of each culture where pearls were traded. They spoke the native language with traders. The best jewelers, like Louis Cartier, sailed to pearling countries and met in person with the sheikhs and princes. From Bombay to the fine jewelers of Paris, London, and New York, the path of the pearl predestined its high worth.

A jeweler named Paul Claudel, a colleague of Cartier's, described the perfect pearl: "I turned it between my fingers on the point of a needle, and observed how it shone from every angle! But not like the diamond, that geometric pentacle with its hard, penetrating fire; no, the pearl is something attractive, charming, delicate, one might almost say—human." Like its ethereal beauty, a pearl's value remained intangible. If a perfect pearl was discovered in the Persian Gulf at the turn of the twentieth century, it depressed other values and could alter exchange rates in the region.

Before cultured pearls entered the jewel trade in the 1920s, it could take years to compile a necklace of pearls similar enough in their shape, color, and quality to fit together. At that point, the worth of the single pearl, now collected as a group, grew exponentially.

In 1903, just such a necklace was in the making. It would take another ten years to find the sixty-one pearls, all of a pinkish-golden hue, to match. Most of the pearls had come from Baghdad and Bombay, but the largest pearl that served as the centerpiece to the necklace had belonged to Portuguese royalty. For a decade, jewelry dealers from around the world had been adding to the collection, looking for the perfect match to create this rare necklace.

A London jeweler named Max Mayer—round-faced, shiny-headed, and heavily mustached—purchased the strand of pearls in Paris in the fall of 1912. He paid an incredible sum and insured the necklace with Lloyd's of London for £135,000 (or roughly $750,000), putting the value of the necklace close to £10 million (or $18 million) by today's dollar—and that's a conservative estimate. The value could have been as high as £81 million (or $121 million) given its share of Britain's gross domestic product in 1913.

It was a wise investment. Pearls had become so valuable that in just a few years, Louis Cartier would be looking to move his New York jewelry store into a mansion on Fifth Avenue in Manhattan, and he would pay for it with $100 cash and a double strand of pearls.

Cartier kept a list of a few impressive pearl trades from that time period. In 1913, the same year Mayer's necklace went on the market, Cartier sold a strand of fifty-nine pearls for just over $170,000. In 1920, Cartier sold three strands of pearls that had belonged to Czar Nicholas I for $100,000. Still, none touched the value of the Mayer pearls at $750,000.

By 1913, everyone in the jewel trade knew of the famed Mayer pearls. As rich in its compilation as in its blushing color, the necklace had made the sprawling journey from the pearl divers to Paris, the pinnacle of pearl trading. Brokers and buyers traveled from all over the world to the gem district in Paris to buy or sell precious pearls. While diamonds and the colored stones dominated the markets in London and Antwerp, Paris remained the capital of pearl sales.

In spite of all the trading on lamp-lit, cobbled streets in Paris, the vast majority of the world's pearling stations were located in or near British-occupied countries: the Caribbean, Australia, India, Ceylon (now Sri Lanka), Bahrain, and many other countries along the Persian Gulf, as well as islands throughout the Indian and Pacific oceans. So while France may have been the world's trading post for pearls, those pearls either traveled through London or were financed by Londoners long before appearing in Parisian jewelry stores.

After all, the British Empire was home to 400 million people around the globe, and London was the largest city on earth. As one historian said, this "archipelago of rainy islands" ruled the world. With free trade reigning and the sun never setting upon imperial Britain, the exchange of goods was at an all-time high. It was only natural that the world's valuables—gold, silver, diamonds, colored gems, pearls—should pass through its largest marketplace as well.

Once in London, all gems made their way to the global gathering place of jewel traders, a few compact blocks known as Hatton Garden. The neighborhood long had a reputation for its gold and silver, as well as diamonds from mines in India, but it really came into its own as the apex of gem trading after the discovery of diamond mines in South Africa in 1867 and the meteoric rise of De Beers. To preserve diamond values during the instability of the Boer Wars, a syndicate of jewelers operated the diamond mines in Africa and controlled the supply and, therefore, the price of the gems. Still, as a rush of buyers descended on the mines, diamonds began to flood the market, and a large diamond was no longer such a rarity. Many diamond traders turned to a more exclusive product and lucrative market—pearls.

By the twentieth century, Hatton Garden brimmed with the business of these precious stones and peerless pearls, attracting people from all over the world—the jewelers, traders, brokers, and cutters. And then Hatton Garden became home to another professional as well: the international jewel thief.

TWO

King of Fences

JOSEPH GRIZZARD WALKED UNDER A CANOPY OF YOUNG TREE limbs still feathered with new spring growth, arching over the sidewalks leading to the Dalston Junction outside of London. At forty-six years old, Grizzard looked like an attractive English gentleman, solidly built and standing nearly a head above the crowd. He had the splinters of age around his eyes, a blond mustache framed his top lip, and he wore typical Edwardian dress—a three-piece suit, waistcoat, single-breasted jacket, shirt studs, derby hat. He always wore nice cuff links, often diamonds, and had a penchant for smoking cigars. In one breast pocket sat the gold chain of a watch draped gracefully across him, and in another, Grizzard carried his calling card, a leather case of cigars, and a cigar cutter.

His outward appearance aside, Joseph Grizzard made an impression on people. Those who knew him tried to pinpoint the elusive quality that had such a great impact on those around him—his height and broad shoulders, his fine clothes and charming demeanor, his reputation—but no one could ever describe exactly what made him so redoubtable. In a photo from the time period, Grizzard appears at ease, complacent even, except for his eyes. They are challenging—the kind of eyes you meet and look away from. In the photo, Grizzard wears a poker face, but his lips and mustache are raised just slightly on the left to reveal the faintest of smiles.

Grizzard, his wife, and son lived in a new home that had been built on Parkholme, a beautiful, tree-lined street in Dalston. The Edwardian era, with its great influx of people and ballooning middle class, produced a number of these wealthy suburbs surrounding London, connected by a web of railroad tracks and train stations. Like many others on the block, the Grizzards' redbrick home boasted dormer windows on a terra-cotta roof with large bay windows and a garden in front. To the back of the house stood a kitchen, scullery, and bath. Upstairs, the house had four or five bedrooms and another bath. The Grizzard home also had the newest conveniences— artificial lighting and plumbing.

Each morning, like every other businessman, Grizzard took the train into London to work. On this particular Sunday, however, the Dalston streets felt quiet, the trains empty of the usual workday crowds. The Dalston Junction's six different platforms, a cage of vaulted steel beams and train tracks, served as the main overground line into London from the east, and that morning, Grizzard's shoes echoed in the great empty station. On weekdays, the train ran every fifteen minutes, but the Sunday train for the North London Line departed just before 8 A.M., and would not return again until afternoon.

Grizzard did not attract much attention as he climbed on board.

To anyone else on the train, he looked like so many other London gentlemen conducting business in the city, even if it was a Sunday. His fine clothing and impeccable manners blended easily into a crowd.

As the whistle sounded and the train jolted to a start, Grizzard sat back and looked through a window mottled with soot and raindrops as the train steamed toward the inner city. Below the tracks, London's suburban streets flashed through the window frames. The tangle of the Dalston Junction train tracks and electrical lines. Then the cheaper box-frame homes built closest to the tracks, followed by the pockets of grass and gardens of the nicer homes. Next, came the wide thoroughfares. Hansom cabs. A horse-drawn omnibus. Advertisements: KINGSLAND GAZETTE and IDEAL MILK. A parade of shops. Streetlamps bent like swan's necks.

Grizzard looked out over the tracks as the train slowed briefly at the Shoreditch station before continuing on. In the distance, his eyes landed on familiar sites from his childhood home in London's infamous East End. There, the streets looked darker, cavernous, with buildings towering over narrow cobblestone roads. Chimneys jutted from the dwellings the way ship masts crowd wharves. Pigeon coops littered rooftops. Crates stood, stacked into tall columns against brick walls. Piles of rubbish collected along the street.

Finally, the train moved on, speeding ahead until it eased into the Broad Street station. The ride wasn't a long one, but it mapped, visibly and unflinchingly, how far Grizzard had come.

⌒

The Victorian and Edwardian eras were not an easy life for most. The population had exploded in the nineteenth century as people moved from the countryside into the city in record numbers, a move made easier by rapidly expanding railroads. Maps of London population from the 1600s through the end of the 1900s look like someone knocked over an ink pot.

In its earliest days, the city mushroomed out of the Thames River, which runs like a garden snake through the metropolitan area. London's street names and neighborhoods are like a linguistic map of that history—a series of gates and churches. Streets like London Wall, Old Bailey, Ludgate Hill, Newgate, Aldersgate, and Bishopsgate hearken back to a time when the city surrounded itself with protective walls and gates. And the wealth of saints— St. Andrew, St. Albans, St. Pancras, St. Giles, and many more—are reminiscent of the churches and parishes that once dominated London. The rest are insipidly practical—Cheapside, Commercial Street, Shoe Lane, Petticoat Lane, Brick Lane, Gravel Lane—but reflect the large amount of trade that has always thrived there.

Throughout its past, the city's development centered on the river. At times, it was said, so many boats crowded the water that someone could walk from one side to the other. People flocked to the docklands for work. Like most modern cities, London soon became weighted down by overpopulation, a lack of waste management, too little fresh water, and diseases like cholera, plague, and typhoid that flourished in the festering atmosphere.

Still, people continued to come. By the late 1800s, London began attracting not only those looking for work, but those seeking asylum as well. Wars and persecution in western Russia and Eastern Europe forced many to flee, landing on the eastern docks along the Thames and moving into the nearest neighborhoods. Immigrant enclaves soon sank from the sheer number of people and overwhelming poverty. As the next century approached, London's population was over six million people—one million of those lived in roughly two square miles of London's East End.

Neighborhoods that make up the East End, like Spitalfields and Whitechapel, became shadowed and gloomy, blackened by coal dust and threads of smoke, pungent with horse manure and pools of sewage. The smell of nearby tanneries and slaughterhouses hovered in the air. If the sun shined yellow elsewhere in England, in the city it broke weakly through the smog, as lifeless and gray as a daytime moon. This was London's Belle Époque—*the Beautiful Age.*

In England, this golden period straddled the stifled Victorian era and the extravagant Edwardian one, ushering in the twentieth century. As Victoria's reign gave way to her son Edward's, it was as though a light had been turned on. Literally. One of the most noticeable traits of the time period was the bright electric lighting in the window frames of buildings and homes. Brightness was only one of the many assaults on the senses, which included piercing train whistles, the lisping of steam, rumbling of the tube, car horns, the shrill of a ringing phone, white light replacing a yellow flame, and the smell of petrol mixed with manure on the streets.

Still, for many, this remained a golden era. E. M. Forster's *Howards End,* one of the most popular novels of the time, showcased society life with its eight-course meals, men's clubs, and ladies' shopping trips to Selfridges or Harrods. While jaunts to the country for the newly termed "week-end"—after all, there had been no need for a weekend when there was not a workweek—were filled with champagne picnics, tennis, croquet, and bicycle rides.

But the Beautiful Age was not beautiful for all, and the feeling of discontent became infectious, spreading virulently in the poorer neighborhoods. One study showed that one-third of Londoners lived below the poverty line. The average pay was only two pounds per week. And poverty, combined with desperation, grew criminals the way scattered seed will sprout and spread toward sunlight. Even people who had steady jobs turned to crime to make ends meet. Some worked alone, while others worked in gangs out of the East End, and so crime continued to rise even as the great divide between real poverty and land-owned wealth gave birth to the new "middle class."

The middle class swelled in London at the turn of the twentieth century, from the lower-middle-class workers such as policemen, shopkeepers, and tradesmen to upper-middle-class professionals like physicians, lawyers, and bankers. Born-to-wealth money in the form of land was being taxed or sold almost out of existence. For the first time, people began to create their own futures in England—the definition of a "gentleman" became fluid. As a result, most people lived well above their means. Members of the aristocratic class tried to maintain their status as the money dried up, while the middle class spent more as they aspired to greater positions and refused to settle for the lifestyle their parents had endured. That philosophy was not lost on the criminal class: why toil in a lower-middle-class job when riches stood just within reach?

London crime created its own social caste system, beginning with the poor whose very survival depended on prostitution, petty theft, pickpocketing, and snatching. Some proved more talented than others—a gifted pickpocket could steal a tiepin while obtaining a light for his cigarette. Or a moll-blazer, with a sleight of hand, could open a lady's handbag, steal the coin purse, and fasten the bag again without notice. From there, smart criminals graduated to other offenses. There were the robbers who stole by force from pedestrians. Further up the ladder were the burglars, who broke into buildings and homes. And there were the unique skill sets like screwsmen, who copied keys and burgled, safecrackers, or smashers, who traded in counterfeit money.

At the top tier were the highly intelligent fences and putter-ups, who masterminded and funded thefts, and the receivers who quickly sold the goods. Once the loot made its way from the burglars and safecrackers to the receivers, it was nearly impossible for the police to trace. One thief, in his memoir, described the receiver this way: "Another class of criminal who appears to be an ordinary gentleman or business man. Has his own house and often his own car. No fear of arrest because there is always a lack of evidence."

The thief went on to say, "Of this class of crook the public knows very little. Apart from an account of his latest coup in the morning papers he keeps entirely in the background, living the private life of an ordinary well-to-do citizen."

Nearly all of these terms could fall under the general category of *thievery,* which was prosecuted as larceny in the courts. But there seemed a subtle sophistication to the persona of a thief. Thieves did not often use brute force. They did not attract much attention. In fact, their very existence was shrouded in secrecy. They were the talented burglars, putter-ups, fences, and receivers—the professionals of their trade.

In the world of London crime, Joseph Grizzard was at the top of the profession. "Kemmy" or "Cammi" Grizzard was well known as a receiver, master putter-up, and London's "King of Fences." One journalist would later call him the "largest and wiliest receiver of stolen jewelry that ever carried on his trade in this country, or . . . in any other country" and a Scotland Yard detective remarked that

Grizzard was responsible for "some of the most amazing coups in the whole history of crime."

Grizzard came from a Jewish immigrant background, but a unique one. His family moved to London in the 1850s from Amsterdam, and this would prove an important distinction. The late 1800s saw a massive influx of Jewish immigrants fleeing the pogroms of czarist Russia in Eastern Europe. Anti-Semitism and anti-immigrant sentiment followed. But Grizzard's family and the other Dutch Jews known as Chuts had settled in London two or three decades earlier when the attitude toward immigrants was slightly more congenial. The Chuts settlement in London was not so much a question of flight from oppression as much as looking for new business opportunities. The Netherlands had a fairly good relationship with different religious groups, so while Jews were often isolated and persecuted in other countries, they were integrated in the Netherlands and acclimated better to life in London.

Most Dutch Jews in the 1850s settled in an area of London's East End known as Tenterground, a small neighborhood named for the tenter machines (as in "on the tenter-hooks") used to stretch fabrics. Tenterground had been built on the wealth of the silk trade and clothmaking shops in the seventeenth and eighteenth centuries. The grand terraced houses lining many streets, and the mansions surrounding Spital Square, stood as testament to the once-rich silk industry. By the time Grizzard's parents, John and Sophie, moved there to start a business and raise a family, the silk trade had long since collapsed, leaving the neighborhood a cheap, poverty-pocked quarter for immigrants recently landed on the nearby docks.

The Chuts settled in the broad-windowed, terraced buildings where they could live upstairs and open shops downstairs. Some Chuts worked as cap or slipper makers. Others made tobacco products. Still others were diamond cutters. Grizzard's father was a "hawker," which meant he sold wares like tin, linens, buttons, cutlery, shoes, and clothing items. The Grizzard family must have been more fortunate than most, or more likely, Mr. Grizzard supplemented his funds by other means, because Joseph and all of his siblings attended school rather than working the streets, and their home had both a domestic maid and manservant.

Tenterground was a small enclave in a larger area known as Spitalfields abutting the Whitechapel neighborhood. Spitalfields, a shunted pronunciation for the "hospital fields" that existed there in Medieval times, had become a Victorian slum. Its cobblestone streets were described as the most dangerous in the city.

Grizzard was born into this crime-ridden, diseased quarter in 1867, in the midst of a major economic recession, and only one year after a cholera epidemic ravaged the area, killing thousands. Often the subject of London's graphic periodicals, his neighborhood was filled with dilapidated tenement housing, where thieves, gangs, alcoholics, and prostitutes abounded. This was Charles Dickens's London. The black mists and mud-slicked streets of Spitalfields were even home to the villainous Bill Sikes when he held Oliver Twist captive.

Grizzard's neighborhood therefore attracted much philanthropic attention. New cottages and gardens had been built as part of a progressive housing movement spearheaded by Prince Albert. Numerous church and charitable organizations graced street corners. The Salvation Army was founded there. And wealthy citizens or reporters such as Charles Dickens, Jack London, Henry James, and

Henry Mayhew were often seen walking the streets to write about the conditions.

The East End was a place steeped in contrasts. While befogged and gloomy, it was also an area full of a variety of life. On the streets, Grizzard would have passed bearded sailors from the docks, speaking different languages, daggers hanging from their leather belts. He heard Irish accents. There were the Dutch broom girls, French singing women, bagpipe players, as well as immigrants from British colonies. Jews, like Grizzard's family, continued to arrive and dominated the clothing trade. From places all over the globe, people were drawn to the vortex of London, making the short trip from the docks into the East End to settle and work.

With few jobs available, they had to make their own—people found a need, no matter how small, and a way to fill it. There were "new milk" sellers. Penny-pie makers. Wild-game merchants. Streets were lined with pungent fish and greens markets, baskets spilling red apples, yellow onions, and purple cabbage. The cat, dog, and horsemeat vendors circled the blocks. Bamboo cages dangled from storefronts, filled with exotic songbirds for sale. Music halls and street performers echoed along the curbstones, while animals bellowed as they were driven into the underground slaughterhouses. Orphaned children, "chance children" who had no fathers, child sweepers, or those just sent out of one-room homes so cleaning could be done, flooded the streets to sell buttons, rags, hairpins. And then there were the lowest of all, "the Pickers," who scavenged the urban wasteland for scraps of coal and cigar butts. Even the bone grubbers found a living, pulling bodies from the Thames River and picking the bones clean of jewelry, cloth, or anything else of value. In this destitute society, nothing went to waste.

*　*　*

From Spitalfields, the Grizzard family moved to Buckle Street in neighboring Whitechapel. Grizzard grew up in this crowded warren of dim alleys, courtyards, and narrow-spaced buildings. He walked Whitechapel Street and, like most kids, cupped his hands over his eyes and stared into the showroom that held Joseph Merrick, the "Elephant Man." He snatched "eating apples" from bins along Commercial Street and grew accustomed to drunken brawls outside the public houses smelling of ginger beer and lager. He watched the card and skittle players, or spent a penny on curbside soda fountains that sold powdered lemonade and colorful effervescents.

Grizzard could easily have been one of those intrepid children Jack London wrote about when he immersed himself there at the turn of the last century and reported about the environment: "There is one beautiful sight in the East End, and only one, and it is the children dancing in the street when the organ-grinder goes his round. It is fascinating to watch them, the newborn, the next generation, swaying and stepping . . . They delight in music, and motion, and color and very often they betray a startling beauty of face and form under their filth and rags."

In spite of that music, motion, and color, children raised in the East End lived with crime surrounding their everyday lives—petty crimes, pickpockets, opium dens, brothels. They also lived with the violence that accompanied it. Grizzard was just a young man during Jack the Ripper's gruesome reign in 1888. Women in the East End, who had been abandoned by their husbands or succumbed to "the drink," often worked as prostitutes to help provide food for their children. All five of the Ripper's canonical victims were single women or mothers who lived or died in Spitalfields and worked the streets of Whitechapel. Mary Kelly, believed to be the Ripper's last victim, was brutally dismembered in her rented room not far from where the Grizzard family lived.

And so Jack London's quaint description of East End children continued on a darker path: "But there is a Pied Piper of London Town who steals them all away. They disappear. One never sees them again, or anything that suggests them . . . Here you will find stunted forms, ugly faces, and blunt and stolid minds. Grace, beauty, imagination, all the resiliency of mind and muscle, are gone." Those broken human beings, he wrote, leave only a hint of the children they once were dancing to the organ grinder.

Pieced together, Grizzard's childhood and young adulthood appears to be one of ambition, street smarts, and enough learned gentility to rise above his humble circumstances. One other important distinction: he was born in the United Kingdom. His parents may have been immigrants, but in an age when mass migration descended on England and the East End was becoming known as "Little Poland," Grizzard was considered a Londoner. What's more, his family did not practice strict Orthodox Judaism. They didn't keep kosher; no one in the family spoke Yiddish. These subtle cultural differences enabled them to blend in even more as Londoners and separated them from what many disparagingly referred to as "foreign Jews."

For someone intelligent and charming, raised in a modest family in one of the city's poorest neighborhoods, Grizzard's future could go one of two ways: he could join the lower middle class to become a shopkeeper, clerk, butcher, tailor, fireman, or policeman, or he could aspire to the ever-expanding upper middle class to work as an apprentice to become a banker, solicitor, or physician.

Grizzard had been schooled, but his real education thus far had been the streets, so the best way to catapult himself into the wealthy middle class was to join a profession he already knew well from a childhood in Whitechapel—crime. Influenced by friends and at least one brother who had already turned to thieving, Grizzard saw his first brush with the law when he was only thirteen years old and served fourteen days for larceny. After that, he managed to escape arrest as he fine-tuned his skills, observing experienced thieves and, more importantly, learning from the mistakes they made. One contemporary described criminals like Grizzard: "He has in most cases been born and bred in the criminal community, has realized very early in life that to make a success of crime he must first cut himself off from them."

Still, it seemed more than just circumstances led Grizzard to choose a life of crime. He, like many other middle-class Londoners during that era, was unwilling simply to accept the society he had been born into. In addition to that, there was a collective, indulgent kind of disregard inherent to interwar generations. England, like America, had not known large-scale war in at least a generation. The British had fought the Boer Wars of the late nineteenth century, and the Americans had fought the Spanish-American War in 1898, but those seemed distant proxy wars under the banner of democracy that would soon lead to a yet unknown phenomenon: world wars. As one historian noted, the years between the violent American Civil War and World War I proved relatively peaceful, so the lives of average citizens were determined by their own choices rather than defined by war and duty as many generations in the past had been, and many in the future would be.

By the time he had his own family, Grizzard had started to branch out in the criminal world. In 1898, when Grizzard was thirty-one years old, he married Sarah Goldstein in the East London Synagogue in Rectory Square. Sarah had been born and raised in Spitalfields as well, and their son, Samuel, was born a year later. Joseph, Sarah, and Samuel Grizzard settled in another area of the East End known as Wellclose Square, an old maritime neighborhood designed by a visionary Londoner whose name suggests his parents had other hopes for him: Nicholas If-Jesus-Christ-Had-Not-Died-For-Thee-Thou-Hadst-Been-Damned Barbon.

When the Grizzards lived there, most of the original buildings had been converted into a hodgepodge of dwellings with affordable floors to let. Grizzard had stayed close to his family, however—his parents and several of his siblings moved into the house next door. When the census taker knocked on the door of Joseph Grizzard's Wellclose home at the turn of the twentieth century, Grizzard listed his job as a "diamond dealer."

Grizzard's trade could appear legal on the surface, while remaining illegal and lucrative beneath it, providing a sort of criminal middle ground. He became acquainted with London's best burglars, forming relationships with them and earning their trust. He spent some time himself as a burglar and saw his second brush with the law in 1903 when his profession seemed well under way. Working with a diamond cutter known as "Sticks," Grizzard was charged with heavy burglary, and in his possession the police found seventy-eight gold watches, twenty-four gold chains, seventy diamonds, and pearl and sapphire rings.

As the constable led Grizzard into the courtroom for his burglary trial, he glanced at the evidence table and said with a smirk, "That's a jolly good bar there. I suppose that's the 'jemmy' I did it with?" In spite of having an eyewitness who placed Grizzard at the scene of the crime, and a woman who testified that she bought a piece of the stolen jewelry from Grizzard, he was acquitted and served no time.

That close call in the courts most likely inspired Grizzard to leave the high-risk stealing to the screwsmen and look into receiving and selling the stolen goods instead. Receiving involved much less chance, and what risk did exist, was controlled by the receiver.

Grizzard's career must have been progressing quickly, because he soon moved his wife and son from their rented apartment in Wellclose Square to a new house on Parkholme in Dalston, a relatively posh neighborhood on the northeastern edge of London. Professionally, Grizzard may have referred to himself as a diamond trader, but he came into his own as a receiver, which led to the logical next step as a fence—planning the heist, organizing the thieves, and putting up the money that would afford him the jewels to receive and sell.

❧

Most of Grizzard's work took place in Hatton Garden, but the quarter was deserted on weekends, so Grizzard often visited the Houndsditch Market in a part of London, as its name suggests, once used as a dumping ground for refuse, sewage, and dead animals. In Grizzard's time, however, items of another kind collected there—gems.

Grizzard left the Broad Street train station and walked a few short blocks to the Houndsditch Sunday Fair or Rag Fair, which traded a wealth of secondhand clothes, hats, bonnets, mismatched shoes, as well as silks, laces, and shawls from abroad. Deep within the rags and tatters of the market and its brood of hawkers and buyers, just beyond the fragrant Duke Street orange market, were the gems. Dark, stooped, and thickly curtained, the shops held board after board of gold, silver, and tiny jewels.

One shop in the orange market stood apart from all others. After entering through a maze of squat doors and dim hallways, it opened up into a grand apartment, finely decorated, hazy with tobacco smoke, and full of trays gleaming with diamonds, rubies, emeralds, and sapphires, many of which had been stolen from their previous owners and broken down, the gold and silver melted, and the gems sold in markets like Houndsditch.

Grizzard wore his diamond stud cuff links and had a fat cigar perched beneath his blond mustache. With his hands clasped behind his back, he perused the gems, though he himself never handled the jewels. He nodded his head toward a gemstone and his assistant stepped forward to offer a price and purchase the goods. Later, Grizzard would travel abroad and sell the gems for a hefty markup.

The police knew of the Houndsditch Sunday Fair, they knew of the trades in Hatton Garden, and they knew Grizzard well, but knowing a receiver and catching him were two different things. Technically, a person is not supposed to knowingly buy or sell stolen goods—but how do you prove he or she *knew* the gems to be stolen? Or as one prosecutor said, "There are those in Hatton Garden today who knew 'Cammi' well, and wondered . . . why no one arrested him, for the trade which all knew that he carried on. The answer is that Grizzard had sufficient brains not to be caught."

Grizzard could not resist the occasional warmth of the limelight, however. For all his criminal genius and business approach to crime, he kept a sense of humor about him. In 1907, England's famed horse race known as the Ascot made news for reasons beyond the Thoroughbreds—the Gold Ascot Cup was stolen. The next morning, the London *Times* combined the two biggest news items of the day into one headline without realizing the obvious and humorous implication: MARK TWAIN ARRIVES—ASCOT GOLD CUP STOLEN. Twain was in London to receive an honorary award, and as he addressed the audience at London's Mansion House, he added his trademark humor to the situation, "I do assure you that I am not so dishonest as I look. I have been so busy trying to rehabilitate my honor about that Ascot Cup that I have had no time to prepare a speech."

The theft was impressive. The trophy, paid for by King Edward, standing over a foot tall and made from sixty-eight ounces of gold, had been taken from the grandstand while under guard. One way or another, the cup ended up in Grizzard's hands. When close friends attended dinner parties at his home, Grizzard liked to serve cocktails in the great trophy and ask his guests if they'd heard about the time he won the Ascot Gold Cup. The trophy was never recovered.

Although Grizzard had been a thief since at least the age of thirteen, and had been picked up now and then, he had never been put away for any real length of time. By middle age, Grizzard had long ago made enough money to retire and lead a respectable life, but the sport of crime proved too addictive.

If the police had trouble understanding Grizzard, Victorian criminologists did not. Although they were slow to catch on to the fact that crime actually does pay—and paid well for men like Grizzard—criminologists had already begun to understand the criminal mind. In the midnineteenth century, they observed two very important facets of criminal life: that crime is not always a product of poverty, and that often criminals can be, in fact, very intelligent. In other words, there need not be a logical reason— poverty, lack of education, low levels of intelligence—that surrounded a life of crime. For a man like Grizzard, it wasn't a question of where he came from, but where he wanted to go.

"Like so many criminals," a prosecutor said of Grizzard, "he was a great man with a twist in his character which made him prefer to go crooked where he might go straight." The prosecutor's statement is an interesting one because, given Grizzard's background and his ambition, it's not likely that he could have achieved what he did by taking that straight route.

For Grizzard, there seemed to be something more philosophically satisfying about a daring life of crime. English poet William Blake once wrote in a letter that "Want of money and the distress of a thief can never be alleged as the cause of his thieving, for many honest people endure greater hardships with fortitude. We must therefore seek the cause elsewhere than in want of money, for that is the miser's passion, not the thief's." Grizzard's passion, whatever it was, lay deeply entrenched in the world of London crime.

❧

As the fence putting up money for a number of different heists at any given time, Grizzard was in control of everything. But he relied on a group of trusted thieves, known as confederates, to put his plans and heists in motion. Grizzard was genuinely admired and respected by his confederates. He never seduced men or women into a life of crime; in fact, he was known to find them honest work if they wanted it.

Most of Grizzard's power and appeal in the criminal world was due to the fact that he was generous, he never used violence, and he was fiercely loyal. Whenever a colleague was put away, Grizzard paid for his defense and helped care for the man's wife and children until he was released. As a result comes one of the most telling details about Grizzard: no amount of legal pressure or jail time ever persuaded colleagues to turn on him. It wasn't out of fear; it was out of respect and loyalty. "His great secret of success in crime," explained one journalist, "is the fact that he trusts his pals and in turn is trusted by them." This group of devoted confederates was known to Scotland Yard as the Grizzard Gang.

THREE

The Grizzard Gang

A GANG OF JEWEL THIEVES AND WHAT NORMALLY CONSTITUTES a "gang" varied greatly. Grizzard's men and women generally did not carry weapons. They did not threaten or intimidate. They were not unified by a single ethnicity, background, or socioeconomic distinction. They existed very much like a business organization of varying skill sets, all under the direction of Grizzard, London's ultimate "capitalist of crime." He and his gang acted as a corporation of thievery.

A twentieth-century criminologist analyzing the Grizzard Gang explained the professional hierarchy: "It is the receivers of stolen goods who are most commonly cited as being controllers of centralized criminal organizations in thieving." In large part, this was due to the fact that the police had become so much more effective at catching criminals—thieves needed to dispose of the jewels as quickly as possible. The criminologist went on to describe the role of the fence: "He usually remains well in the background, the man with the purse, and perhaps more important than that, the man who knows too much for any of his trusted confederates to betray him . . ."

Joseph Grizzard, as the head of his crime syndicate, worked patiently and meticulously to plan every heist. A genius with details, he spent months studying maps, shops, behaviors, and various getaways. He put up the money to cover hotel stays for weeks at a time to case a situation and paid for travel expenses to shadow jewelers abroad. A thorough businessman, after a successful pull, Grizzard even assigned gang members to watch police headquarters and the offices of insurance underwriters for signs that they might be on the hunt.

Grizzard had succeeded in a number of impressive heists like that at the Café Monico. Another brazen pull he masterminded involved planting two of his confederates in the employment of a gentleman's home. The thieves waited until the gentleman left town for the weekend. Then they studied every drawer, cabinet, wardrobe in the house, as well as the owner's safe. After they reported back to Grizzard, he told them to wait to burglarize the house until the owners returned—it would appear as though outside thieves had been responsible and keep the police from suspecting housemaids and butlers. The plan itself was not so brazen, but the house in question was. Grizzard had chosen to steal from the son of the city alderman, who just happened to be a close friend of the prosecutor Richard Muir.

In the end, the detectives never fell for the ploy. They recognized signs of falsified burglary, and they began looking into current and past employees with knowledge of the home. When confronted by detectives, the two thieves confessed. The prosecution and the police knew that Grizzard was the putter-up, but could never convince the two confederates to give up his name. The men accepted twenty-one months penal servitude instead.

For the few notorious crimes attached to Grizzard's name, his real genius remained the ability to stay in the shadows, out of public view. His name only appeared in the London *Times*, the weeklies, or the court dockets a few times in his life, but the Metropolitan Police had long believed Grizzard had some part in every major theft in Edwardian London, either helping to plan the heist, fund it, or receive the stolen gems.

Grizzard's gang of colleagues and confederates was extensive—too extensive for any police record, newspaper article, or historian to follow. At any one time, and regardless of how many gang members might be in prison, Grizzard always had many others at his disposal, including his most talented and trusted confidant, James Lockett.

If Grizzard held the title "King of Fences," James Lockett was the undisputed "Prince of Thieves." Lockett's pursuits were considerably more risky, and therefore, he needed more names to hide behind. At various times, Lockett was known as William Preston, Harry Graham, Jim Lockhart, James Howard, and on the streets, Lockett-the-Lionhearted.

As fixed as a person's identity would become in the future, in that day and age, identity could be fluid. Without photo identification or fingerprints, how would one person prove who he says he is? Or, for that matter, who he's not? In fact, the fingerprinting system originally was created to address this problem in the justice system. The police, prisons, and courts had a hard time proving or even keeping track of repeat offenders. So, each time Lockett was arrested, he went before the court with a different name—his sentences remained relatively short since he was a first-time offender so many times over.

At fifty-one, Lockett was a few years older than Grizzard and had put those years to good use as a youth. Lockett grew up as a member of the Elephant and Castle Gang, which operated out of South London. Reputably well dressed and intelligent, the gang worked with a sister group known as the Forty Thieves, a highly skilled, well-organized gang of women thieves under the direction of the Queen of the Forties. This band of men and women thieves had special clothes designed—fashionable garments that would blend easily into London's most expensive stores—with hidden pockets in hats, skirts, cummerbunds, and coats. The Elephant Gang and Forty Thieves frequented the stores on Regent and Knightsbridge, as well as in tourist towns along the coast.

Under the tutelage of the Elephant and Castle Gang, Lockett quickly graduated to Continental thievery and became a master screwsman. One of Lockett's better-known thefts included a Parisian jeweler visiting Birmingham, England. While the jeweler waited in line at a chemist's shop, Lockett and his partner stood at the counter ordering pills and some licorice. When the chemist handed them the packages, Lockett and his partner bantered and argued about receiving the wrong orders. They passed the packages of pills and licorice back and forth to each other, and then back to the chemist. Exasperated, the jeweler standing in line set his bag down at his feet and waited patiently.

When the argument subsided, Lockett turned and asked the

jeweler if he knew the way to New End Station. As the jeweler gave him directions, he noticed that Lockett was clean-shaven and very well spoken. Lockett politely thanked him and then walked out of the chemist shop. When the jeweler picked up his bag, he realized it was considerably lighter. Still convinced by Lockett's gentlemanly behavior, he assumed the bags had been switched by mistake and ran to catch the two men before they boarded the train. The jeweler hurried down the street toward the station, but to no avail. The men and the jewels were gone.

Within the month, Blonde Alice Smith had sold the majority of the gems to buyers in the United States. The police picked up Lockett—who was always suspected in clever thefts and burglaries—and put him on identity parade, but no one from the chemist's shop recognized him.

In another daring burglary, Lockett knew of a home with a heavy safe full of jewels and coins. He and his men broke into the house next door while the family was away for the weekend and, from inside the basement, tunneled their way into the other home, cleaned out the safe, and took £4,000 worth of jewelry.

By 1910, the police kept Lockett under constant surveillance.

Lockett was married to a woman named Becky Cohen. They had one daughter and lived in a home in Golders Green on the outskirts of London—appropriately, in a house with several electric alarms. Lockett was part owner of a local cinema and had opened a motorcar garage. It was a smart business venture. As more and more Londoners purchased motorcars, their town homes and flats had no place in which to park them. Most Londoners paid rent to a garage to house their auto.

Lockett's wife, Becky, was a talented thief in her own right and had pulled off many notable thefts. Thieves like Becky Cohen Lockett and Blonde Alice Smith are an interesting commentary on the role of women in Victorian and Edwardian London. According to the all-male "experts" of the time, socially, politically, and biologically, women remained inferior to men, caught in a desperate cycle of dependence. They were born dependent on their fathers for the first half of their lives, then bartered, traded, and placed with a husband for the second half. The Edwardian Age marked the first time in history when middle-class women had a choice other than marriage or house service—they could train to become shopkeepers, seamstresses, secretaries, milliners. They could support themselves independently. In fact, the most dependent, socially imprisoned women remained those who belonged to the highest social class.

Thievery proved very egalitarian for the era. Women thieves could work alongside or even lead men in a time when that happened nowhere else in society. The Forty Thieves Gang of women exemplified that business model. They operated succinctly and lucratively for as many as two hundred years—one of the longest-running, most successful gangs in history.

Following most of his impressive thefts, James Lockett needed a way to dispose of the goods quickly, and that way proved to be Joseph Grizzard. Time and again, Lockett cracked a safe, robbed a mailbag, stole from hotel rooms, and snatched jeweler bags only to have handed the bounty over to Grizzard by the time the police caught up to him—if they caught up to him. One of the perks of being an international jewel thief was that travel did not yet require a passport. After a theft or heist, the jewel thief just hopped on board an ocean liner or train and disappeared for a while. Needless to say, Lockett was a well-seasoned traveler.

A Scotland Yard detective later said that the pair, Lockett and Grizzard, possessed a dangerous combination of brains and executive ability that ruled the criminal underworld.

While Lockett was undoubtedly Grizzard's most gifted gang member, there were others who served purposes as well. One of those men was Simon Silverman, a diamond broker who had a small office in Hatton Garden. Although Silverman had no criminal record, he had known and worked with Lockett for ten years or more, so it's likely that he had meandered into some illegal work at one time or another.

Silverman was a tediously polite and apologetic person, an accommodating people-pleaser. He had neither the charm nor the respect held by men like Grizzard and Lockett. Most people were unfriendly if not openly rude to him. Some of this was due to his appearance—he was unusually short and curved his shoulders forward, earning the nickname "the hunchback" of Hatton Garden. His thin face had a sharp jawline and cheekbones that beveled into a pursed frown. But some of the prejudice was due to his heritage. Although he had lived in London's East End for most of his life, Silverman had not been born there, and noticeable bigotry toward immigrants still existed. His mother, sister, and he had fled persecution in Eastern Europe, and they remained outsiders in spite of the decades they spent in London.

*   *   *

On a chilly afternoon in the winter of 1913, Silverman stood alone among the crowds of traders and brokers at the merchant's market known as the Diamond Club. He overheard a conversation between two well-known Hatton Garden jewelers—the men had apparently not noticed or simply did not care about his presence there. One of the jewelers was Max Mayer, and he was discussing an extremely valuable necklace he had recently purchased. When Silverman finished his business, he left the club, placing his hat atop the few wisps of hair on his head and pulling on a morning coat that was one size too large. The pall of a winter day hung overhead as he walked back toward his office. His head hunched downward, eyes on his feet, Silverman mulled over what he had heard. An opportunity had presented itself. There was nothing about Simon Silverman that suggested gumption or audacity, so he decided to take the valuable knowledge he had just learned to someone who had both.

FOUR

Hatton Garden

WHEN AND HOW GRIZZARD DECIDED TO STEAL MAX MAYER'S pearl necklace remains a mystery. Word of the necklace spread rapidly after Mayer purchased it in 1912—not only of its incomparable beauty but of its great worth—and news of expensive jewels traveled as quickly among the illegitimate traders as it did among the legitimate ones.

Mayer was one of the most respected jewelers in London. He was a portly, bewhiskered, self-satisfied gentleman of good repute, and he had conducted his career honestly—beginning with costume jewelry and working his way up to diamonds. Mayer gained an international reputation as a diamond dealer during the height of mining in South Africa. He then traded in his expertise, believing that "diamonds were gradually going out of fashion in favor of pearls." Mayer liked to say, "If rich parvenus wanted to make a display a few years ago, they gave their women diamonds, but by the time a woman has adorned herself with a hundred thousand pounds' worth of diamonds she looks garish. She can, however, wear two hundred thousand pounds of pearls and remain dignified and in good taste." As he shifted his focus from precious stones to pearls, Mayer's fortune followed him from the former to the latter—and only the most refined jewelers handled pearls.

When Simon Silverman approached Grizzard with details about Mayer's latest purchase and the necklace's many trips between a shop in Paris and Hatton Garden, Grizzard couldn't resist. Normally, he preferred to work with diamonds because they were easier to cut down and sell for a nice profit—but the precious stones provided him with very little in the way of a challenge. Any accomplished receiver or fence could deal in diamonds or the colored gems. A necklace like Mayer's was historic in both its rarity and value. In fact, the *New York Times* would later put forth the theory that Mayer's necklace became a target *because* it was considered the "Mona Lisa of Pearls." As the *Times* theorized, "the theft was committed just for the 'glory' of the thing and . . . the purloiner ranked among the great criminal artists, of whom, till now, the lifter of the Ascot Gold Cup was the most brilliant ornament."

Stealing pearls, however, proved a much greater risk since they could not be altered or recut. The longer the pearls remained in London, the higher the probability that detectives could track down the necklace and the thieves. It came down to the art of timing.

As early as March 1913, Scotland Yard detectives reported seeing Grizzard meet with James Lockett and Simon Silverman at a pub in High Holborn—by then Grizzard was under constant surveillance, which made even the simplest meetings all the more complicated. Every gesture, every conversation, was monitored, so it was important not only to conceal certain things, but also to reveal others in order to keep detectives guessing.

Grizzard and his gang members convened at prearranged locations like a Lyons or Lipton tea shop, where they took a bus to a nearby pub. Then the men walked separately around the corner to yet another pub, entering both the front doors and back, until they could be sure no police shadowed them. Finally, the four men sat at a quiet table together somewhere in the back of a faintly lit dining room with a clear view of the door. Lockett's eyes moved back and forth, watching both entrances to the pub, while Grizzard stared intently at the confederates across from him and discussed business.

After hushed words at the corner table of some establishment along High Holborn, the men would leave, prompting the string of detectives who had just caught up to them to start moving as well, and the whole lot would make their way toward the small tic-tac-toe board of Hatton Garden.

One of the oldest neighborhoods in the city, Hatton Garden had been an axis of jewel trading for centuries but, as its name suggests, had a history in blooms before gems. Built on the magnificent garden belonging to the bishops of Ely, it was famous for its roses and berries, especially after William Shakespeare visited the area and took notice of the "good strawberries." Christopher Hatton, a favorite of Queen Elizabeth I, leased some of the land from the bishop in the sixteenth century, although not entirely by choice. At the queen's steely insistence, the bishop handed over the property, which became "Hatton's Garden." It has held his name ever since.

As time passed and London grew, the street Hatton Garden became a wide and treeless spoke off the carriage-choked round about of Holborn Circus. As a neighborhood, Hatton Garden consisted of a few square blocks with smaller streets like Leather Lane, Vine Street (now Kirby), and Saffron Hill running through it. Charles, Cross Street, and Hatton Wall were narrow roads threaded through the others. At the very end, as a perpendicular boundary to the area, ran the much rowdier Clerkenwell.

Tucked within the quarter, as a sort of alcove, was Ely Place, a long-standing reminder of the bishops' palace, entered through guarded, grand gates off Holborn Circus. Even today, Ely Place feels quiet and cloistered with solemn rows of offices and the Gothic St. Etheldreda Chapel, its incense and painted saints the only surviving remnant of the bishops' influence there. Its strong historical connection to the Hatton Garden neighborhood is now only a narrow isthmus leading from the bishops' retreat to the livelier commercial street with a quaint pub, the Mitre Tavern, hidden in the center. The old tavern even houses a carved piece of the cherry tree supposedly used by Queen Elizabeth I as a maypole.

In spite of its picturesque history, Hatton Garden had some darker moments as well. Legend says Lady Elizabeth Hatton, in 1626, held a ball at her home and was seen by many guests dancing with a mysterious stranger. The next morning, her body was found "torn limb from limb, heart still beating." The vividly named "Bleeding Heart Yard" still exists today as a quiet courtyard off Charles (or Greville) Street.

Over time, Hatton Garden sank into decline as residences gave way to small businesses, the neighborhood's proximity to urban slums contributing to the morass of dubious businesses. Charles Dickens lived in nearby Holborn and frequently remarked on the area in his writings—Oliver Twist found his way to Fagin's den of thieves on Saffron Hill and was later taken to a police court on Hatton Garden to face the dreaded Mr. Fang. Dickens and his family found it a vibrant world where all types of people communed, whether fashionable gentry, famous solicitors, or those just up from the Cape with "a hatful of diamonds."

By the nineteenth century, the wide lanes once lined with town homes three or four stories high had been converted to offices with the obvious pockets of progress—modern, geometric buildings— sprouting up between them. The buildings sat close to one another, adjoining shallow curbs and paved streets broad enough to allow several horse-drawn hansom cabs, and later motorcars, to pass. With the influx of South African diamonds and demand from the rising middle class, business in Hatton Garden grew as bountiful as the blooms and berries once did.

❧

Grizzard did not have an office or shop, so he moved easily among the professionals in Hatton Garden, stopping along curbstones, tipping his hat at traders, shopping at the tobacconist, treating dealers to lunch at one of the many public houses. He also kept a drawer and mailing address at the Globe Pub, which stood right in the center of the neighborhood, at the intersection of Hatton Garden

Street and Charles. Fences like Grizzard could pick up more business one afternoon in his favorite pub than the legitimate jewelers would make in a week. Nonetheless, it was the large deals—the heists—that created the kind of wealth Grizzard enjoyed.

Grizzard did enough trading and selling to satisfy the prying eyes of detectives, but his real income came from knowledge—he served as a conduit of information for the many thieves under his employ. He visited shops, hobnobbed with jewelers, and in any number of locations might pause beside a jewelry shop to light a cigar or cigarette and quietly observe the comings and goings of a particular place of business. On that afternoon, it was Max Mayer's office at 88 Hatton Garden.

Grizzard stood at the busy corner, singeing the tip of his cigar with the open flame of a match and breathing in deeply until it reddened. Through the haze of fragrant smoke, he watched the traffic outside Mayer's office. Hatton Garden was unlike any other market—all of its business took place not inside, but out, as shopkeepers and curb traders negotiated publicly in different languages. Yiddish. German. Dutch. French. Rarely English. The men, dressed in pressed suits, looked to be in casual conversation with one another, except for their hands. They gestured abruptly as they agreed on prices and trades. After a few minutes, a hand would retrieve a handkerchief or crumpled cloth from a pocket and a glint of sapphire blue or emerald green or ruby red would catch in the daylight, veritable prisms of profit. Not long after, the jewels would appear—for two or three times the price—on necks, hands, or cuffs in the West End.

By nightfall, when the neighborhood became all shadow, gilded streetlamps, and flickering firelight, the traders returned to their offices and closed up shop. Some of the largest safes in London weighted the floors of these buildings, and most safes sat in a maze of locked rooms and bolted windows. Throughout the night, watchmen walked the streets and guarded the stores until the weekend when jewelers locked their precious stones in banks. In spite of the many riches within reach, Hatton Garden shops were not easy marks.

Grizzard turned, letting downy ash from his cigar flutter into the gutter, and walked several paces back to the Globe, looking ahead toward Holborn Circle. Hansom cabs and autos circled the statue of Albert astride his horse. Even the occasional zebra-drawn taxi carriage trotted by to advertise the zoo. Roadster bicycles, sold just around the corner at Gamages, snaked in and around traffic. Businessmen hurried by, fingertips on the brim of their hats to protect against wind gusts, while women in their ladies' coat suits and laced boots wide-stepped puddles and horse manure.

Among the hive of activity, Grizzard watched the uniformed postal workers in their tall walking boots and navy uniforms with radiant red collars and trim. They filed out of the Holborn post office and began their walk slowly up Hatton Garden, lugging heavy canvas mail sacks over their shoulders.

FIVE

The Plan

ON MARCH 13, 1913, GRIZZARD AND LOCKETT MADE THEIR WAY toward the Charing Cross train station. The multistoried, redbrick building faced the Strand, and the two men crossed through crowds of cabs, double-decker buses, and pedestrians swarming past the ornate Eleanor Cross, a touch of the medieval among all the modernity. Inside, the South Eastern and Chatham Railways linked London to the coast, and farther, to the Continent. Grizzard and Lockett entered the grand station and headed for Lyons tea shop, where they joined an "unidentified gentleman." The police shadowed the thieves for three hours, but Grizzard and Lockett did nothing more than enjoy their afternoon tea at a leisurely pace.

The next day, the police again watched the train station, where they witnessed the same unidentified gentleman arrive once more, but this time to meet with Simon Silverman before boarding the 2 P.M. train for Paris.

Grizzard's typical mode of operation was to rely on well-placed, well-paid informants, so most likely the unidentified gentleman was a Parisian reporting to Grizzard news about the pearls. A necklace that valuable and expensive would garner a lot of attention. It would also be shown several times in Paris and London before finding a buyer.

For many fences, the success of a heist depended on the amount of money put up for planning and paying off. For his newest heist, Grizzard was personally putting up £4,000, which would have the purchasing power of £290,000 or $440,000 today. In an age when the average workingman made £100 per year, that was an impressive amount of money. He clearly considered it worth such a hefty investment.

Grizzard had any number of methods from which to choose for the heist. With his decades of experience, he had worked as both a burglar and receiver. Broker and dealer. Jeweler and thief. He and his gang members had stolen jewels in elaborate ploys, raided hotel safes, snatched cases from traveling jewelers, tunneled into homes and banks, cracked safes, copied keys, robbed hansom cabs and train cars, and posed as everyone from domestic servants to wealthy buyers to policemen.

In order to choose the best course of action, Grizzard needed to learn where the weak point in the jeweler's plan lay—did the jeweler drink, did he have a mistress stashed in London or Paris, did he have a weakness for gambling, did he frequent the same hotels and pubs, did he travel often to the Continent, did he have much experience with jewels, could he recognize fakes or altered pieces, was he cautious and shrewd or loud and boastful?

So far, Grizzard knew only that the necklace belonged to Hatton Garden's well-known pearl dealer Max Mayer, and when Mayer had an interested buyer abroad, he mailed the necklace to his Parisian colleague, Henri Solomans. Mayer made frequent trips to Paris, but he worked primarily out of his Hatton Garden office, so he relied on Solomans to represent him in negotiations with French buyers. As Paris remained the world's center for pearl trading, the necklace would be shown there most often.

Mayer rarely carried jewels with him, and usually counted on the mail service, which was the standard way to deliver valuables at the time. Sending jewels with paid couriers was far too risky because they made such easy marks for watching thieves, and jewels were at risk even in the hands of the jeweler—as evidenced by the Café Monico heist—so the post office appeared the safest option.

Both Mayer and his Parisian liaison were extremely cautious—they kept the necklace locked in a safe in the bank at all times. They only agreed to show the pearls to reputable buyers well known in the trade. Which meant the only time the pearls were ever left alone was in transit through the mail service.

It was a serious offense to attack and rob the Royal Mail Service, and mail tampering carried a stiff penalty in the United Kingdom. The post office and mailing system stood as a mark of progress and civility. In the past, the recipient, not the sender, paid the postman for delivery. Therefore, few packages were mailed and only to those who could afford to receive them. By the nineteenth century, with the invention of the Penny Post, purchasing a stamp and mailing a letter or package had become mainstream and affordable to many. Securely sending mail and packages symbolized modern communication and civilized trust.

Still, that trust had been breached a few times when mail had been intercepted, though nothing even close to the value of the Mayer necklace. Several months before the pearl heist, a package with a few stray pearls went missing, either the work of a dishonest postman or thieves.

In fact, so many small items began disappearing in transit that the post office decided to change its procedures. In the past, valuables shipped through the mail had been sealed in a large, highly visible red bag—an absolute bull's-eye for thieves. The post office quickly realized its error and began enclosing valuables deep within the regular mailbags, making it far more difficult for thieves to discern which among three hundred or so mail sacks might contain something worth stealing.

The jewelers therefore trusted the mail completely—because of the sheer difficulty and planning it would take to intercept a valuable package. Few criminals would attempt it; even fewer might pull it off.

Like a game of chess, organizing a heist required not only envisioning a plan, but also anticipating the opponent's moves well in advance and knowing how to respond. Grizzard still had very few essential details—a valuable package would be mailed from London to Paris and back to London sometime over the summer. He knew it would come from Henri Solomans' office in Paris to Max Mayer's in Hatton Garden. But he didn't know exactly when it would be done. That's where his confederates became most useful—pawns in the larger game.

Throughout the spring, as cold rains fell, daffodils sprouted, and

London's bleak parks greened, Grizzard outlined the details of the heist. For the first part of the plan, he relied on a familiar tactic. He fronted the money for Simon Silverman to change offices in Hatton Garden. The new office, on the third floor of a small building at 101 Hatton Garden, stood between the post office and Max Mayer's shop. Silverman's sales were slow, to say the least, but he kept up enough business to seem respectable and have a few pieces of mail delivered each week.

Silverman began his own research by watching the mailmen who delivered in Hatton Garden. He noticed what time they left in the morning, how long it took them to cover the block, how many mail sacks they needed on average, and with several delivery times per day, what time jewels and larger packages typically arrived. He then befriended the postal worker on the Hatton Garden mail run, a man named W. E. Neville.

While Silverman focused on how and when to get hold of the necklace, Grizzard began planning how to dispose of the pearls as quickly as possible. The key to the heist depended not only on acquiring the package and extracting the jewels, but also on selling the goods before the police could trace the gems to the thieves. For that purpose, Grizzard needed one more participant.

The fourth person who would become involved in the theft of the Mayer necklace was a man named Lesir Gutwirth. He was a small, black-haired jeweler from Austria who had immigrated to London as a child. With a slight build and short stature, he was the sort of man always trying to compensate for his minor appearance with a big presence. He spoke too much and too loudly and, in general, tried too hard to attain the attention of others.

In the Hatton Garden hierarchy, Lesir Gutwirth was at the bottom. He didn't work in a shop, and instead, traded directly on the curb. He rented a drawer and key at the Viennese Café, known as the "Flea Pit," where he also had his mail delivered.

Although Grizzard found him to be a boastful thief "long on tongue," Gutwirth also traveled to the Continent often, especially Antwerp, to trade. So, Grizzard hoped to use Gutwirth's connections there to unload the pearls—they would attract far less attention in Antwerp than they would in either Paris or London.

What's more, Gutwirth had never been arrested, so he was not under police surveillance and could slip easily out of the country. Neither Gutwirth nor Silverman had ever been picked up by the police, while Lockett and Grizzard were veritable celebrities of the criminal world and frequently featured in *Illustrated Police News*. With little else to offer, it may simply have been Gutwirth's anonymity that appealed to Grizzard.

❧

In late spring, Silverman walked toward the Leather Bottle, a pub on the corner of Charles and Leather Lane, a street so narrow that "the houses almost meet above your head." It was an intersection of public houses frequented in the jewelry quarter—the Leather Bottle, the Viennese Café, and across the street, the Pewter Platter. Every day, during lunchtime, one of London's oldest outdoor markets opened on Leather Lane, creating a loud crowd among barrows of cheap fruit, vegetables, and wilting wildflowers. Mary Angela Dickens, daughter of the famed London author, described the market as "another epoch, another world," where "swarthy Italians stand at the doorways of the image shops; dark-eyed Contadini show their pearly teeth in smiles." The variety of fruits, vegetables, flowers, and trinkets filled the market in tented stalls, infusing the neighborhood with an unpredictable mix of people, noises, and smells.

Silverman pushed his way slowly through the crowded market, which buzzed with blackflies, while children ran beneath the stalls, pelting fallen roses at one another. When he reached the corner pub, the Leather Bottle, he left the bright chaos for the quiet interior. The smoke-filled tavern smelled of cinder, stale lager, and fried cod. They were not fresh smells, but the kind that gather, layer upon layer, over time. Silverman looked toward the back of the pub and soon found the man he was looking for—Peter Robertson Gordon. Gordon worked as a hammersmith, and he and a friend were enjoying a couple of pints when Gordon pulled an engraving out of his pocket to show to his companion, a card printer.

An important part of a jeweler's word was his card and his seal. In a business traded on curbs through brokers or dealers, nods and promises took the place of receipts and ledgers. As packages of gems traded hands, the jeweler's crimson seal pledged that the contents represented an agreed-upon price and authenticity. The seal also ensured that the jewels had not been tampered with.

Silverman awkwardly approached the corner table as Gordon still held the engraving.

"Oh, you are an engraver, are you?" He asked the question casually enough.

"Yes," answered Gordon. "This is a bit of my work." He held the engraving in the palm of his hand. The low lights picked up the lines and etchings of a name.

Silverman looked the engraving over before asking Gordon for his name and address. Then he promised to call on him soon and disappeared into the rowdy Leather Lane market.

Silverman and Gordon met a few days later at the Crown Public House—it seems business in Hatton Garden was often conducted over a pint. Silverman's eyes darted along the street, nervous and twitching. When he felt confident no police had followed him, he opened the door to the pub. He found Gordon and pulled a piece of flesh-colored wax from his pocket with the initials *MM* on it.

"Can you cut a die like that?" Silverman asked.

"What do you want it on, metal or wood?" Gordon held it up toward the window and examined the twin letters in the light.

"Wood will do."

"You will have to get boxwood," advised Gordon. "Any other wood would be too soft to get an impression."

The next day, Silverman returned to the same pub—once again to meet Gordon over drinks—and handed over the wax and boxwood.

"How long will it take you to do it?"

Gordon shrugged, "About half an hour."

Silverman either gave a false name or claimed to want the engraving made for an employer, so Gordon suspected nothing of the initials. Silverman waited patiently at the pub until Gordon returned with the engraving, then paid him a shilling for his services. Silverman returned to Gordon's store a few more times that summer, paying for additional parcel seals with various initials or designs like a shield and locket. He also requested several more MM seals in varying sizes. Every now and then, the two men would pass each other on Charles Street or Hatton Garden and give the other a friendly nod or wave.

With the planning of the heist well under way as warmer days approached, spring proved a relatively quiet time for Grizzard and his gang, but it also marked a time of loss for their friend Lockett. In early May, Lockett was credited with an impressive burglary at the Berkley Hotel in Piccadilly—there wasn't any evidence, and no one was ever arrested, but the police suspected Lockett nonetheless. In reality, he could not have been involved. That month, his wife, Becky, died after a long illness. Her sister moved in with the Locketts and helped nurse her through the worst of it. When Becky finally passed away at the age of forty-three, Lockett, their daughter, Grizzard, and Silverman, among others, stood graveside for the funeral.

In hopes of raising his spirits, two friends of Lockett's, Lorenzo and Lizzie Moore, invited him and his daughter to spend the Whitsun holiday, a bank holiday celebrated at the time of Pentecost, with them at Scullard's Hotel in Southampton. Lorenzo Moore had been a friend of Lockett's for over twenty-five years, and he treated Lockett and his daughter to a quiet weekend away motoring in the country-side. As a thank-you, Lockett invited the Moores to return with him in August—his treat—to a weeklong vacation for the Glorious Twelfth, when the London social season officially ended, and the country shooting parties and red grouse season began.

Lockett must have been depressed after the loss of his wife, and he now had a nine-year-old daughter to raise alone. When he returned from Southampton, he arranged to sell his motorcar garage and told the new buyer that with his wife gone, he had nothing to stay in London for. He planned to move with his daughter to Canada. Still, he was a loyal friend and sharp businessman, so he continued to work with Grizzard on the heist. This one last pull would allow Lockett to retire once and for all.

Grizzard continued to visit Silverman's office frequently as May turned to June, fine-tuning details. Any talented putter-up was a micromanager by nature, so undoubtedly, Grizzard wanted frequent updates. Lockett, however, didn't like to show his face in Hatton Garden too often, so Grizzard met with him only when necessary.

A few weeks after his wife's death, Lockett arrived at the Globe to meet with Grizzard. Both men wore well-tailored suits for the meeting. They sat at a small round table, dark wood beams hanging low overhead, beer steins hooked above the bar, Grizzard's cigar smoke amorphous around them.

In spite of his attire, everything about Lockett's face portrayed hardened experience—from his advancing age to the occasional scars marking rough-hewn cheeks to a bristled mustache, broad chin, and a wide, solid neck. Still, this tree trunk of a man had learned what only a few other thieves had—that nothing camouflaged a criminal better than gentility.

A thief described the social Darwinism of crime: "Of course, the reason for the elimination of what for want of a better term I will call the uneducated criminal is his inability to be anything but himself." Victorian thieves stood out in a crowd with their Cockney accents and poor manners. But the progressive era marked a change in the criminal world. Through the 1910s and 1920s, fences either educated their thieves in the appropriate ways to talk, walk, and act, or they started recruiting from the upper classes, where inheritances had begun to fade and cash became scarce. A thief at the top of his game could pass easily from the East End to the West End without attracting any attention. Lockett's rough exterior and Cockney accent had been transformed into a finely dressed, well-spoken gentleman.

The two men soon left the Globe to eat lunch at the nearby Diamond Club, located a few doors down from Mayer's office. Hatton Garden taprooms were generally quieter during the daytime hours when the local jewelers lunched there over kidney pies, macaroni au gratin, or jellied eels. As the thieves ate lunch, they listened intently to the conversations taking place at nearby tables. Max Mayer and another jeweler were discussing the trade, and Mayer mentioned his valuable strand of pearls coming from Paris, soon to return to London.

Henri Solomans had contacted Mayer on June 6 about borrowing the pearl necklace. Mayer had not been willing to send the necklace to Solomans unless this was a serious buyer, and so Solomans contacted him again midmonth to tell him there was, indeed, a buyer who seemed genuinely interested.

Mayer had no idea that he was in the company of thieves, nor did he know that they had been shadowing his movements for weeks. Grizzard and Lockett, as always, kept quiet and in the background. Jewelers may have spoken too loudly over lunch; jewel thieves did not. And, while there is a long list of thieves who turned from crime to writing fashionable memoirs about their escapades, neither Grizzard nor Lockett ever traded their secrets for a royalty check. Whatever passed between two of London's most brilliant criminals has never been recorded.

To an outsider, Grizzard and Lockett looked like innocuous businessmen having lunch—but they had just learned that Mayer had placed his pearls in the registered post express for Paris.

A Perfect Crime

JUNE 1913 WAS A DISQUIETING MONTH FOR LONDONERS. THE violence started when Emily Davison, a suffragette with the Women's Social and Political Union banner in hand, threw herself in front of a racehorse at the Epsom Derby. The racehorse, the king's horse no less, trampled her at full speed, injuring the jockey and fatally wounding Davison. It was never determined absolutely whether Davison jumped in front of the horse deliberately or accidentally, but she died a few days later from a fractured skull.

Only days after Davison's tragic end, the Balkan War broke out. Or, more accurately, the Second Balkan War. London had just hosted the peace treaty to end the First Balkan War—the peace lasted less than a month. Many Londoners tried not to notice the unrest in Europe rising like a squall line ahead of thunderclouds, and the summer social season, along with the sensational death of

Davison, and a state visit from Russian royalty, provided the necessary distractions.

As suffragettes began flooding the streets near Holborn to wait for the massive funeral procession of Emily Davison to St. George's in Bloomsbury, Silverman arrived early at his office, pushing his way through crowds and cutting through the busiest streets. Hatton Garden was quiet until 9:30 or 10 A.M., but in June, Silverman began arriving well before then and waiting for his morning delivery—as mail had become the most popular form of communication, there could be as many as a dozen deliveries in a day, but the first always arrived by 8 A.M. Silverman stood outside along the curb and greeted the postman cheerfully as he waited for his mail.

Typically, Silverman only received about three letters per week and never any packages. Nonetheless, on June 27, he sent the neighborhood post office an official notice.

101-2 Hatton Garden, S. Silverman and Co.,
London, E.C. Pearls and Precious Stones
Hol. 2865, Te. No.

Secretary, General Post Office.

I should esteem it a favour if you will instruct your postman to deliver my correspondence on the first post in the mornings to my office personally, and not to give to lift attendant under any circumstances.

> *Thank you,*
> *Yours faithfully,*
> *S. Silverman.*

The request seemed a little odd. In all previous months, Silverman had been content to have the lift operator sign for his mail. Now he asked to have the postman climb three flights of stairs and deliver the mail in person. Then again, with so many valuable packages delivered to Hatton Garden, Silverman's request could not be considered out of the ordinary. What did seem odd, however, was that Silverman only requested this of the first mail service of the day—the one that Postman Neville delivered.

Soon thereafter, Silverman and Gutwirth cultivated a friendship with Neville. Gutwirth even drank with the man after work on occasion. Neville had a long and distinguished career as a postman, but he was "fond of the drink" and often missed work because of his frequent trips to the pub. In retrospect, Neville was probably not the right man to be trusted with London's most valuable packages.

One afternoon that June, Gutwirth took Neville to the Cock Public House—undoubtedly over a few pints—to meet with Grizzard and Lockett to discuss a business offer. Postmen like Neville were not paid well, making only a few pounds per week and some tips. And, after thirty years on the job, with advancing alcoholism, a substantial nest egg might be very tempting. True to form, Grizzard offered a price that would be hard to turn down, £200, to leave his mail sack unattended for a few minutes on a designated date at a designated time.

The bag carrier, however, proved a little trickier. Bag carriers showed up early in the mornings to volunteer to help carry the heavy mail sacks for the postman as he walked the neighborhood. It earned him a little extra money, and once the bag was empty, the bag carrier left for his other jobs. Bag carriers volunteered unannounced at the post office and held a bag while it was filled, so they were never assigned a particular postman in advance. Grizzard had no way of knowing who would serve as Neville's bag carrier on a given day.

Finally, the gang also approached an acquaintance named Arthur Spain, a mail sorter who often worked the ferry between France and England, to be on alert for the package as well—in case he found himself alone and with opportunity. It was the least likely scenario, but Grizzard preferred to cover every angle.

As the month of June came to an end, all of the details for the heist were in order. Grizzard knew that the necklace was currently in Paris and soon to be mailed back to London. Silverman had moved to an address on Mayer's mail route in Hatton Garden. He had parcel seals in several sizes engraved with MM, as well as the dark red sealing wax. The thieves also had a detailed map for the Hatton Garden mail delivery, and a postman and ferryman willing to cooperate. With all of the pieces in place, it was time for Grizzard to book passage to Paris.

Grizzard frequently made trips to Paris on business, staying at his favorite hotel on Rue Lafayette. The thoroughfare of shops ran from the Paris Opera House to the Gare du Nord, although, like Hatton Garden, much of the jewel business was conducted on the curb among trusted brokers and dealers. As most deals were made in good faith, dishonesty quickly moved a dealer from the curb to the gutter—literally.

In order for the heist to work, Grizzard would have to know the exact date Solomans planned to return the necklace, so he began shadowing the jeweler. He may have visited the shop or asked about the necklace. He may even have posed as an interested buyer in order to have the pearls sent to Paris. But mostly, Grizzard just waited patiently.

On July 3, near Solomans' shop, a Parisian waiter noticed an unidentified Englishman sitting in a café. There was nothing unusual about the tall gentleman except for how many cups of coffee he ordered. Each time the coffee was delivered to the table, he slipped the three cubes of sugar into his pocket and continued to read his French newspaper. No one noticed which paper, but a safe bet would be the *Écho de Paris*.

About a week later, Silverman arrived in Paris to meet with Grizzard. He only stayed a couple of days, but upon his return, Silverman's housekeeper noticed that he appeared ill at ease. When asked about it, Silverman complained that it had been a rough passage. Somewhere in Silverman's luggage, however, was the scrap of French newspaper, several cubes of French sugar, and pale blue linen wrapping paper that Grizzard had given him.

Finally, the call came. Mayer planned to leave for vacation, so he contacted Solomans and asked that the pearls be returned before he left.

❧

On the morning of July 15, 1913, Solomans sat in his shop on Rue de Provence wrapping the most valuable necklace he had ever handled. Solomans gently surrounded the necklace with cotton wool, then tissue paper. He placed it in a small, Moroccan, plush-lined case, nailing the box closed. He then wrapped the case itself in his signature pastel-blue linen paper. The pearl necklace, with all of its protective layers, was placed in a cardboard box, covered in brown paper, and tied with a string. Solomans held a flame to crimson wax, and with the smell of match tips pluming the office, sealed the package in several places with the initials *MM*. He addressed it to *Max Mayer, Esq., 88 Hatton Garden, London.*

Solomans and his wife walked together to the nearest post office to mail the conspicuously large package. Anyone watching, especially a seasoned thief, would know a box that large mailed from a jeweler's store contained something very precious. Solomans then sent a telegram to let Mayer know that the pearl necklace was on its way back, along with three other pearls valued around £1,500 for his consideration.

The pearls made their way from Rue de Provence into pigeonholes for the mail train to Calais, where the English representative signed for them and put them on the steamer for Dover Quay. The rain fell steadily that night, streaming along the ship's lights, as the necklace traveled through the whitecaps toward the windy shore. And at 3 A.M., the French night mail arrived at the Dover pier.

The superintendent for the foreign mail supervised as workers unloaded the bags from the ferry. The sealed bags of registered mail and packages were sorted immediately in a special room. A man named Edward Allen sorted the package addressed to Mayer, and after inspecting it, he reported to his superior that it was still intact. He then placed the package on the Town and Country train carriages, where it went into the registered mail car and remained under guard by special postal workers—regular mail carriers could not even enter the registered package train car. Then special sorters began organizing the packages into sealed bags to go to the country or those headed for town. The pearl necklace sat deep within the registered mail sack destined for London's Eastern Central District Office.

A dull dawn broke around 5 A.M., the rain clouds still hanging heavy over the Thames on the morning of July 16. The weather was unusually cool and hazy, even for London. It was one of the coldest summers in recent memory. Nonetheless, the city was already full of morning activity. Distant whistles signaled the arrival of morning trains. Men in rubber boots hosed down the streets, clearing them of horse manure and petrol. Factories along the river ignited soft coal, sending billows of smoke skyward.

At 6:20 A.M., the pearls arrived at the Eastern Central District Office, where they were assigned to the "32 table" for the Holborn neighborhood. Postal worker John Sinclair noticed the Mayer package because it was too large for the standard pigeonhole. He noted it on his log and, like those before him, found the package to be fully intact.

Exactly one hour later, Sinclair handed the mailbag containing the Mayer necklace to Postman Neville, who, dressed in his bright red-and-blue mail carrier uniform, walked out into the colorless, brisk morning to deliver the mail in Hatton Garden.

Neville's volunteer bag carrier that day was George Hollands; the two men had never worked together before. Hollands did not officially work for the post office and was not on the payroll. He held no allegiance to the post office and planned to be married in a little over a week, which probably made him an easy mark for bribery if the need should arise.

By 8 A.M., Silverman sat in his cramped office on the still-quiet Hatton Garden street with Gutwirth. It looked like a jeweler's office with tabletops of brooches, lockets, chains and gems, cardboard boxes holding paperwork, reels of silk for wrapping jewels, and a glass bottle of aqua fortis, a solution used to dissolve silver. He kept a close eye on his pocket watch. After weeks of observation, Silverman knew that Neville began at the bank at 112 Hatton Garden, on the corner of Holborn Circus. From there he walked up the block delivering to several of the shops until he reached 101 Hatton Garden. Silverman waited anxiously, and finally he heard the front door open.

Hollands stood outside on the sidewalk, holding the second mailbag. It was still early, quiet enough to hear the swallows chirping and watch the swifts fly out of eaves on scissor wings. Neville entered the building and, avoiding the lift operator, stomped wearily up three flights of stairs to hand Silverman his mail—including a large box wrapped in paper and tied with string. Neville was in the building for no more than two minutes before leaving and continuing up Hatton Garden with Hollands to deliver mail to another fourteen or so addresses, including Mayer's.

Quickly, Silverman moved inside his office, where he worked with Gutwirth to slice the package open and extract the pearls. The men worked quietly and rapidly, adept at the sleight of hand and focus needed by fingersmiths. One man rewrapped the box in fresh blue linen paper and reaffixed the torn mailing paper covered in stamps and French writing. The other set a ladle across a flame to melt the crimson wax. Then the men pressed the seal, MM, several times across the end of the package covering the tears where the mailing paper had been opened. The switch took only minutes.

Neville and Hollands continued up Hatton Garden. The first mailbag was empty by the time they reached the corner of Charles, and by 93 Hatton Garden, the second mailbag was considerably lighter. Neville stopped. He pulled a bundle of mail out and considered the weight of it. "I think you can go now," he said to Hollands. He thanked him for his help, and Hollands handed the empty bag back to the postman, turned, and headed back toward the post office for his pay. Neville walked on toward Mayer's office alone, switching the cumbersome bag from one shoulder to the other, and dropping back to a slower pace.

Meanwhile, Gutwirth pulled the door closed to Silverman's office, looked to be sure the lift operator did not see him, and hurried down the back staircase, walking swiftly up to Max Mayer's office at 88 Hatton Garden. No one took note of Gutwirth that drizzly morning, but then, the Hatton Garden neighborhood was a labyrinth of buildings, passageways, and back entrances. Since most of the buildings had once been residences, nearly all had rear doors through small alleyways and old stable yards. Gutwirth entered Mayer's building and stood in the dark hallway waiting for Neville. Once the postman arrived, Gutwirth silently slipped the package back into the mail sack before Neville knocked on Mayer's door to deliver the mail to the clerks. Then Neville left the building to make his way through the thickening yellow fog to deliver the last of the morning mail and return to the post office—perhaps with a stop at a pub on the way.

By then, Silverman had already handed the necklace over to James Lockett, and the pearls were on their way out of Hatton Garden.

❧

Max Mayer walked toward his office at nine-thirty that morning. The early morning rain had mosaicked the street with slick gravel, mud, and blackened cobblestone. Window washers cleaned glass storefronts streaked with raindrops and frosted with filth.

Mayer crossed over Charles Street and approached his building.

His office was four stories of simple, Edwardian architecture with blocks of stone and squared windows. A waist-high iron gate netted the front entry. Mayer raked his shoes across the boot scraper and opened the door to his office. He was met by two of his clerks, Mr. Dell and Mr. Woodward, both of whom had worked for Mayer for twenty years or more.

The package from Paris had arrived as planned, delivered by registered post, wrapped in brown paper and string, sealed in several places with *MM*. One of Mayer's clerks broke the red seals with his letter opener, unwrapped the light blue paper, popped the nails, and gingerly opened the small box while Mayer shuffled through other letters from the early morning post.

"Look," the clerk complained as he pulled out a piece of wrinkled newspaper. "What a dirty way in which to pack up the necklace. And why the sugar?"

Mayer looked up from his letters and peered into the package. Inside, the box was empty except for eleven cubes of French sugar and a scrap of newspaper, the *Écho de Paris*.

SEVEN

The Hunt Begins

MAYER PACED THE FLOOR OF HIS OFFICE, ORDERING HIS CLERK to send a telegram to Solomans in Paris: *Box arrived, but no pearls.* His impatience got the better of him, and almost as soon as he'd sent the telegram, Mayer had the other clerk place an expensive, static-filled long-distance call to Paris. Solomans, as nervous as Mayer, assured him that he did send the pearls—this was no dummy package.

Solomans and his wife left immediately to travel to London and help with the search. Solomans had at one time enjoyed a reputation much like Mayer's in the jewelry world, but he fell victim to one of the greatest scams of the time. Madame Thérèse Humbert, a poor French villager, managed to convince most of Paris society that she was a wealthy socialite awaiting her inheritance. She and her husband borrowed enormous amounts of money, services, clothes, and jewels from various people in Europe, as well as in America, all to be paid back by an inheritance that would never come. Solomans, like many others, lost most of his fortune to her in 1902. He had spent the last decade trying to earn it back by working as Mayer's Parisian liaison. He owed what business and livelihood he had to Mayer and could not afford to have his loyalties questioned.

Mayer's next call was to his underwriter at Lloyd's of London. Frank Beaumont Price of Price and Gibbs Assurance Assessors left as soon as he hung up the phone. His office was in a stately building at 1 Ely Place and the corner of Hatton Garden, so Price arrived at Mayer's office within minutes. The necklace was insured by a floating policy, meaning several investors had pooled money together to create the coverage. Now they were on the hook for a necklace—one they'd never even seen—insured for £135,000.

Price brought Alfred Leach along with him. Leach, who now worked as a consultant for Price and Gibbs, was a former superintendent from Scotland Yard. For nearly a decade before his retirement, Leach had held the Hatton Garden beat, and he'd followed Grizzard most days. Every now and then at a pub, Grizzard would shout over to the publican, "A cigar and a drink for Mr. Leach, please!" Leach would politely refuse, and Grizzard's smile would stretch thinly beneath his mustache.

At Price's urging, Mayer also called Scotland Yard directly and asked for the detective with the most experience in jewel heists: Chief Inspector Alfred Ward. After Leach retired, Ward had taken up many of his old cases as a "cruncher" for a number of jewel thieves, including Grizzard.

Ward seemed the antithesis of the suave detectives recently made famous in short stories and novels. In fact, one colleague remarked, "There is nothing Sherlock Holmes about Mr. Ward except his profession and his results." Ward had a milky-complexioned, cherubic face with flushed cheeks and a mouth flanked by a dark, walrus-tusk mustache. He looked more like a young banker than one of London's greatest detectives. Or as one newspaper described him, he seemed like someone who "belongs in a Parish and keeps a rose garden." In fact, the description wasn't too far off; there was something almost monastic about Ward's detective work. The descriptions didn't bother Ward—his appearance made it much easier to shadow suspects.

Ward called his closest Yardman in the area, Sergeant Cornish, who promised to meet him at Mayer's office as well. Ward left Scotland Yard's headquarters on the Victoria Embankment armed with his bulldog revolver, manacles clanking, wearing his navy uniform with three silver diamond patches sewn onto the sleeve. He headed toward Holborn Circus and Hatton Garden, entering a beat the Metropolitan Police knew well. He came up Holborn, passed Gamages' mishmash of department stores and the symmetrical buildings of new construction husked in scaffolding. He waved to a few "blues" making the rounds from Bow Street.

Holborn Circus was a wide thoroughfare surrounding a small circular center with a statue portraying Prince Albert on horseback. By midmorning, the roundabout was crowded with cars, a few horse-drawn carriages, double-decker buses, bicycles, and pedestrians, men prodding the ground with canes as they walked, ladies dragging their skirt trains across the mud.

The fog grew jaundiced as the smoke from river factories slowly made its way across the city. By afternoon, on bad days, it could become so dark that the streetlamps in Holborn Circus had to be lit. It lent London a feel of near-constant dusk. Ward could barely see from one street corner to the next amid the unfurling smog that greased windowpanes, blackened buildings, and made the air smell of fire smoke.

In spite of the smog, Ward looked for familiar faces or conspicuous characters carrying Gladstone bags or silk pocket purses as he turned onto Hatton Garden and walked beneath the serrated shadows of architecture, past the clock tolling time and its twin calendar clock. St. Andrew's Church chimed eleven times as he arrived at 88 Hatton Garden.

Entering the office, Ward greeted Mayer and Price. Cornish and Leach were already waiting as well and stood as Ward approached. He pulled out his notebook and ink pen and began to look over the evidence on the table—so far he had nothing more to go on than sugar cubes and a scrap of newspaper. He could not even be sure that the heist took place on English soil. The newspaper clipping from the *Écho de Paris* certainly pointed to French thieves. He used his handkerchief to collect the evidence—the scrap of newspaper, sugar, red wax seals, pale blue wrapping, mailing paper, and string— careful not to touch it with his own hands.

As a preliminary measure, Ward also wanted all avenues through which the necklace might be disposed of closed, and he sent detectives out to question local "smashers" and receivers who might try to sell the pearls. If the necklace had been stolen in London, he wanted to keep the pearls from disappearing into the criminal pipeline of the city's underworld.

Before leaving, Ward had a reward poster drawn, depicting the necklace, its dimensions, and a £10,000 reward. Thievery was a business, and rewards often enticed one thief to turn in another. And then he had two of his men, Sergeants Cooper and Haymann, begin distributing the reward posters and questioning pedestrians in Hatton Garden.

The curb traders crowded the streets, and as lunchtime approached, the pubs along Charles began filling with customers. The air carried the scent of bunched bluebells and lilac, ripened fruit, and various foods from the Leather Lane market.

One of the first men the police encountered was Lesir Gutwirth, who was standing outside of the Globe, leaning casually against the brick wall.

"Hullo, Haymann," he said cheerfully. "What are you doing around here?"

"I am looking for the pearls that were stolen from Mr. Mayer," Haymann answered.

Gutwirth smiled and shook his head. "You know they were never pinched. I suppose they were insured?"

How Gutwirth knew about pearls stolen only hours ago did not seem to bother the policemen. Nor did it occur to Gutwirth.

That night, Henri Solomans and his wife arrived in London on the ten forty-five train into Charing Cross. Mayer, Price, and Ward met them at the station and took them by motor down Whitehall, toward the Victoria Embankment, where New Scotland Yard headquarters stood. The streets were quieter late at night, the air had cooled even more, and the orbed streetlights glowed in the gauzy London air. The inquiry lasted all night; not until the early morning light bruised the sky did Ward, Solomans, and Mayer leave Scotland Yard.

That same day, Joseph Grizzard boarded a train in Paris and returned to London.

PART TWO

THE STING

EIGHT

New Scotland Yard

ON THE MORNING OF JULY 17, 1913, SCOTLAND YARD HEADQUAR-
ters cast a dim, geometric shadow against the street below. It was
cloudy, and the weather still felt unseasonably chilly, twenty degrees
cooler than a normal summer day. Ship masts moved sluggishly
inward, riding in on the high tide of the brackish Thames. Across
the river, the factories tufted morning coal smoke, and the clouds
of smog gathered and moved toward Westminster, wreathing the
buildings.

New Scotland Yard, made up of two buildings connected by a
sky bridge, was an intimidating fortress of dark red brick with white-
trimmed, angular dormer windows overlooking the river. Its Gothic
architecture, turrets, and spires gave it a castlelike, ominous appearance that was matched only by its grim beginnings—as construction
began along the Victoria Embankment in 1888, the dismembered
remains of a woman, rumored to be a Ripper victim, were found

wrapped in black cloth. No one was ever charged with the murder. In that sense, an unsolved mystery was literally the foundation upon which the world's most famous detective unit was built.

As the name *New* Scotland Yard implies, it was not the original location for the Metropolitan Police. The first police department sat between Whitehall and Great Scotland Yard—believed to be named either for the location where Scotland's diplomats used to stay or for Adam Scot, who owned the land in the thirteenth century. The Metropolitan Police became known as Scotland Yard, even when their headquarters moved and no longer warranted the name.

Alfred Ward entered New Scotland Yard through the back door. Already, a line of omnibuses and taxi motorcars sat idling, waiting to enter the ground floor to be examined for licenses. If the auto did not run properly or proved too noisy, it failed inspection. Ward climbed a flight of stone stairs and walked through the wide, bleak corridor to the offices of the Criminal Investigation Department, or CID, which was the detective unit of Scotland Yard. Only the chief commissioner and superintendent had their own offices; the rest of the CID's officers shared a large, oblong room echoing with the absence of furniture, rugs, artwork, or any other types of comfort. Desks sat up against the wall like a schoolroom with one large table at center, straight-backed wooden chairs surrounding it. It was an atmosphere of contrast—Gothic architecture and spare furniture paired with the greatest technology available at the time.

Ward sat at his desk and looked over the *Informations,* a newspaper printed on Scotland Yard's own on-site printing press to publish the latest news for the police and detectives. The fresh ink left stains on his hands. Upstairs, Ward could hear the faint, yet constant, ticking from the telegraph room as wires went out through London and abroad reporting and receiving information about crimes. The Yard also had its own photography unit, forensics lab, ballistics room, and the new fingerprinting division.

Ward stared at the notebook in front of him and pages of interviews from Henri Solomans and Max Mayer. Methodically, his mind outlined the gangs of thieves who worked out of Hatton Garden, the men or women currently serving time, and those working freely on the streets. He could have resorted to a long list of small-time jewel crooks among the crowds of buyers and businessmen in Hatton Garden; but for a job like this, he knew of only a handful of men experienced enough and clever enough to accomplish so brilliant a pull from one of London's best-known jewelers. If the thieves were even British—there was still a distinct possibility that the theft occurred in France. Ward had decades of experience in detection, but he had often insisted the most difficult cases to solve were not murders, but burglaries. Stolen jewelry had become so common that the police often filed it as "lost property" rather than theft.

Finally, Ward gathered his paperwork and headed to his superior's office for the "Council of Seven" meeting, where the six chief inspectors and superintendent met. The council was an elite group of the finest detectives, and they sat around the table and brought their unsolved cases to discuss, hoping collective thought could compass a solution. Oftentimes, a case could be solved before the men left the room.

This set of men, including Ward, became the most talented detective unit Scotland Yard ever produced. During their tenure, wireless telegraph was used for the first time to capture Dr. Hawley Harvey Crippen, who fled London after the murder of his wife; the fingerprinting system was created and later perfected by a Yardman; criminal profiling came into use; undercover work and shadowing became an art form; and forensics and ballistics flourished. And on that July morning in 1913, Ward undoubtedly carried under his arm a new file to present to the council—*The Pearl Heist.*

For all its progress, Scotland Yard's detective unit had a rough start. In 1829, home secretary Sir Robert Peel first opened the Metropolitan Police force to great opposition and wariness. The public considered it an infringement on personal liberties, and they were not entirely wrong. The primary need for a police force arose out of anarchist plots and political protests, which peaked in the mid-nineteenth century. In fact, the original location for Scotland Yard would be bombed during a Fenian anarchist attack in 1884, requiring relocation to a new building.

The other reason for a police force, however, simply came from the ever-expanding population and its growing criminal class. London had outgrown itself, spilling over the edges, past boundaries and any measure of control. Londoners acknowledged, with trepidation, that some organized, protective force was needed to serve as a floodgate.

The Metropolitan Police, also known as "bobbies" or "peelers" as a nod to Sir Robert Peel, served the public primarily by patrolling streets and the river as a deterrent to crime. In order to earn public trust, however, the Metropolitan Police had to lead exemplary and disciplined lives—they wore their uniforms even when not on duty to keep an open identity; they had to pass literacy and physical fitness tests; they were not allowed to grow beards, so many opted for the wide, bristled sideburns that became a trademark; they needed character references; they could not swear or consort with servants or drink to excess. In other words, they had to be above the criminal class in order to have the right to arrest them.

Soon, however, there came a need for a type of policeman that went beyond the current standards. Though police could often catch a criminal, there was rarely any evidence with which to convict him. It presented a chasm between the crime and the punishment for it. What was needed was a middleman to *solve* the case. This new type of special police would be trained to investigate the crime scene, put the pieces of the crime together, and establish a plausible chain of events to hand over to the prosecution. The term for these new investigators came from the Latin word *detectus,* which meant "to uncover," or "reveal." These trained officers henceforth became known as *detectives.* Although the word existed for some time, the term, as it applied to law enforcement, was an entirely new concept. The detectives would become the critical joint in the chain linking criminality to justice.

The public remained deeply suspicious, however. After all, this represented a significant intrusion on people's personal liberties—the idea of a gentleman knowingly deceiving people, prying into private lives. So, the first detectives at Scotland Yard were kept a secret. A handful of them infiltrated the public sector in plainclothes during the 1840s in order to follow anarchist activity. Despite the secrecy, the notion of a detective continued to gain clarity and garner attention.

In what became a sort of "detective fever," British novelists began to romanticize the concept. Edgar Allan Poe published the first real detective tale in "The Murders in the Rue Morgue" in 1841. Wilkie Collins's *Moonstone* in 1868 and Sir Arthur Conan Doyle's tales of Sherlock Holmes were not far behind. Charles Dickens, an admirer of London detectives, wrote an inspector into *Bleak House*. And Charlotte Brontë first wrote of a "sleuth-hound." While police certainly had their skills, the detective mind fascinated the public because it required a keen sort of intellect to unravel a mystery.

In spite of the literary endorsement, it wasn't until 1878 that Scotland Yard's detective unit finally became an official entity known as the Criminal Investigation Department. The acceptance standards for the CID proved substantially more difficult than the height requirements, good spelling, and solid character required for police. New recruits had to be over twenty-one and under twenty-seven years of age; must stand clear five feet nine inches without shoes or stockings; must be able to read well, write legibly, and have a fair knowledge of spelling; must be generally intelligent; and must be free of any bodily complaint such as flat foot, stiff joints, or deformities of the face, which were too recognizable to criminals. Often, the CID recruited directly to the detective unit rather than requiring applicants to work the police beat first—it stamped the CID with a perception of elitism that has persisted.

Alfred Ward never explained why he became drawn to a career as a detective, but he knew at a young age that he wanted to be a policeman. Perhaps it was the literary influence of the time, or maybe it simply arose out of his surroundings. His life, similar to Grizzard's, began in the 1860s in a poorer section of London known as

St. Pancras. Both Ward and Grizzard sought to rise above their circumstances.

Ward's father worked as a blacksmith, and his mother was a dressmaker. His father, however, discouraged Ward from pursuing a career in the Metropolitan Police, so Ward worked as a city clerk until he was of age. In 1881, Ward applied and was accepted to the police department and soon began patrolling the East End in his neatly ironed blue uniform. Incidentally, that would place Ward in the East End during the years a young Joseph Grizzard fine-tuned his criminal skills.

Ward never looked the part of crime-stopper. He had a round face and youthful appearance. Off duty, he wore a well-tailored morning coat with a modest hat and a gold chain in his waistcoat. One contemporary of Ward's wrote, "The real detective is a common place man. You would not pick him out of a crowd. He avoids large mannerisms. He is genial, but somewhat mysterious. He does not wear policeman's boots. He is a plain businessman with shrewd common-sense, trained to detect." But Ward's exterior belied a tenacious, bold, daring mind that impressed his superiors.

Ward showed an unusual talent for policing and for Sherlock Holmes's famed deductive reasoning. One day, while patrolling his beat, Ward saw a known thief hurrying down the street. The thief wore the customary shabby clothes, but Ward noticed a nice pair of polished boots on his feet.

"Where did you get those boots?" he asked the young man.

"Bought 'em with my own money two days ago!"

"Let's have a look at them," Ward said as he took the man back to the station for questioning. The thief continued to decry his innocence, insisting that he purchased the boots himself.

Ward grabbed the man's shoes and held them up to his superior. The price of the boots was still chalked on each sole. The thief reasoned that it was entirely possible for chalk to stay on the bottom of shoes for two days.

"Not when it's been raining," answered Ward.

In another case, Ward found the damning piece of evidence against a suspected murderer—a cloakroom ticket to a parcel left in the railway station—sewn into the silk lining of the killer's bowler hat.

Ward became one of the finest criminologists in the Metropolitan Police. It didn't take long for his superiors to take notice, and in spite of fierce competition, he was promoted to sergeant in the Criminal Investigation Department, entering their six-month training program. In addition to teaching the art of detection, the six months also kept future detectives off the street long enough that they would not be as easily identifiable from their days of patrolling. Every day, Ward took classes in safecracking, use of explosives, picking locks, fingerprinting, even learning to draw faces and features. He practiced "imprinting" or memorizing particular facial features.

Scotland Yard headquarters held a "Make-Up Room" for wigs, greasepaint, and accessories for its shadowers; but the CID had moved well beyond that, teaching detectives how to embody the character of a hawker, drunken diner, milkman, or street singer to blend into the neighborhood. Cheap theatrics and false wigs would not only put the detectives at risk among clever criminals, the costumes would be a hindrance during a struggle or arrest. So, playing the part became more organic. The plainclothes detectives didn't shave for several days or bathe. They wore down the heels of shoes and roughed up their clothes until they became the part they played.

Finally, the detectives in training took a written and oral exam in which physical descriptions were given, and the detectives had to home in on the most noticeable and identifiable traits, recalling any number of fine details about an individual's appearance.

As a matter of fact, Scotland Yard's pioneering of so many skillful detective techniques would inspire a similar unit across the pond called the Federal Bureau of Investigation.

One of Ward's first cases with the CID also became one of his most famous: the case of Thomas Neill Cream. A number of prostitutes in London's Lambeth area were turning up dead, poisoned with strychnine. Criminal profiling did not have its own department or even designated parameters at the time, but the detectives employed it as common sense in an investigation. Due to the length of time between murders and the proximity of the crime scenes to the Thames, the detectives reasoned that the murderer was most likely a seafaring gentleman or a foreigner who traveled to London often.

Around the same time, an American physician named Thomas Neill Cream began inserting himself into crime scenes and contacting police. He claimed to have an interest in the crimes as a medical man. However, in secret, Cream had been blackmailing other prominent citizens—including doctors—threatening to expose them as the "Lambeth Poisoner." In one of those letters, he specifically referred to victim Matilda Clover. When the physicians turned the letters over to Scotland Yard, the police soon caught on. Matilda Clover's recent death had been listed as the result of natural causes—Cream could not have known her death was a murder unless he was involved.

Sergeant Alfred Ward began shadowing Cream and later

reported that the American doctor "was watching women very narrowly indeed." Finally, the detectives asked the home secretary to have one of the bodies exhumed for examination to prove poisoning once and for all. And true to the Victorian attitude toward scientific accuracy at all costs, the forensic scientists tasted some of the residue from the body and found it to be bitter like poison. They then injected a frog with the substance to prove it was lethal. The detectives also contacted the American police, who, as it turns out, had already imprisoned Dr. Thomas Neill Cream after several of his patients died following suspicious operations he performed. When he was released, Cream had immediately fled the States for London.

In 1892, Cream was sentenced to death and hanged. It was widely rumored that his last words as he climbed the gallows were "I am Jack the . . ." Many believe Cream attempted to take credit for the Jack the Ripper murders, but as he was in prison in the United States at the time of several of the killings, there doesn't seem to be any truth to it. In all likelihood, it was Cream's last vain attempt at notoriety.

The idea of a criminal inserting him- or herself into a case or coming in contact with the police can be used as a tool in profiling, and it happened often enough that Scotland Yard began viewing any anonymous sources with skepticism. In one instance, a gentleman visited the headquarters to offer information on a crime. He was led into a waiting room until a detective could interview him. While he waited, he noticed several other business gentlemen and clerks in the room either working or reading the newspaper. What he did not notice was that they were all actually plainclothes detectives, lowering the pages of a newspaper every so often, to study and imprint the features of the "anonymous gentleman" should he turn up to be involved in the very crime he was reporting.

Ward's star continued to rise. He proved instrumental in yet another poisoning case when Frederick Seddon convinced a tenant to sign over her finances, and in return, he promised to take care of her. And that he did—with arsenic. Ward traced Seddon's purchase of poisoned flypaper as part of the evidence. Like Cream, he was convicted and hanged at the gallows.

Ward's talents went beyond shadowing and deductive reasoning, however. He also knew how to trap a criminal. In a case involving anonymous, slandering letters, Ward had every postage stamp sold within a certain area marked. He also had two local stationery stores mark their papers and envelopes as well. When the next anonymous letter arrived, it didn't take long to trace it to a local woman. It was a woman the police knew; she had inserted herself in the case, complaining about letters *she* had received in an attempt to throw off the police.

By the end of the year, Ward was awarded the Howard Vincent Cup for "the most meritorious piece of work in connection with the detection of crime." Vincent, a barrister, had been one of the leading forces in developing a detective unit at Scotland Yard. He studied French police practices and wrote an argument in 1878 in favor of creating a detective branch in the UK. The cup named for him was awarded each year to the most successful detective. It was a great honor for Ward and a unanimous decision among his colleagues. A detective in the unit described Ward as "one of the keenest, most subtle brains at Scotland Yard." Another said that Ward handled more famous cases in a year than most detectives handled in a lifetime. And, soon, Ward was promoted to chief inspector.

～

As forensics continued to flourish, so did criminology—a scientific study of how criminals think and behave. Detectives had to follow disparate sets of clues and think not as English gentlemen but as criminals. That was Ward's strong suit.

Criminal profiling was one of the newer methods detectives employed—it meant using a system of clues from a crime scene to evoke a criminal type. It would later evolve into a tool used to hunt down serial offenders who left an individual "signature" behind at each crime scene.

One of the earliest examples of criminal profiling involved the case of Jack the Ripper. The profile Scotland Yard put together claimed that at least five of the Whitechapel murders had been committed by the same man. They believed the Ripper was a raging misogynist based on his violent treatment of the bodies and the fact that all of his victims were women. The profile described him as a physically strong man who would appear harmless and neatly attired to anyone who passed him on the streets. He wore a cloak in order to disguise the blood on his clothes when leaving the crime scene. The profile also stated that, in addition to being mentally unstable and a loner, the Ripper could not be a surgeon or a butcher because his cuts were too rudimentary. As the Ripper case remains unsolved, there's no way to know if the profile is accurate or not.

Profiling changed detective work, putting the focus on the criminal rather than the crime. With a profile to work with, detectives could narrow the choices and focus on a few select individuals. This generalized thinking could at its best establish patterns of behavior and, at its worst, become patently prejudicial. The latter is obvious in some of the detective notes from the time period. A top investigator who would later become one of "The Big Four" at Scotland Yard, wrote that "The cleverest criminals in a broad way are Jews. The cleverest thieves are, in my opinion, undoubtedly born Cockneys."

As was typical with the Victorian and Edwardian eras, profiling was also steeped in science or pseudoscience, some of it questionable at best. It often involved unusual physical features like ear size or skull shape and unattractive personality traits. Illustrations of Victorian criminals show them to be obviously disfigured, caricatures more than reality. Foreheads are noticeably large, ears look swollen and protruding, eyes bulge with lids at half-mast, mouths hang open awkwardly. They look like partially evolved humans.

The caricatures extended beyond facial characteristics as well. A leading scientist of the time profiled criminals in general as deficient in many qualities, physically unattractive, lacking sympathy for others, and bearing no sense of duty. Criminals, he believed, were inherently selfish and did not possess the self-control necessary to maintain family relationships or live within normal society.

Interestingly, Joseph Grizzard defied every attribute given in criminal profiles.

NINE

News

THE THEFT OF THE PEARL NECKLACE IMMEDIATELY MADE THE front page in the newspapers. Mayer, indignant but more than a little flattered by the sudden attention, fanned his feathers and told the *Daily Sketch,* "Don't ask me a word about it, for I can neither confirm nor deny the report. As a matter of fact, I am pledged to say nothing until tomorrow morning."

Grizzard undoubtedly followed the story. One of his favorite places to spend an afternoon was London's famed Café Royal on Regent Street. It carried not only the English papers, but the French ones as well, and as the restaurant had been opened several decades before by a Parisian fleeing the law in France, Grizzard might have felt particularly at ease there. The decor was opulent and gilded, the lunches long and wine-laden, and the clientele included Oscar Wilde during his lifetime, Home Secretary Winston Churchill, as well as a number of London aristocrats and travelers from the Continent—including several who worked as international jewel thieves.

In the days following the heist, with the London social season well under way and the Royal Garden Party only days later, the newspapers teemed with sensational stories. The daily papers had a large London following during the Victorian and Edwardian Ages—there were hundreds in circulation at the time. They gave special focus to crime, with gruesome stories of bodies found in cellars, white slavery in the East End, murders of jealous spouses, even a corpse discovered by a cat. The papers also covered some less weighty matters such as an editorial in the *Daily Sketch* "Debating the Sinfulness of Sunday Golf."

The summer of 1913 had its fair share of frivolity. The papers reported on the "tango teas," afternoon parties designed around the Latin dance. Gray proved to be the fashionable color of the season, and the hats became more extravagant with osprey feathers and tulle. There was also a growing fascination that summer with the Russian Romanov family—Czar Nicholas, his wife, their charming children, and pet wolf. And much attention was paid to the fact that the Americans were winning at Wimbledon.

There were more foreboding headlines as well. Tensions in Europe continued their steady boil when war broke out between Bulgaria and Serbia, but most disconcerting was news from Germany. In recent years, Germany's economy had caught up to Britain's, their population soared, and now the German Empire had the ability to mobilize 4.5 million troops, while England could count on less than a million. Britain had long feared Germany would invade the United Kingdom and headlines continued to reflect that. The *Illustrated London News* reported on the new 450-foot "air-ships," designed by Herr Zeppelin, displayed in Germany, and the latest science news heralded AIR SCOUTING BY WIRELESS. But the fear became palpable as news coverage focused on new battleships, all part of the growing naval arms race between the United Kingdom and Imperial Germany.

On June 16, however, as Grizzard thumbed through the dailies, the theft of the pearl necklace dominated headlines: LOST PEARL NECKLACE. THE GREAT PEARL MYSTERY. THEFT OF THE PEARL NECKLACE. THE MISSING JEWELS. The *Daily Chronicle* reported that "It appears certain that the pearls were abstracted on French soil, as the lumps of sugar were of the shape generally used on the Continent." The *Star* came to the same conclusion: "The sugar was of French manufacture, and this with the presence of a scrap of French newspaper makes it clear that the robbery took place in Paris." Even the London *Times* seemed to agree. A few papers suggested the possibility that the French clues were part of a ruse. Still others believed the substitution took place before the package even made it to the post office.

As news of the theft spread, one clever detective remarked that the pearl necklace would probably be found sitting around the neck of the missing Mona Lisa portrait, which had been stolen in 1911 and remained at large. Grizzard must have found that one especially amusing.

❧

Ward spent much of that week poring over the headlines as well in the sparse, desk-lined office of the CID with clippings about the theft spread out in front of him or tacked onto the walls. He also kept the scrap of the *Écho de Paris* on display as evidence. On the wooden tabletop, plans of Hatton Garden were drawn and mapped. Detailed photos of the dark red seals and torn package wrapping were printed and labeled. Copious notes were made. Ward dispatched officers to the train stations and docks to watch for known thieves, while he continued interviewing witnesses.

Ward began by investigating the path of the necklace and focused on the likelihood that the theft took place in the French mail system. After tedious interviews, inquiries, and notes—with much irritation on the part of the French—Ward finally ascertained that the necklace was never alone or vulnerable to theft while on French soil. That meant, in all probability, that British thieves had stolen the pearls in London. Beyond that, Ward had almost no evidence to link the theft to any particular burglar or receiver.

What's more, the evidence he had sent to the anthropometric department for fingerprint analysis turned up nothing. By the time of the pearl heist, fingerprinting had been in use for some time at Scotland Yard. Sir Edward R. Henry, who later worked as the head commissioner of the CID, invented a numerical system for identifying fingerprints that expanded on the earlier one known as the Galton System. Essentially, Galton, a cousin of Charles Darwin, identified fingerprints by three distinct patterns: the arches, loops, and whorls. Henry used those classifications and took them one step further—he added a mathematical formula pigeonholing those patterns into separate groups that could be used to catalog fingerprints and suspects.

In the case of the pearls, however, problems existed. For one thing, the package had traded hands at least eight times before arriving at Mayer's office. For another, any prints lifted from the box would have to match prints already on file, and the system was too new to have a large enough collection of prints. With all of the collected evidence organized before him, Ward began to fear that none of it would lead to the necklace.

Ward's meetings with the "Council of Seven" continued daily as he discussed the case with his most qualified and talented colleagues. As an acquaintance of Ward remarked, "The detective of fiction relies upon individual brilliance; the detective of fact relies upon teamwork and routine." Another detective later wrote, "The order in which those facts are collected is of small importance compared to adding them together so that a conclusion may be formed. It is in getting *all* the facts that a detective proves himself."

A superintendent named Frank Froest, who had been Ward's mentor in several cases, often boasted that he did not find Sherlock Holmes very impressive—in spite of the fact the two were often compared to each other. For Froest, the emphasis in detection was on the criminal himself, a theory that he had used to great success. As a detective, Froest proved something of an enigma—bullish-looking, yet charming and "a great dresser." He was described as brutish, yet also had "delicate hands." His talent, however, was undisputed. Froest had been the lead officer in the capture of Dr. Harvey Crippen. He had also been involved in bringing down several international jewel thieves.

In focusing on the criminal rather than the crime, Froest believed that detectives could capitalize on errors made. Criminals, he argued, were too egotistical to pay attention to the details and, therefore, often made mistakes. "We of Scotland Yard are much indebted to them," he once said.

Ward hoped that sooner or later one of those mistakes would come to light in the pearl case.

On July 23, the skies over London darkened, the window light in the CID grayed. Wind whipped the flags and rattled tree limbs. The Thames whitecapped. Gale-force winds blew, creating "a cyclonic disturbance." It was one more instance of the strange weather affecting the city that summer.

Two days later came the first break in the case—a response to the reward bulletin circulating the neighborhood. An anonymous letter arrived at the insurance offices of Price and Gibbs, marked *Strictly Private,* and read: "Gentlemen, I am an engraver and was asked some weeks ago to engrave a seal. I have no doubt it was for the purpose of the pearl robbery. Not wishing my name mentioned, kindly put an advertisement in the personal column of the *Evening News* to-morrow as to my procedure in the matter. Yours faithfully, Engraver."

At the bottom of the page, he added in pencil, "Enclosed find the impression of one I did from verbal instructions, but was, I think, not used. Did another, which I think was used. Have just seen reproduction in *Lloyd's News.* Put an ad in such a way that no one else will understand as I have reason to think I'd be in danger if known. I am giving you this information because I know the people who gave me the instructions and their whereabouts."

The next day, the *Evening News* carried the following personal ad: *Will engraver please give full particulars or some address or make appointment for confidential interview? P and G.*

The man in question—Peter Robertson Gordon—arrived at

their offices a few days later with a detailed recounting of his meeting at the Leather Bottle and the seals he created for a local jeweler whose name he did not remember. The insurance assessors turned over the information to the police, who promised to investigate it further. The detectives were overwhelmed with tips—too many turned out to be misunderstandings at best and attempts at slander at worst.

After that initial break in the case, hope for the return of the jewels waxed briefly and then waned once again. Mayer lamented that thieves clever enough to steal the pearl necklace probably had sufficient funds to lie low for some considerable time until the police search died down. At that point, the thieves would be free to escape London and the pearls smuggled through the Suez Canal to India, where the necklace would be broken down, sold, and lost for good.

TEN

Decoys

AUGUST 4, 1913, BEGAN THE DUSK OF ENGLAND'S GOLDEN ERA—
exactly one year later, Britain would declare war on Germany, changing London—and the world—forever. The Belle Époque would
wither away. It also became a fateful date in the jewel heist.

On August 4, the French police officially posted their investigation results and found that the theft had not taken place in France.
A French inquiry agent assigned to the case spoke publicly about
the lost pearls and the handsome reward. When asked, "Whom do
you suspect?" the agent laughed and said, "Everybody. That is my
business!" Throughout France, word of a 250,000 franc (or £10,000)
reward spread.

On that same day, a twenty-seven-year-old French jewel trader
named Samuel Brandstatter walked through the old-world streets
of Antwerp. Brandstatter was a smaller man, but well dressed with
a clean-shaven face and a new, stylish fedora tipped rakishly to the

right. He made his way through the city with its fortresses, walls, and elaborate skyline of sharp points and steep angles like a mountain range of architecture. In the distance, smoke gathered in the breeze coming off the harbor and hollow-sounding ship horns bellowed. In addition to all its topographical beauty, Antwerp had a long history as one of the world's finest diamond and gem centers. Jewelers from all over the world traveled there, much like Hatton Garden in London and Rue Lafayette in Paris. As Brandstatter strolled through the diamond district, he came face-to-face with a distant cousin of his named Lesir Gutwirth.

Brandstatter and Gutwirth had conducted business a few times over the past four years, and they were pleased to see each other. Gutwirth, talkative as ever, chatted about the jewel trade and possible sales, though he seemed to have something else on his mind, and he cryptically referred to a secret he would like to discuss with Brandstatter. Finally, the two men agreed to meet at the Terminus Hotel the following day.

It was then that Gutwirth became more direct, asking Brandstatter if he ever purchased gems on a large scale. Brandstatter told him that he could purchase merchandise only up to 200,000 francs. Gutwirth scoffed at the amount and bragged that he was looking for someone willing to pay a million francs or more. Leaning in, he added that it had to do with the Max Mayer necklace stolen almost a fortnight ago. When Brandstatter pushed for more details, Gutwirth answered, "The pearls are in the hands of friends in London." The two men parted ways, and Gutwirth promised to send Brandstatter "further particulars."

In spite of their relationship as cousins and colleagues, Brandstatter apparently felt no allegiance toward Gutwirth, and almost immediately he made plans to collect on the £10,000 reward money. He returned to Paris and discussed the plan with his wife. If their motivation was anything other than money, it never came to light. Brandstatter, who spoke almost no English, realized he needed an ally in this plan, so he contacted yet another cousin named Myer Cohen Quadratstein, a calculating and clever man, who soon took over the plans.

Quadratstein, like Brandstatter, was in his late twenties and also part of the diamond industry. He had been born in London, but lived mainly in Paris, where he frequently did business with Brandstatter. As closely knit as the jewel trade was, Quadratstein had also done business with Gutwirth before, acting as an intermediary in the sale of sapphires to the infamous "Cammi" Grizzard.

Two weeks after the Antwerp trip, Brandstatter had still heard nothing from Gutwirth, so he wrote to him pretending to have an interested buyer in France. Gutwirth sent him a telegram the next day in German and told him that a letter would soon follow. The letter arrived, written in Yiddish, which was then translated for the French-speaking Brandstatter.

2 Charles Street,
Hatton Garden

My dear Samuel,

I am now writing to you explicitly that you shall leave to-morrow for London and send me a telegram when you are leaving. I will then meet you at the station and we can arrange matters. Bring with you 1½—you know what I mean—what we have spoken

*about. Now, dear Samuel, about what you have told me that you
can get the 1½. If you can come yourself I shall be very pleased,
but if the man does not want to give it to you he can come with
you, but be sure that the man is all right. Bring with you what I
am asking you . . .*

Yours always loving,
Lesir

Brandstatter read it aloud to Quadratstein, who thought about
the next move, one that would prick Gutwirth's ego. He told Brandstatter to respond immediately with the following message: "Please
send a photograph of the necklace or a few pearls on approval so
that we should be able to convince our would-be buyer that it was
really the string belonging to Mr. Mayer."

Gutwirth sent him a wire in response:

COME AT ONCE. TELEGRAPH IF LEFT.

Brandstatter and Quadratstein discussed the matter and decided
to keep the police out of the plan for the moment. Instead, the two
men packed quickly and took the ferry, then train, arriving in Charing Cross at 10:45 P.M. on August 15—exactly one month since the
pearl necklace itself made the fateful trip from Paris to London. The
whistle echoed as the train pulled into the station, which was nearly
empty at that time of night. Through the ridge-and-furrow ceiling,
a full moon cast blue-white light across the floor. Waiting for them
in the doorway was Gutwirth.

The next morning, Brandstatter, Quadratstein, and Gutwirth

had a typical English breakfast together—eggs, tomatoes, mushrooms, toast. Then the three men took the electric tram from Islington to Hatton Garden, dropping off their luggage at a nearby cloakroom en route. The men wore their finest suits, cuff links, and hats. They carried calling cards and other tools of the trade common among jewelers.

Making their way up Holborn, the men turned onto Kingsway, London's widest street and one of its most modern. They walked beneath newly planted trees beside a broad roadway. Electric trams passed by them on the streets, and the Underground quaked below. While much of the architecture remained neoclassical along the block, some, like the new Kodak building, was starkly contemporary. It was a street that would impress any foreigner.

At half-past ten, the men arrived at the Lyons tea shop for the arranged meeting. They sat at a small iron table and ordered coffee from the "Gladys," or tea-shop waitress. Then they waited for whomever it was Gutwirth seemed so anxious to see—he still had not given them any details as to whom they would be meeting. Though the pastry and sweets display in the front window obscured some of the view, through the glass the men saw a gentleman walk casually by the front door. The man strolled by, blasé, but he stood out in the crowd—noticeably taller than those around him, with broad shoulders and an expensive suit. Wisps of cigar smoke caught the breeze behind him.

Gutwirth nervously stood and stepped outside to meet the gentleman while Brandstatter and Quadratstein remained inside watching cautiously, stirring coffee, picking at pastries, and pulling out coins for the check. After a few minutes, Gutwirth signaled to the other two men to join the stranger on the crowded sidewalk, and that was the first time they met the legendary Joseph Grizzard in person. It unnerved both Brandstatter and Quadratstein, who had heard much of the "King of the Underworld." If they appeared nervous, however, it didn't bother Grizzard, or he had grown used to it. He stared them in the eyes, looking downward at the two shorter men. His manner was polite, professional, cordial. Then he directed the men toward the corner stop as a red, boxy omnibus approached, and the four men climbed aboard, headed up Holborn.

The men remained quiet on the ride, saying nothing to one another, looking out the window at the advertisements, which seemed to cover every upright surface with words of all sizes and scripts. It must have been disconcerting for Brandstatter especially, who could not read English, much less follow the conversations around him.

The bus came to a stop on a chaotic corner busy with morning commuters, traffic, and street peddlers. Below, the Tube grumbled and steam billowed out of the grates. Grizzard suddenly stepped off the bus into a cloud of steam, and the other three men jumped off to follow. Neither Brandstatter nor Quadratstein knew what to expect, and Grizzard seemed intent on keeping them guessing.

Under the great arched windows of a Lipton tea shop, the men followed Grizzard as he entered through glass doors silvered by the overcast sky. The restaurant had tile floors and iron tables, so noise from other customers echoed loudly through the tea shop. Grizzard greeted the proprietor warmly and asked if the smoking room was available. He was told that it was not, but that the gentlemen were free to smoke in the main dining room.

Following Grizzard's lead, Gutwirth, Brandstatter, and Quad-ratstein chose a corner table, farthest from the door, and ordered tea and coffee. While they waited to be served, Grizzard continued to look casually around the room—almost bored—watching ladies in their broad-brimmed summer hats hook porcelain teacups on gloved fingers and gentlemen sit straight-backed, buttoned up. Smiling nonchalantly at Brandstatter, he remarked, "Beastly weather we're having, isn't it?"

When Grizzard seemed confident that no detectives or police were present, he reached into his jacket and fished out a cigarette, tapped his pockets for a lighter, and after finding none, looked around him for a light. He turned to a stranger wearing a tweed cap and a white silk scarf sitting at a nearby table.

"Have you a match?" he asked graciously.

Without a word, the gentleman pulled a box of matches out of his coat pocket and tossed it onto the table in front of Grizzard. Grizzard thanked him, lit his cigarette, and then leaned over the table toward Brandstatter and Quadratstein as he opened the Bryant & May matchbox completely.

"A pretty piece of work," he said with a smile.

Inside the box, resting on a tuft of cotton, sat three of the largest, most beautiful pearls the men had seen in their years of jewel trading. Fleshy pink with a warm golden glow to them, the pearls lived up to their reputation.

"Are you convinced it is the string?" Grizzard asked.

"Well, are you satisfied that they are real pearls?" Gutwirth added proudly.

"I'm satisfied that they are genuine pearls," Quadratstein answered, "but there's no proof they belong to Max Mayer."

Gutwirth held his hands up in mock offense and said, "Don't call him that—call him MM!"

Quadratstein ignored Gutwirth and continued: "I can't be sure until I weigh them and see if they match the weight published in the paper."

Grizzard was quiet for a moment, and then added, "That seems reasonable."

His eyes still on the Frenchmen, he said to Gutwirth, "Take them someplace nearby with jeweler's scales to weigh the pearls."

As Gutwirth led Brandstatter and Quadratstein outside, he looked around him, edgy and birdlike. He led the men quickly down a dark walkway toward the George public house, where they could weigh the pearls upstairs in a private room. But first, he handed the matchbox to Brandstatter to carry. He didn't want to be caught holding the pearls if any detectives stopped them. While Gutwirth and the two Parisians weighed the pearls nearby, Grizzard and Lockett—the man in the tweed cap and white silk scarf—waited patiently, sipping their coffee.

When the pearls were weighed, Quadratstein recorded the weight in his notebook and then threaded the three pearls on a strand of silk, sealed on one end with Brandstatter's seal and on the other with his own. It was the usual way to identify pearls sent on approval. He boxed them up, tucked them in his pocket, and the three men walked back out onto Holborn just after noon.

On their way back toward the tea shop, Brandstatter and Quadratstein remained nervous. They were in a foreign country, playing a part, attempting to deceive London's most notorious fence—Grizzard's reputation and vast number of gang members would intimidate any amateur. As the two men made their way back, the lunch crowds gathered on the sidewalks, and Brandstatter and Quadratstein pushed their way through the sea of boater hats and parasols when, suddenly, a familiar face appeared among them. Grizzard stood firmly there, the crowds parting around him, and held his hand out, waiting for the return of the pearls. Quadratstein pulled the box of pearls out of his pocket, handed them to Grizzard, and doing his best to sound confident said that he believed they belonged to the Mayer necklace after all.

Pleased, Grizzard answered, "The price is one million francs, nonnegotiable." He added that an American buyer was also interested if the price proved too steep for them. The 1-million-franc price tag was still a substantial sum, comparable to about £40,000. Though it represented close to only one-third of the necklace's real worth, it could still provide a nice sum for Grizzard. As receiver, he put up £4,000, would sell the necklace for £40,000, pay his three gang members about £3,500 each, and pocket £25,500 in profit. Today, that amount would be worth almost £1.6 million (or $3 million)—not bad pay for six months of work and little risk involved. He gave the men time to travel to Paris, discuss the price with the buyer, and return to London, where they all agreed to meet at the First Avenue Hotel on August 22.

Still a little unnerved, and undoubtedly surprised that their plan had worked, the two Frenchmen walked back to the cloakroom to collect their luggage and then took a taxi to the Charing Cross station just in time for the Continental boat train's departure. They waited in the station for a long time, conversing only in German or French, looking cautiously around them for any signs of Gutwirth or members of the Grizzard Gang. When Brandstatter and Quadratstein felt sure they were not being watched, they took a cab back into the city to the Great Eastern Hotel near the Liverpool Street station. It was another of the great railroad hotels for travelers, but this one was farther east, near the East End, but still several blocks from Hatton Garden and Holborn.

As their taxi approached the colossal Victorian hotel, the two men pulled out the flyer they had hidden in their luggage to contact Price and Gibbs about the reward offered. The Frenchmen checked into a joint room, and Brandstatter sat down to the desk and wrote to his wife, enclosing a letter registered express. He asked her to post it from Paris, addressed to Gutwirth. Meanwhile, Quadratstein stayed behind in the lobby, closing the privacy door to the phone box and dialing the phone number for the insurer of the necklace. By the time Quadratstein set the earpiece back on its hook, he had an appointment scheduled for Tuesday morning.

Frank Beaumont Price of Price and Gibbs assurance assessors was young and very successful for his age. Tall, thin, well mannered, and impeccably dressed, Price would have been called dapper or even debonair by his contemporaries. Price had spent the last four weeks interviewing any and everyone who might know something about the missing necklace, and the phone call from Quadratstein was the first credible clue since the theft.

On Tuesday morning, Price arrived at the Great Eastern Hotel, climbing out of the taxi in the cool shadow of massive architecture and sepia-colored brick. He entered the lobby unimpressed by its ornate moldings and Oriental rugs as he strode across the marble floors to meet the two men in their private room.

Price sat patiently upright, wearing his round, wire-rimmed glasses, listening to their story, and taking copious notes—he liked detailed records on every aspect of a case. Quadratstein did most of the talking since Brandstatter spoke so little English, but even without the language barrier, Quadratstein seemed the gentleman with all the ideas. As he listened, Price remained wary, but still interested in their plan. The two Frenchmen wanted to lure the thieves into a trap by offering to buy the pearls, or at least part of the necklace, like a normal jewel trade. They had earned the trust of Gutwirth, who had intimate knowledge of the heist and the whereabouts of the necklace.

As Price left their hotel, he climbed into a waiting taxi and used the short ride down London Wall to his office on Holborn Circus to think through the situation before him. He realized that the gang of thieves holding the necklace would spare no expense in protecting themselves, which meant all of his future dealings with Brandstatter and Quadratstein might be observed by any one of Grizzard's gang members. Once he arrived at his office, Price phoned Max Mayer to give him the good news and to ask who should pose as the interested French buyer offering 1 million francs for the pearl necklace.

In the meantime, Brandstatter contacted his wife and asked her to post the letter he had sent her, addressed to Gutwirth, from a Parisian post office. The letter informed Gutwirth that the two Frenchmen had met with a buyer, and he seemed confident that the pearls were genuine, but expressed doubt that the thieves might hold the entire necklace in their possession.

Gutwirth was indignant. He telegrammed back in Yiddish: *London. I have received your letter and am astonished that your man should believe that I have only what you have seen. Therefore, my dear Samuel, you must come, and send me a wire. Bring one, and we shall only ask the money of you after you have seen the whole thing. I wish to remark that if you play about with me you will be sorry, as I can dispose of it at once to a foreigner today. Your friend, L. Gutwirth.*

Brandstatter and Quadratstein replied that they would return to London immediately—which in reality would be a simple trip across town. The next morning, the two men quickly checked out of the Great Eastern Hotel and hurried toward the equally stunning First Avenue Hotel on Holborn. The three-hundred-room hotel was grand and fashionable, with towering fluted columns, stained glass, marbled floors, and deeply beveled Venetian mirrors. The men hurried through the lobby taking brief notice of the fragrant spray flowers, large tropical plants, and colorful glazed tiles.

Upstairs, the two Frenchmen settled into their suite and dropped their valises in the wardrobe just before Gutwirth arrived in the lobby at noon. He took the wide, rounded staircase up to the next floor and knocked on the door to room 197, where Brandstatter and Quadratstein, breathless, sat waiting for him.

All of the rooms in the First Avenue Hotel were spacious suites with one or two bedrooms and elegantly decorated sitting rooms with silk fabrics and mantled fireplaces. Gutwirth moved quickly through the doorway into their suite, closing and locking the door behind him. Brandstatter and Quadratstein did their best to appear calm and professional, betraying no sense of uncertainty. As Gutwirth sat down in one of the plush chairs, Quadratstein explained in greater detail that they had found a buyer in Paris who wanted to begin negotiations. Gutwirth listened and smiled—not only did he have a buyer barely a month after the necklace had been stolen, but he was getting the price Grizzard wanted.

Then he leaned in to ask a very revealing question: Had Quadratstein made it clear to the Parisian buyer that an additional 5 percent commission would be needed for Gutwirth?

Both Brandstatter and Quadratstein remained silent at that comment. Gutwirth, never particularly adept at perceiving subtle or awkward silences, ignored their blank looks and underscored the tempting offer once again.

"You shall have it for a million francs," he whispered. "Also, I shall want one hundred thousand francs for myself as a commission. It is not every day that you get a chance like this." He kept his voice low and leaned in uncomfortably close. "Just think, it is a necklace for which you will get a hundred thousand pounds. For a million francs, it is yours."

Leaning back and smiling coyly, he emphasized that his partners, including Grizzard, could know nothing about the commission.

ELEVEN

The Expert

AS THE GLORIOUS TWELFTH OF AUGUST ARRIVED, MOST OF THE upper echelons retreated to the countryside in northern England and Scotland for the beginning of the red grouse shooting season. The grouse are driven from the moors, fluttering on young wings into the sky. Red grouse are followed by partridge and pheasant seasons, which keep the gentry in the countryside among shooting parties for most of autumn. That year, King George V himself would bag over a thousand grouse. For the Britons not wearing tweed and carrying sidelocks, the Glorious Twelfth marks the last weeks of summer holiday and drives an impressive covey of Londoners into the countryside or to the shore to enjoy cloud-dappled skies and landscapes papered in greens and blues.

Jim Lockett decided to return a kind favor to several friends and family members who had helped him during the months of his wife's illness. His friends the Moores had taken him and his daughter to the country shortly after the death of his wife in May. This time, Lockett treated the Moores to a two-week reprieve from the city in Southampton. Lockett also invited his in-laws, the Atkinsons, on the extended holiday. Mary Ann Atkinson was Becky Lockett's sister. Not only had the two been close, but Mary Ann had also nursed Becky through much of her illness and was with her when she finally passed away. And Lockett included among the group his niece Catherine Finn, the daughter of his sister. Catherine helped take care of Lockett's nine-year-old daughter, Ellen, called Nellie.

Lizzie Moore took Nellie Lockett and her own daughters early to Southampton, settling in on the twelfth. Lockett, however, had business in the city and promised to join them in a few days. The traveling party occupied several rooms along the first floor of Scullard's Hotel on Above Bar.

Southampton was a popular tourist destination, known best as the port from which the *Titanic* sailed the year before. It was a maritime town with quaint shops and air brined by the sea. Above Bar, a street named for its relative position to Bar or Barre Street, had large T-shaped light posts running through the center of a broad cobblestone road lined with shops. The Alexandra Cinema stood next door to Scullard's Hotel, though Lockett's party spent most of their time outside of the city rather than at the movies or shopping.

Although he remained vague about his travel plans, when Lockett could get away from his business, he took the train to Southampton and joined the motoring party. Each day, the group, including a chauffer Lockett hired named Lloyd, left the hotel to go motoring through the countryside or to take ferry trips to the

Isle of Wight. The guests didn't return until seven or eight each night, when they "garaged" the car nearby.

Scullard's Hotel most likely had a safe. Or perhaps there was a secure bank nearby. Or maybe the screwsman himself proved an impenetrable vault. But somewhere in Southampton, Lockett had hidden the pearl necklace.

A few times over the following week, Simon Silverman visited Lockett there. Another associate joined the motoring party for a few days as well, a charming, finely dressed gentleman named Mr. Goldsmith. Only later did Lockett's sister-in-law and niece learn that Mr. Goldsmith was also known as Joseph Grizzard.

∽

While the thieves continued to travel between London and Southampton, Max Mayer and Frank Price searched for the right Parisian "buyer" to work with Brandstatter and Quadratstein in their negotiations with the thieves. It would take someone who could be discreet, tactful, and able to pass as a Parisian receiver. And, more importantly, he had to have enough knowledge of pearls to be able to ascertain if the thieves actually held the real Mayer necklace. They settled on a man named Max Spanier. Spanier was Latin in heritage, born in France, raised in England, and he would be required to speak German to the thieves. This cultural amalgam of a man also operated a jewel shop on Rue Lafayette in Paris. He was the perfect choice.

Price wrote to Spanier explaining the delicacy of the situation, "Above all things you must not come to my office, because I am being shadowed, and it would spoil everything if it were known that you and I were in collaboration." Price was right to be concerned about shadowing thieves. Grizzard already had gang members watching the offices of the underwriters to see whether or not any suspicious activity or meetings with police inspectors had taken place.

The following night, Price met Spanier as he arrived into Charing Cross station on the last train of the night. From the start, and with thinly veiled arrogance, Spanier informed Price that he did this as a favor to his close acquaintance Mr. Max Mayer. He went on to add that he would not act as detective on either an amateur or professional level. "I am not a policeman—I am an expert!" Spanier repeatedly said.

Price took Spanier to a nearby hotel to stay hidden away until the following morning when the all-important meeting would take place. He went through the plan in detail: who the players were, how he was to act, and what *not* to say or do that might arouse suspicion among the thieves. Price also explained that he would put up £4,000 to purchase the stray pearls, earn Grizzard's trust, and string the thieves along.

After settling the irritable Mr. Spanier into his room for the night, Price then met discreetly with Brandstatter and Quadratstein to issue more instructions. He handed the men an identity card bearing the number 123437 on it with directions to meet Spanier in the hotel lobby. They would identify him by his similar calling card numbered 123438.

When everything was in place, Price returned to his office late that night, lit the Tiffany lamp, casting the walls in color, and took notes on the day's events. He outlined details in his leather book with a fountain pen. In careful script, he wrote that he had met

Spanier, who seemed a "good chap," and that he was confident in Spanier's ability, in spite of his "Southern temperament."

The next morning, Spanier arrived at the First Avenue Hotel, walking through its arched doorway through the lobby and all of its pilasters, taking note of the fine "Oriental" decor and the painted pagoda entrance to the restaurant on his right. Spanier walked up to the hotel desk and with an air of self-importance instructed the clerk to call Mr. Quadratstein.

While he waited, Spanier asked for a table in the hotel's fabled grillroom, where he ordered French coffee and looked around at the other patrons, businessmen traveling to London, enjoying table d'hôte items off the menu. The grillroom was an expansive restaurant, nearly three hundred feet long with arched ceilings, floor-to-ceiling windows, glazed-tile walls, and mosaic-tile floors—it was like stepping inside a piece of artwork.

Moments later, Spanier saw a young, "foreign" gentleman obviously looking around the hotel lounge for someone in particular. Spanier stood, greeted the gentleman, and showed him the green identity card. Quadratstein did the same, looking around to see if any of the thieves he recognized might be nearby. Finally, the two men sat down at the table together and sent a message to Brandstatter to join them.

After the initial introductions had been made, the three men sat around the lounge table discussing plans. As always, Brandstatter remained quiet, counting on Quadratstein to translate, as Spanier discussed the amount to be offered to the thieves in exchange for a few pearls. The three men scarcely knew one another, and

Spanier undoubtedly felt uneasy about trusting them, jewelers well below him in experience and expertise, in what could be a dangerous situation. One mistake, and things could go very wrong for the decoys.

Finally, Spanier instructed the gentlemen to remain at the table while he retrieved the money Price had changed into francs for the exchange. Spanier left the grillroom, walking swiftly through the marble lobby and mahogany doors, setting his hat atop his head and making his way back onto High Holborn. He carried a leather case with him, and elbowed his way through the crowds. Hawkers called, street artists performed on corners, sweepers brushed past, pavement stencilers painted advertisements. Spanier kept his eyes open for anything that looked out of the ordinary while he stepped into a taxi to take him to a nearby hotel where Price would be waiting.

Inside the Holborn Viaduct Hotel, Spanier took the lift to the room. Price handed over a bundle of French notes, carefully numbered and marked, and Spanier stuffed them into his leather valise before quickly leaving again. The ride back toward Holborn with a bag full of cash made Spanier even more edgy. At a clipped pace, he hurried out of the taxi and into the hotel.

When Spanier strode through the doors of the First Avenue Hotel once again, he was unnerved to see that one of the thieves had already arrived and sat visiting with Brandstatter and Quadratstein at the lounge table. As Spanier approached, Gutwirth stood to meet the jeweler and, with his usual tactlessness, almost immediately added that he would require a confidential 5 percent commission separate from his partners. If Spanier had any doubts about the type of people he was being forced to negotiate with, Gutwirth had just confirmed his low opinion.

"That's absurd," Spanier answered.

"Well, there is no harm in asking," Gutwirth replied.

"Well," Spanier said disdainfully, "as I can see that I can make you an offer and that you would be satisfied with less, I shall not forget you."

The entire conversation took place in German, as Price suggested. Spanier had been instructed to pretend he could not speak English—it was a long shot, but Price and Spanier hoped it might lull the thieves into speaking openly in front of him.

A few moments later, a very short, frayed man in his midforties, with shoulders hunched forward, suddenly sat down at the table across from Spanier. As was customary, no introductions were made, no names were used, but Silverman was there to finalize the deal, and Brandstatter, Quadratstein, and Gutwirth left the table and moved to another corner of the lounge, leaving Spanier and Silverman alone.

Silverman, still not offering his name, assured Spanier that he would see the necklace soon and be able to finalize the purchase, but not on that particular day. He went on to explain that a friend was holding the necklace for him, and at present, the gentleman was motoring near Southampton with "some girls." He said this last part with a twinge of knowing sarcasm and, by way of explanation, added that his friend had recently lost his wife and was forgetting his sorrows by "leading a fast life."

Spanier feigned frustration with the delay, although it probably required little acting. He had hoped to have played his part and already be on his way back to his August vacation spot. Spanier threatened to call off negotiations if the meeting could not be conducted immediately, telling Silverman to contact the friend holding the necklace and induce him to return to London at once to finish the transaction. Silverman told the agitated jeweler that he needed to talk to his associates first and agreed to meet with Spanier later in the afternoon.

All of the gentlemen left the First Avenue Hotel, none of them satisfied with the stagnating state of affairs. Spanier slipped quickly out of the hotel lobby and hurried back toward the Viaduct Hotel, where Price sat waiting for an update. Silverman, on the other hand, took Gutwirth, Brandstatter, and Quadratstein in the opposite direction toward the Lipton tea shop on the corner of Holborn and Kingsway.

Brandstatter and Quadratstein did their best to appear at ease, but when they entered the tea shop and found Grizzard sitting at the table waiting for them, it became a harder facade to maintain. Grizzard, as always, wore a fine suit and sipped his coffee, appearing considerably calm and cool by comparison. Brandstatter and Quadratstein knew that the more time that passed, the more likely Grizzard would sense that something was awry with the plan or the two Frenchmen. This delay in selling the necklace put them on edge.

Gutwirth and Silverman explained the situation to Grizzard— the meeting had taken place as planned, but Spanier was in a hurry for the necklace and irritated by the delay. Grizzard was quiet for a moment, pulling his silver cigarette case from his pocket while Silverman lit a match.

Negotiations of this kind were typical in the sale of jewels, but Grizzard had been doing this for a very long time. Anyone who grew up in the East End and managed to profit from that life knew how to haggle. He also understood human nature. Grizzard knew he could negotiate the terms better than his confederates could, and

Spanier would feel more comfortable dealing with a gentleman. What's more, it would give Grizzard a chance to meet Spanier in person and get a feel for why he was in such a hurry to make such an expensive purchase.

Grizzard turned to Quadratstein and in a low and steady voice instructed him to return to the hotel. The weekend was approaching, so the meeting would be set for Monday. Silverman, who still planned to meet Spanier later that afternoon, would relay the message—the meeting had been arranged for Monday, August 25, 11:30 A.M., at the First Avenue Hotel.

Spanier was not happy with the news. That evening, several blocks away, he met with Price, who was anxious for a report. Spanier, growing tired of the situation, also announced that he would return to his vacation at Folkestone, where, coincidentally, Mayer was also on holiday. Price protested. If Grizzard had gang members shadowing Spanier, seeing him with Mayer would end all negotiations. But Spanier was adamant. So, with an abundance of caution, Price had Spanier leave his luggage at the Carlton Hotel, where he was ostensibly staying, and buy a valise from a shop on Old Kent Road. There, a car would wait for him and drive him to Folkestone for the afternoon mail boat. Anyone shadowing Spanier would be watching main terminals, not the mail boat. Two days later, rested but no less anxiety-ridden, Spanier repeated the convoluted travel arrangements and returned to London.

As Spanier hopped through cabs, trains, and mail boats that weekend, Silverman traveled to Southampton to meet with Lockett and "the girls"—Lockett's nine-year-old daughter, Nellie, and his two nieces. Lockett and Silverman dined alone at Adelaide's Restaurant at Scullard's, quietly discussing the business at hand. The bartender noticed the two men whispering to each other and obviously engaged in a private conversation. Silverman explained to Lockett that the necklace needed to be returned, in the safest fashion possible, to London by Monday morning. And on Sunday night, August 24, the two men took the train together back to London for the meeting.

On Monday morning, Silverman entered the familiar lobby of the First Avenue Hotel and walked through the painted pagoda doorway to the lounge. Brandstatter, Quadratstein, and Spanier were all present, and Silverman told them that "his associate" had returned from his motoring trip in Southampton early with the necklace in hand. Silverman politely invited the agents and buyer to meet him in a private residence where they would not be disturbed during the transaction. He instructed the men to watch him leave the hotel, wait several minutes, and then follow him up Holborn.

In this convoluted exchange, the thieves were pretending to be legitimate jewelers while the actual jewelers pretended to be thieves, and with no one wanting to slip up, few questions were asked. The group waited for Silverman to leave and then followed him as instructed.

As always, the streets festered with activity—omnibuses and carriages, people hurrying past on the sidewalks, dodging the costermongers pushing rattling carts and the bootblacks calling for shoeshines. The three men looked west for Silverman and followed him as best as they could through the throngs of pedestrians. Suddenly Silverman turned around and walked east, back past the First

Avenue Hotel, toward the Chancery Lane tube station. Brandstatter, Quadratstein, and Spanier scrambled to keep up.

When they hurried into the station after Silverman, he was already at the counter purchasing four tickets. The three decoys looked around, confused. No plans to leave the area had ever been discussed. In German, Spanier quietly told Brandstatter and Quadratstein to try to find out where they were being taken.

His back still turned to the men, Silverman answered in English: "A friend's house in Golders Green." Then Silverman collected the tickets from the booth, faced the group, and looked over their shoulders toward the door.

When Spanier turned around to see what caught Silverman's attention, he saw the silhouette of a tall, imposing gentleman standing in the doorway, backlit by the outside daylight. Though the man's face was obscured by the shadow of his hat, Spanier knew immediately who it was. Price had already briefed him as to the principal players involved, and Joseph Grizzard's intimidating height, cool confidence, and infamy preceded him. Spanier was already very wary of the famed thief, and the silhouette of the renowned "King of the Underworld" only added to the theatrics of the situation.

Grizzard, with his usual unruffled disposition and understated voice, spoke directly to Spanier. "I assure you the home is quiet and stylish, and most importantly, private."

By now, Spanier's wariness had blossomed into high-pitched fear. Price had warned him not to follow the thieves to any unknown or private meeting places, and Grizzard's unexpected presence there signaled that even more importance had been placed on the transaction, or perhaps, that the thieves had grown suspicious. Although none of the thieves had any history of violence, with this kind of money at stake, their behavior was unpredictable. Reminding himself of the part he played—illegal receiver from Paris—Spanier decided to play up the role. He raised his chin toward Grizzard.

"I have never seen you before. How do I know that you will not lure me into a trap and then betray me to the police?" Spanier asked petulantly. "How do I know you are not policemen in disguise?"

Silverman translated Spanier's statements from German to English, and Grizzard began laughing as he listened.

Stalling, Spanier added, "You pretend to be suspicious of me. It is I who am far more afraid of you!"

Grizzard stood watching Spanier for several seconds, then he and Silverman stepped away from the group and whispered to each other. Silverman nodded, returned to the counter, and sold back the tickets. Grizzard rescheduled the meeting for that afternoon back at the First Avenue Hotel, where Spanier would feel more at ease. They all agreed to meet at 1:45 P.M., in the billiards room. Then Grizzard and Silverman turned and disappeared back up the stairs and onto the busy street.

Spanier, Brandstatter, and Quadratstein quickly met back at the Holborn Viaduct Hotel to give Price yet another update about the change in plans. Three of the gentlemen went downstairs to have lunch, but Spanier, still nervous that he might be under surveillance, chose to lunch alone upstairs.

⁓

By one forty-five, Spanier had returned to the First Avenue Hotel for the meeting, and as he, Brandstatter, and Quadratstein approached the billiards room, they saw Grizzard leaning against the doorframe, arms folded, placidly watching a game of pocket billiards. Gutwirth stood nearby—although both Gutwirth and Spanier had been present at previous meetings at the hotel, they still had never been formally introduced.

"I know your friends Mr. Quadratstein and Mr. Brandstatter, but who is this?" Spanier protested, once again playing the part of the wary jewel receiver.

Amused, Grizzard assured him that Gutwirth was fine. And, a few moments later, Silverman arrived for the meeting. All five men instinctively turned toward Grizzard to ascertain what the next move would be. Grizzard leaned forward and told Gutwirth to wait in the billiards room while the rest of them went upstairs. Gutwirth looked surprised. Grizzard rarely offered up explanations, but perhaps he wanted Gutwirth to watch the lobby for detectives, or it may have been that already he felt Gutwirth could not be trusted.

Grizzard gestured to Spanier and the other two jewelers to go ahead of them to the room. He and Silverman would join them in five minutes. The jewelers climbed the stairs to the next floor, passing the water closet at the end of the hall and making their way to the hotel suite. A few minutes later, they heard a faint knock on the door, and Grizzard and Silverman entered the room quickly, shutting and locking the door behind them.

Brandstatter and Quadratstein had dragged a side table toward the window for the best natural light and pulled up five chairs. Grizzard and Silverman immediately chose the seats closest to the door, positioning themselves between the other three men and their only exit. Spanier remained nervous and agitated. He kept his right hand in his pocket, hoping to convince the thieves that he carried a revolver—in reality, he was the only man in the room *not* carrying one. Although it's not likely that Grizzard needed a revolver—if his reputation alone was not intimidating enough, he was almost twice the size of the other four gentlemen seated around the table.

Grizzard then reached into his pocket and pulled out a brown paper bundle and handed it to Silverman, who unwrapped the paper and placed on the table a small tin box and two Bryant & May's matchboxes. One matchbox contained the pearls that Brandstatter and Quadratstein had examined and sealed with their initials. They began looking over the silk strand, making sure the seals were still securely in place. The other matchbox held a beautiful, blush-colored drop pearl and two round ones. And there in the small tin box, with little fanfare, was the remainder of the Mayer pearl necklace in its entirety.

Spanier picked up the drop pearl and the smaller ones that had been encased with it. He pulled out an examining glass, looked over them carefully, and measured them. He recognized the two small, round ones as pearls he'd sold to Mayer over a year ago. Precious gems left an infallible mark on a jeweler's memory, especially pearls.

"You're right," he said, "these are the pearls. You have kept your promise."

"Of course, we always keep our promises," answered Silverman.

The room felt close, warm in the afternoon heat, and so quiet that the silence pounded. On the table sat pearls worth more money than any of the men in that room had ever handled at one time—it was also a necklace that all of Europe was now looking for.

So, it startled all five gentlemen when they suddenly heard a knock on the door. Brandstatter and Quadratstein jumped to their feet. Spanier looked up anxiously and found Grizzard's eyes boring into him. Silverman glared at the other two men, who paced the floor, unsure as to whether a bevy of police stood on the other side or criminal reinforcements.

Spanier's fear must have been palpable because Grizzard leaned over, patted him on the shoulder, and said, "There, there, I will protect you. Have no fear."

Finally, Quadratstein walked toward the door, cracked it open, and a hotel page handed him a note. Quadratstein read the message aloud—it was from Gutwirth, who was waiting in the hallway downstairs and wanted to join the group.

Grizzard, still seated, answered over his shoulder curtly, "Tell him that we're busy. He can come back in an hour or two."

After the anticlimactic interruption, the five men returned to the business before them. Spanier debated what to do next. He had no intention of buying the entire necklace, and the underwriters had given him a finite amount to spend. But he would have to buy at least a few of the pearls to keep the thieves on the hook.

"How much?" he asked again.

"A million francs for the lot," Grizzard answered evenly.

Spanier thought for a moment and then offered 100,000 francs for the three pearls already weighed and sealed by Quadratstein. He promised the thieves that he would return to Paris for more money to buy the rest.

Silverman took a notebook from his jacket pocket and looked over it. "I can't do it. Those three pearls cost me more than that!" Knowing full well how Silverman acquired those pearls, Spanier tried to keep from smirking. He bartered back and forth with Silverman, who stood firm in his position. Silverman may not have had the experience Grizzard had, but he was shrewd. Spanier refused to budge, however, and sensing an impenetrable offer, Silverman finally agreed to the price.

Spanier pulled from his pockets notes from the Bank of France and handed them to Grizzard, who immediately handed them to Silverman to be counted. Then Grizzard put the money in his pocket while Silverman collected the rest of the pearls, sealing them closed in envelopes. The five men agreed to meet again the following week after Spanier procured more French notes and could purchase a larger portion of the necklace. Grizzard took the envelopes from the table and slid them into his front breast pocket before standing to leave. The room still smelled of matches and melting wax.

Following his lead, the other gentlemen stood from the table as well, brushing off the burned matchsticks, scraps of sealing wax, and remaining envelopes from the tabletop. Quadratstein picked up a piece of paper on which he had written the descriptions and weights of the three pearls after measuring them. When he looked up, Grizzard was watching him.

"You don't want that anymore," Grizzard said pleasantly. "It's of no use to you now." He stood there, unmoving, clearly insistent that Quadratstein destroy any evidence of the meeting and of the pearls. Having no reasonable excuse for keeping the measurements on him, Quadratstein acquiesced and tore up the paper. Grizzard turned toward the door, hat in hand.

Spanier, grateful to have the meeting over and anxious to get out of a locked room full of thieves, moved quickly toward the door as well.

"One moment, Mr. Spanier, please."

Spanier didn't have to turn around to know whose voice it was. He heard Grizzard's purposeful footsteps coming toward him. Grizzard turned to face Spanier and his partners with his usual steely stare. And then, with the nonchalance of a gentleman on his way for a stroll around St. James's Park, he slid his hand into his right trouser pocket where the revolver sat.

"No one leaves this room for ten minutes after we have left. Do you understand?"

He motioned toward Silverman, and the two men stepped through the door and moved quietly through the hallway, disappearing down the staircase.

Spanier sat there with Brandstatter and Quadratstein for a full ten minutes, checking his pocket watch diligently. He was acutely uneasy and just wanted to escape the confines of the hotel room. When the time was up, he hurried through the hallway, down the stairs, and out the front door without even saying good-bye to the other two Frenchmen.

Outside, the air felt fresher than the stale, sultry, tobacco-filled hotel suite. An empty taxi stood waiting at the curb, and Spanier stepped straight in, giving the driver an address at the corner of Hyde Park. As the taxi sped up Holborn, however, Spanier's nerves began to get the better of him. Why had an empty taxi been waiting right at that moment in front of the hotel? Had it been coincidence or by design? He fingered the three pearls in his pocket. Could the taxi be taking him to some undisclosed location where he would be robbed of the very pearls he had just paid for?

As the taxi eased into traffic along Southampton Row, Spanier pushed the door open and jumped onto the street, shoving cab fare through the front window to the driver. He hurried onto Kingsway, flagged another taxi to take him toward Hammersmith, and looked repeatedly out the back window as the taxi moved slowly among the other autos and the occasional horse-drawn carriage. At

Hammersmith, he paid the fare and took yet another taxi to the Midland Hotel in North London. Entering the lobby, he hurried toward the dining room, left through a back door, and returned to the street to grab another taxi to take him to his final destination, the Holborn Viaduct Hotel, to meet with Price. When he finally made it up the staircase and knocked on the hotel door, Price looked at the man and sent for a glass of brandy.

Spanier's paranoia may not have been unfounded. Lockett remained in London all of that day, unaccounted for, before returning to Southampton late that night. As he never took part in any of the meetings, Lockett most likely shadowed Spanier, Brandstatter, or Quadratstein through most of the day or stood watch outside the underwriter's office.

Spanier handed over the pearls, and Price smiled broadly. He called Max Mayer to arrange a time to meet with him, examine the pearls, and confirm if they were indeed part of the original necklace. Up to that point, Price had only been operating off tips, assumptions, and the questionable opinion of two Frenchmen. Now, however, he held the proof in his hand—for the first time in weeks, they were close to getting the entire necklace back. It was time to contact the police and get them involved.

Price sent for his consultant, Alfred Leach, the former superintendent of Scotland Yard, who had spent so many years patrolling Hatton Garden as well as shadowing Grizzard. Leach then called Alfred Ward.

In the meantime, the frazzled Spanier left Price, took another four taxis through various London neighborhoods, and finally arrived back at the Carlton Hotel. He rushed through the lobby, stopping at the front desk to ask who was renting the room directly beside his. Upon hearing that it was "a lady," he relaxed some and went upstairs to retire for the evening. But the night proved no quieter than the afternoon had.

As he lay in the still darkness and tried to fall asleep, he heard scratching through the wall next door. He sat up and turned on the light, pressing his ear up against the "communicating door" separating the two rooms. Nothing. He returned to bed and turned out the lamp. A moment later, he heard the scratching again and bolted upright in the bed, listening intently.

Finally, he gave up trying to sleep, and instead sat in the armchair across the room all night, making sure that the bell for the front desk was within reach. He stayed this way as the moonlight crossed his ceiling, the darkness gave way, and at last, morning's blue-gray light pooled beneath the windows.

Exhausted, edgy, and frustrated, he washed and dressed for the day and went downstairs to the front desk to demand that a hotel page unlock the door and search the room adjoining his. As the room was empty for the time being, the hotel page accompanied Spanier upstairs and unlocked the door. The room felt dark, except for the anemic light coming through the nearby window. Spanier looked toward the "communicating door" searching for signs of nefarious behavior or clues as to what the suspicious neighbor had been doing all night. Instead, he found that the bed had been placed directly against the door connecting to his room, so that each time the lady moved or rolled over during the night, the wood scratched harmlessly against Spanier's door.

TWELVE

Playing the Fish

"PLAYING THE FISH" IS A TECHNIQUE USED BOTH IN FISHING AND in poker. In the former, the fisherman repeatedly reels in the fish before letting the line slack, giving the fish room to swim and exhaust itself before the fisherman reels the line in farther. In poker, the term is used for very experienced players at the table with novices. The amateur poker players, excited by the game, are too quick to act. The expert players "play the fish" by waiting patiently for the novice to make mistakes—which, invariably, he will. In poker, as in fishing, success goes to the man with the ability to sit still and allow his opponent to believe he is the one in control until the critical mistake is made. In that sense, "playing the fish" became a very effective detective tactic as well. The only remaining question then was which one was the fisherman and which one the fish?

[Tuesday, August 26, 1913]

Alfred Ward, pencil and notebook in hand, sat and listened to Spanier and Price relay the events thus far: how Brandstatter, lured by the reward money, had come to meet Gutwirth; why his cousin, Quadratstein, joined him; how they came to be in London meeting with the thieves; how they joined forces with Price and brought Spanier into the ruse; and why they now had three of the Mayer pearls in their possession. What gave Ward pause was the name of the mastermind behind the heist: Joseph Grizzard.

There was something of an intimate history between the thief and the detective, even though they had met only a few times— Ward had stood in the bay-windowed dining room of Grizzard's home in Dalston. He had met his wife, seen photos of his son. Ward had first learned of Grizzard from his predecessor, Alfred Leach, who had unsuccessfully pursued Grizzard for decades. Then, in Ward's first major dealing with Grizzard, in 1909, he had failed to recover the stolen jewels from the Monico heist or put away Grizzard for acting as fence in the crime. Knowing that Grizzard was at the helm of this heist would change the chase.

The two men also shared similarities. They were the same age. Both had grown up in impoverished neighborhoods in London. Both had transcended that lifestyle to better themselves, one through joining law enforcement, the other through evading it. Both were intelligent men, schooled on the London streets. Both were settled, married, and had one child at home. And both were generally decent men devoted to their families and respected by a loyal following of colleagues.

Ward knew that Grizzard, a seasoned criminal with finely tuned instincts, was unlikely to be careless or make mistakes lesser criminal minds would. He wanted to find a way to put Grizzard in his professional zone of comfort, where he felt in charge and at ease. The easiest way to do that was to go with what had worked before and turn the pursuit into a sting operation. A sting would involve using civilians or trained police as insiders to earn the trust of the thieves and set them up to be arrested by plainclothes detectives on the scene.

A sting operation was a highly successful detective technique that was still relatively new, but it was not without its critics. Londoners, who still seemed wary of law enforcement trampling on personal liberties, found the idea of manipulating a person's trust and trapping them to be ethically wide of the mark. On some level, civilians still wanted the police only to catch the criminals once a crime was committed or prevent the crime before it happened, but not to lure and trap criminals in the process. The police, as far as the public was concerned, shouldn't sink to the level of the criminals.

At Scotland Yard, however, patience with the gentlemanly way of detaining criminals had long since run out. The professional gangs of thieves had spent so many years so far ahead of the detectives chasing them that it didn't even seem a fair fight. Ward had been part of the original, talented criminal investigation unit that decided to turn detective work into a science. They used their forensics labs, fingerprinting, plainclothes observers, insiders, sting operations, and any other techniques necessary to keep up with the thieves.

For the sting operation to capture Grizzard, Ward recommended that Spanier, Brandstatter, and Quadratstein simply duplicate the meeting they had held Monday at the same location, in the same room, with the same type of negotiation. Keep it simple and straightforward and lull Grizzard into that comfortable zone. When all the players were in place, the police would storm the hotel and arrest the thieves with the pearls in hand. They would also arrest the decoys in order to protect them. Spanier, Brandstatter, and Quadratstein would be quietly released at a later date. Ward outlined the plan for Price and the three main players. All agreed to it, except Spanier, who reiterated his mantra.

"I am not a policeman. I am an expert!"

Refusing to be arrested as part of the plan and sully his reputation, Spanier agreed to all other points.

Price briefed Spanier at the Holborn Viaduct Hotel. The plans were essentially the same as before—Spanier would meet with Quadratstein at the First Avenue Hotel, just a few blocks away. There, Silverman would join them to discuss further negotiations and to set the new date and time for a meeting.

Spanier left the Viaduct, walking out beneath its arches and immense columns onto the street. Businessmen in black suits rushed around him entering the Viaduct train station, where the South Eastern and Chatham Railways shrieked by on the lower track, connecting passengers to South London. Spanier walked west toward Holborn Circus. As he did so, he saw Grizzard crossing the street. He paused and panicked for a moment, trying to think of an excuse as to why he was leaving the Viaduct Hotel. Then he realized with relief that Grizzard had not seen him.

Spanier walked slowly in the crowd several feet behind Grizzard and watched the gang leader in action. A sailor swiftly turned the corner, moved through the crowds toward Grizzard, and then walked in step with him for about a block. The sailor kept his hands in his pockets and his head forward, but he was saying something. He looked as though he was talking to himself. He lost step with Grizzard, pulled back, and walked away. Next, an elderly woman walked up. Still looking straight ahead, Grizzard slowed his pace to keep step with the woman, who, like the sailor, kept her eyes forward and seemed to be talking to herself. After a few moments, the woman disappeared, and Grizzard kept going—just a typical businessman, dressed in a suit, making his way down a busy street. It was called the "human chain," and it was the way Grizzard's gang members delivered messages or warnings to him.

Spanier slowed down and watched as Grizzard descended the stairs toward the tube station. It occurred to Spanier how vast Grizzard's gang of thieves was. These were not small-time thieves caught with a valuable necklace to unload; these were professionals who thought through every single detail with precision.

※

As the detectives worked out the details of their plan, it occurred to Ward that Grizzard or one of his gang members must still be holding the pearls so soon after meeting with the decoys. Grizzard had planned to sell the entire necklace then and there at the First Avenue Hotel, but Spanier had stalled, asking for more time to obtain the full amount of money. That left Grizzard, or one of his men, with the pearls in hand.

Ward and several of his detectives spent the afternoon watching one of the few addresses they had for Grizzard Gang members—a house in Highbury, a neighborhood of new, terraced homes built just north of central London. Several of Grizzard's men routinely came and went from that address, so Ward and his detectives discreetly hid in motorcars, buildings, or bushes nearby and watched the house for Grizzard on the off chance that they might catch him with the pearls in his possession.

The extra measure proved futile. Grizzard never appeared at the house. In fact, the only person they saw that afternoon was an old man, a hawker, who came out balancing half a dozen potted flowers in his arms to load onto his wooden cart.

Finally, Ward and his men gave up and left, never knowing how very close they had been to the necklace. Inside one of those pots, the Mayer pearls had been buried beneath the soil and flowers. The hawker made his way innocuously through the neighborhood and eventually got the pearls back into Grizzard's pocket.

That night, Grizzard left London on the evening train for Southampton. He spent the night at Scullard's, dining downstairs with Lockett and tweaking the details for the next meeting with Spanier. Lockett was one of the men he trusted most, and the two discussed their growing concern with Gutwirth.

That same evening, at the same time, Price met Max Mayer at Folkestone, along the coast. Mayer had taken the wind-whipped ferry back to England for the very important, mysterious meeting. Price opened a package and placed two pale pink pearls on the table in front of Mayer, giving him very few details about how he had obtained them. Mayer held the familiar pearls in his palm, gently rolling them through his fingers and smiling. He confirmed excitedly that the pearls belonged to the original necklace. Mayer signed a paper presented by Price verifying that statement, then took the ferry back again to continue his vacation. Price, meanwhile, wired

Scotland Yard from Folkestone to tell Ward that the identification had been made, and they should proceed with the sting operation the next morning.

[Wednesday, August 27, 1913]

Grizzard, Lockett, and Lockett's niece took the 8:47 A.M. train to London, arriving at the Waterloo Station. The threesome took a cab to the Strand to have breakfast at Cows Restaurant, and shortly thereafter, Grizzard left.

Lockett and his niece, Catherine, walked up Kingsway around eleven-thirty, to the Opera House, where they booked seats for the revue that afternoon. After buying a train ticket at the British Museum tube station, Lockett left his niece, explaining that he had some business to attend to for a couple of hours, but would return to meet her for the afternoon show.

Across town, Ward felt confident that all involved understood the plan and could play their parts accordingly. Price had taken out another thousand French notes for Quadratstein to take with him to the meeting that morning, scheduled for eleven-thirty at the First Avenue Hotel. Price had also given detailed instructions to Spanier.

Spanier left the Charing Cross Hotel, where he was now staying, and made his way toward Holborn as planned. Sergeant Cooper shadowed the jeweler, who was growing more nervous and unpredictable with each new meeting. It was a sunny morning full of yellow light and reflected sky, prompting gentlemen to pull their hats farther over their eyes and ladies to open lace parasols that speckled the ground with sunlight and shadow.

Outside of the First Avenue Hotel, Ward had several of his men in plainclothes as street cleaners, hawkers, and businessmen patrolling the neighborhood. He also positioned a delivery van full of police on a corner near the hotel. The uniformed police sat in the hot, closed van with their bulldog revolvers and manacles, ready to pounce when the group of thieves entered the hotel. The trap was set.

When Spanier arrived at the hotel for the meeting, he found Brandstatter and Quadratstein standing in the lobby talking to Silverman. Gutwirth was not present, and more importantly, neither was Grizzard. It immediately struck Spanier as odd. In all other transactions, Grizzard had no qualms about being present or, at the very least, arriving suddenly and disconcertingly out of nowhere. The arrest could not be made without Grizzard's presence at the meeting.

Silverman extended his hand warmly to Spanier, greeting him. Spanier told him that he had been able to raise the rest of the money, in two different envelopes, to purchase the remainder of the necklace. Silverman was obviously pleased and agreed to the price then and there. He also suggested that the group retire to a room he had rented at another hotel for the private exchange. The extra measure of caution was more out of practiced habit than suspicion. The Grizzard Gang kept on the move constantly, making it harder for the police who regularly shadowed them to keep up.

Spanier, however, insisted on staying at the First Avenue Hotel, or at the very least a public restaurant—nothing too private, he added warily. It was the only way to spring the trap. The more Silverman protested, the more Spanier accused him of having ulterior motives.

From inside the van and along the streets, Ward and his police watched the exchange taking place in the hotel lobby. Ward could see Spanier through the glass and waited for the signal, but none came. Without it, Ward could not be sure if they had the necklace in their possession or whether or not Grizzard was present, and he certainly didn't want to tip off the thieves prematurely. For all they knew, Grizzard had entered from a back way or was already sitting in a room upstairs. Without Grizzard and the pearls, the plan was useless. Ward continued to watch Spanier carefully for any signal and kept an eye on his plainclothes detectives on the streets.

At last, he saw the man himself. Grizzard's tall frame walked swiftly up the block from the south. He kept his head low, his bowler hat pulled over his eyes, trying not to attract undue attention. There was no doubt, however, about his intentions. He walked with purpose and directness right toward the First Avenue Hotel. In moments, Ward would have exactly what he needed: the thieves together, the pearls in their possession, and the decoys to testify as to the purpose of the meeting. Ward was a cautious, well-tempered man, but he must have felt some satisfaction. He would finally have Grizzard in his possession, and his failure after the Monico heist would be supplanted by this much greater victory. Once Grizzard entered that hotel, the police had more than enough cause to arrest him and the other men present.

As Grizzard came up the sidewalk and approached the hotel, however, he suddenly stopped. He lifted his head slowly and looked around him. Ward searched the scene for what might have caught his attention. There was absolutely nothing out of the ordinary. Hawkers yelled from their wooden carts filled with trinkets. Some sweepers picked up rubbish nearby. A newsboy called from the corner. A few taxis lined up outside of the hotel, along with several delivery trucks and vans—including the one with detectives hidden inside. An omnibus pulled up to a stop, and men and women climbed aboard. Pedestrians walked by, looking through the glass at the shiny tiled floors of the hotel and the giant palms and ferns pluming out of Chinese ceramic pots. Ward had trained his men to blend completely into a street scene—they wore the right clothes, used flawless Cockney accents, muddied their boots, smudged their faces, and took on the entire persona of the part they played.

Still, Grizzard had sensed something. He turned around, facing the street, and stood there for a long moment. Then he rested a cigarette against his lips, pulled out a match, cupped his hand against the wind, and lit the tip. He drew in a long breath and let the smoke bleed out before walking up to the van where the police sat hiding. Grizzard leaned against the mudguard, crossed his ankles, and smoked the cigarette down to his fingertips. From inside the van, where the warrant for Grizzard's arrest sat folded, the smoke seeped through cracks and scented the hot air with tobacco. Finally, Grizzard flicked the cigarette onto the ground, put his hands in his pockets, and walked away.

Inside the hotel, Silverman thought about what to do next. The thieves had arranged for a private meeting elsewhere, as was their usual mode of operation. Now Spanier was refusing to cooperate. Silverman told the three gentlemen he would need to discuss this with the others and promised to return soon. Brandstatter, Quadratstein, and Spanier stood in the lobby waiting.

While Ward and the police were still trying to decide whether to follow Grizzard, Silverman walked outside, crossed the street, and met Gutwirth on the sidewalk as though the two men had just bumped into each other. They spoke quietly, looking around them in all directions, though Gutwirth was obviously excited by something. He told Silverman that Grizzard had recognized at least four Yardmen on the street, and he had a message for Silverman to deliver to the dealers.

Inside the hotel, however, the scene had changed. Spanier's choleric temperament got the better of him, and irritated to have been left waiting so long, he refused to remain a moment more. He strode out of the front doors so quickly that the doorman barely had time to pull the handle ahead of him. Ward, still hidden along the street, watched as Spanier stomped off in the direction of Hatton Garden.

A few moments later, Silverman entered the lobby. By then, Quadratstein too was frustrated and began yelling at Silverman, blaming him for taking so long and for Spanier's hasty departure. The entire operation seemed to be unraveling before them. Tempers flared. Silverman, trying to be as conciliatory as possible, promised to wait in the hotel smoking lounge while Brandstatter stepped into the telephone box to try to reach Spanier.

Quadratstein was pacing nervously back and forth in the lobby when Gutwirth came through the doors and eagerly relayed the events outside, explaining that Grizzard had recognized Yardmen. Quadratstein stood still and willed himself to stay calm—if the thieves knew of the police presence, sooner or later they would wonder how the detectives learned about the meeting. Gutwirth rambled on, explaining that Grizzard demanded to see the jewel dealers outside the hotel at some other location.

Before Quadratstein had time to react, he heard a commotion and looked toward the doorway. Spanier had returned, strutting through the front doors, and now stood among the pilasters berating Silverman for leaving him waiting for too long. The deal was off, he shouted. A few heads in the lobby turned to watch the commotion, and Silverman seemed to shrink, even farther, turning his face away from the onlookers.

In all likelihood, this temper tantrum of Spanier's was not an act—his nerves were threadbare. He had abandoned his vacation, spent sleepless nights fretting about notorious thieves following him or spying on him. And now it seemed the transactions would be delayed even further. Defeated and determined, he told Silverman that he was returning to Paris at once and that Quadratstein could act as his agent in all future negotiations. With that, Spanier left, went directly to the Holborn Viaduct Hotel, and told Price the same thing. Spanier was on the train to the coast by that afternoon.

Brandstatter, Quadratstein, and Silverman stood in the lobby of the First Avenue Hotel debating what to do next. Negotiations stalled, a meeting was set for the following day at J.P.'s Restaurant when the men could reconvene with cooler temperaments and make the trade without Spanier's presence. There was no reason to call off negotiations now.

As the three men left the hotel, Ward and his police waited until they were out of sight and then disbanded, disappointed and frustrated.

Just before two o'clock that afternoon, Lockett hurried from the direction of Holborn, up Kingsway, to meet his niece outside of the London Opera House. The building, only two years old, was an incredible feat of architecture in the French Renaissance style. It took up an entire city block with its massive stone and meringue masonry. Inside, the lavish theater housed over 2,500 people on three levels of balconies. Lockett continued toward Portugal Street, arriving just in time to join his niece to see the highly successful revue *Come Over Here.* Three hours later, around five, Lockett and his niece had tea before taking a taxi to meet her parents at the Waterloo train station. The whole group boarded the train and returned to Southampton for the weekend. Lockett never explained where he had been during those few hours apart and no one asked.

THIRTEEN

The Sting

NOW THAT THE POLICE KNEW OF THE THIEVES, AND THE THIEVES knew of the police, a "follow-my-leader" ensued. Ward's detectives watched Grizzard, Lockett watched the detectives, and plainclothes police watched the gang members watching the detectives watching the thieves. On any given block in Holborn or Hatton Garden, the swarms of pedestrian men and women might be made up entirely of police or thieves disguised and following one another. The next morning, the procession of those shadowing and those being shadowed set out for J.P.'s Restaurant.

[Thursday, August 28, 1913]

At eleven o'clock, Silverman met Brandstatter and Quadratstein at J.P.'s on Holborn. The meeting was short, as Grizzard, now very suspicious, had sent Silverman alone to relay a new meeting time and place, an hour and a half later at the Lyons tea shop directly next door. The interval gave Grizzard's men a chance to see if Brandstatter and Quadratstein had detectives following them.

When the two Parisians arrived at Lyons at twelve-thirty, they found Silverman once again alone. He explained Grizzard's reluctance and apprehension about the detectives shadowing them.

"Your chief's suspicions are absurd!" Quadratstein protested.

"It is no business of mine," Silverman said calmly. "You had better come and see Grizzard in person."

The three men set off for their third meeting place that afternoon. They walked up the road toward the Lipton tea shop where they had met Grizzard several days before, and there they found him sipping coffee beneath clouds of cigarette smoke. He looked rigid, keenly aware of the other people in the restaurant, fearful of who might be listening.

"You have had a very narrow escape," Grizzard whispered to the two jewelers. "The police are on our tracks on account of Spanier drawing so much French money, and we must be very careful. All negotiations are suspended for a month, and I will not sell to another buyer in that time." He stubbed out his cigarette and stood, gathering up his hat and buttoning his coat.

Brandstatter and Quadratstein had no idea what to do next. On the one hand, they felt relief that Grizzard did not suspect them or Spanier of working with the police. On the other, another month set the whole operation in jeopardy.

"You two had better return to Paris," Grizzard continued as he set his hat firmly on his head and looked around him. "Tell Spanier to return the notes to his bankers in London and draw fresh ones in Paris and return in a month's time, when you can buy the remainder of the necklace in one lot." He promised to meet them at the train station when they returned in order to be sure no detectives followed them.

"How will we get the pearls out of London, then?" Quadratstein asked.

"That's easy," said Grizzard. "Bring your wife over with you and she can wear the pearls going back."

Quadratstein told Grizzard that he would speak with Spanier about the plans and asked where to contact him in the meantime.

Grizzard offered up an address: Mr. Levi, c/o Mr. Goldberg, 45 Hatton Garden. He added, "But the letter must be registered."

Grizzard felt uneasy about the breach to the fortress of his professional endeavors, and he clearly felt Gutwirth to be partly at fault. He told Brandstatter and Quadratstein that in the future, they would not be dealing with Gutwirth, who had "too long a tongue."

"From now on," he said ruefully, "you will only have to deal with gentlemen."

Grizzard also removed Silverman from future negotiations because he did not want the police shadowing them to recognize or suspect him. Silverman did not have a criminal record, and up to this point, his name had not even been revealed to Price or Ward. Although Spanier, Brandstatter, and Quadratstein had met with Silverman several times at the hotel, he never introduced himself, and Gutwirth never mentioned his name.

Before leaving, Quadratstein tried to ascertain where the pearls were being kept, but Grizzard would not offer any details. He said only that the necklace was in a place as safe as the Bank of England. With that, Grizzard left the restaurant, looking swiftly in both directions as he stepped onto the crowded sidewalk.

As the remaining gentlemen stood and prepared to leave, Quad-ratstein mentioned that he still owed a little money on his hotel bill. Silverman handed him two five-pound notes and some change to cover the cost. Quadratstein later cashed one at Victoria Station and gave the other over to Price as evidence.

All in all, Grizzard's instincts were correct. Although he didn't know exactly who was at fault, he applied his usual intelligence and high level of caution to the situation—suspending negotiations, sending the Frenchmen back to Paris, changing the money, and putting the pearls back into hiding. If his gang members deferred to his instructions, the heist, though taking longer than originally planned, would be a successful one and all would profit handsomely.

❦

Unlike the chilly month of July, August had been hot, sultry. As London grew quiet and her residents left for shooting parties and coastal resorts, the air became stifling and claustrophobic with the smell of the brackish river hanging over the city. Undoubtedly, the two gentlemen who answered the reward poster nearly a month before were beginning to feel the suffocating closeness as well. Brandstatter and Quadratstein went immediately to Price and Ward to discuss what to do next; they were within hours of losing the necklace and Grizzard.

Ward sat thinking quietly. At this point, Grizzard knew he was under surveillance for the pearl necklace. His guard was up, and he was not going to make any careless or aggressive moves. By nature, receivers were careful. They relied on the protection of ignorance—a receiver could always claim he did not know the goods were stolen—and a lack of evidence. Usually, a receiver's weakness was his greed and desire for money, but Grizzard was already a wealthy man, he didn't need the money. However, Grizzard was not only a receiver, he was also a fence, the putter-up, the leader. A leader's weakness was his confederates.

Ward instructed Brandstatter to send Gutwirth a letter, in Yiddish, to set up a meeting for eleven the following morning, at the nearby Inns of Court Hotel. He told Gutwirth to ask for "Monsieur Dubois," the name Brandstatter would use to rent a room. Brandstatter wrote the letter, as directed, and had it dispatched by special messenger to Gutwirth. Ward also instructed Price to use the alias "Mr. Bloch" and wait near the telephone box to call the police if necessary. Ward then outlined the plan for Brandstatter and Quadratstein as well.

In order for Grizzard to agree to any further dealing under such intense police pressure, the situation would have to be very persuasive. Ward surmised that by presenting Grizzard with the perfect buyer—someone who could pay the right price and would remove the pearls from the UK in a hurry—Grizzard might be tempted to unload the necklace immediately. But as cautious as Grizzard was, it would take some additional pressure as well.

[Friday, August 29, 1913]

At eleven o'clock, Gutwirth strutted up High Holborn toward the smog-blackened Inns of Court Hotel. He was very pleased that he had been brought back into the negotiations after Grizzard had shut him out. When he inquired at the front desk about a "Mr. Dubois,"

he was sent upstairs to the appropriate room, where he found Brandstatter and Quadratstein waiting for him.

Quadratstein, becoming a natural at duplicity, explained to Gutwirth that they had found an Indian rajah who was anxious to
purchase the pearl necklace, but needed it immediately, as he
planned to travel back to India soon. It was a clever ruse and presented a perfect situation for a thief. While the pearls could be traced
back to Paris, New York, or possibly Antwerp, once they traveled as
far as the Middle East or Asia, they would be lost amid the massive
gem trade, cultural disconnect, and daunting geography. Further-
more, Quadratstein threatened, if this potential buyer fell through,
it could be a very long time before another came forward. To solid-
ify the deal, he promised Gutwirth a special commission of £1,000
in addition to the 5 percent he was already seeking, if he could
facilitate this sale as quickly as possible. With the extra incentive
and no thought as to why it had been given, Gutwirth jumped at
the offer. Quadratstein smiled and asked to see Silverman as soon
as possible to officiate the deal.

That afternoon, Silverman, Gutwirth, Brandstatter, and Quadratstein took the offer to Grizzard, meeting him at a bun shop near
his favorite Lipton café on High Holborn. They looked around the
restaurant and saw him sitting at a back table. He looked pensive,
and there was a mound of discarded cigarettes sitting before him.
Although he did not want to enter into any more negotiations under
such heavy scrutiny from the police, Gutwirth and Silverman pres-
sured him to accept the deal. Outnumbered and genuinely relieved
to rid himself of this problem once and for all, Grizzard reluctantly
agreed. A meeting was set for Monday, September 1, at 2 P.M., in
the Lyons tea shop on Holborn.

[Saturday, August 30, 1913]

Gutwirth, feeling self-congratulatory and elated by the impending windfall, was in a chatty mood by the time the weekend arrived. He decided to stop by Brandstatter and Quadratstein's hotel for a surprise visit. Once there, Gutwirth just couldn't contain himself. He began bragging about "getting the pearls." The brilliant plan. The bribe to two postmen. It was the first time there was any real mention of *stealing* the pearls.

Quadratstein, feigning confusion, asked why they needed to bribe the postmen and for how much. In answer, Gutwirth whipped out a notebook and began reading off the amounts of money spent in acquiring the pearls—£100 to two different postmen, another £200 pounds to each, he continued rattling off, £400 and £800 for other expenses.

He didn't stop there. Gutwirth began bragging about where the pearls were hidden and who had possession of them. He promised the two Parisians that the pearls were perfectly safe since Grizzard and James Lockett were looking after them for the weekend. Gutwirth went on to say that Lockett's brother-in-law, a man with "a pointed black beard," had been holding the pearls all along. Up to that point, Lockett's name had never been connected to the pearl heist.

[Monday, September 1, 1913]

Lockett and his niece Catherine boarded the 8:48 A.M. train in Southampton for London. Lockett's daughter, his brother and sister-in-law, niece, and the Moores took motorcars back to London. The train felt muggy and the station crowded as Lockett and Catherine arrived with many other Londoners returning to the city. Torrents of rain fell that morning, leaving the curbs awash in overflow and puddles pooling along the sidewalks.

Lockett checked their luggage into a cloakroom, and the pair hurried into a taxi to the new Strand Palace Hotel for breakfast. From there, they pulled their umbrellas close and walked farther up the Strand to the post office, where Lockett needed to send a telegram.

There's no explanation as to why Lockett always traveled to and from London with his niece, but it's likely that he wanted to blend into the crowd as "a couple." His niece was almost eighteen years old, so in the right traveling clothes, broad-brimmed hat, and parasol, she could look like a young woman traveling with her older spouse. Detectives, who regularly watched the train stations for the comings and goings of Grizzard's gang, knew Lockett was a widower, so they would look for him either traveling alone or with his little girl, Nellie.

Of course, the other reason Lockett always came and went from London with his niece in tow might be as a means of transporting the pearls. The strand worn around her neck or tucked in the collar of her lady's traveling coat would be the perfect way to hide them.

After Lockett and Catherine left the post office, they walked up the Strand to catch a bus and crossed the river to visit Catherine's home in the Peabody buildings in Bermondsey, a series of flats surrounding boxy courtyards. They visited her father for about ten minutes, and strolled around the property, giving Lockett the chance to see if they were being shadowed—and perhaps drop off the pearls for safekeeping.

Around eleven-thirty, the two crossed the river once again and made their way up Kingsway toward Holborn and Hatton Garden to meet with Silverman. This gave them ample time to watch for detectives or plainclothes cops, although the large number of black umbrellas worked in their favor, lending a feel of anonymity to the busy sidewalks that day.

At 101 Hatton Garden, Lockett and his niece took the lift up to Silverman's cramped office on the third floor. Catherine stood aside looking around at the various scales, jewels, sealing waxes, and bottles of solutions. Her uncle and Silverman spoke in low voices in the corner so that Catherine could not hear the conversation. After a few minutes, all three left the office. Lockett and Catherine walked back down Holborn and stopped for lunch while Silverman continued on until they lost sight of him.

Gutwirth arrived at the Inns of Court Hotel on Monday, midmorning, and was met with good news. Quadratstein told him that by afternoon he would have the 900,000 francs to purchase the rest of the pearls.

"And when can you have my commission?" Gutwirth asked.

"This evening . . . if I safely buy the pearls," answered Quadratstein.

The two gentlemen left the hotel for the nearby Lincoln's Inn Fields, a large park of damp green grass and walking paths off High Holborn and Chancery Lane. The weather felt crisp after the heavy rainfall, so Londoners walked the grounds, enjoying the reprieve from wet weather. Silverman arrived in the park next, clearly on edge as he studied the crowds looking for Gutwirth. He had just come from his meeting with Lockett and Catherine, and whatever had been said unnerved him. He located Brandstatter and Quadratstein and asked, or demanded, that they follow him back up Holborn to his office in Hatton Garden. Silverman wanted to show them a back entry to his building in case the meeting place had to be moved and the exchange needed to take place in some other private location. He wanted to cover as many aspects of the plan as possible.

By 2 P.M., the Lyons restaurant in Holborn was surrounded by shadows and prying eyes. Ward had at least a dozen disguised men along the street watching for the Grizzard Gang's approach.

Brandstatter and Quadratstein arrived at the restaurant first. Soon thereafter, Grizzard arrived, followed closely by Gutwirth. Ward and his detectives kept their sights on Grizzard, who sent Gutwirth outside to keep a lookout—apparently not his strong suit since he failed to see the twelve or so detectives surrounding the place. As Brandstatter and Quadratstein sat down to the table, Grizzard skipped the pleasantries and went directly to the point.

"Have you got the money?" he asked.

Quadratstein stalled. He explained that the buyer had changed his mind and did not want so much money on one man in one location. London, as he well knew, had no shortage of thieves. Instead, he'd rather buy 200,000 francs' worth of pearls in installments. To reassure Grizzard, Quadratstein asked if he could choose the pearls at once to purchase for the first installment.

The two Parisians sat patiently waiting for a reaction. If Grizzard produced the pearls, they would give a prearranged signal to Ward, and the police would swarm the restaurant, arresting Grizzard on the spot. Ward too must have watched the scene—from a distance—with a sense of urgency. But Grizzard was not so easily swayed, and Ward was fully aware of the fact that at every meeting, in a myriad of locations, the four thieves had never been together at the same place at the same time. Grizzard was too smart for that. Grizzard sat back in his seat, relaxed, looking out the restaurant window at a street stenciler, a beggar, a hawker selling tin toys, and then he looked in the direction of Ward and smiled as he took another sip of milky tea.

"I would rather wait until Silverman is present," Grizzard answered coolly. "He is the only one who can properly value the pearls, and I might give you too much."

Quadratstein sensed Grizzard's mistrust, and he suspected that contacting Silverman was just a stalling tactic. For whatever reason—whether he'd been tipped off by a gang member more adept at noticing plainclothes cops than Gutwirth, or whether he himself had noticed detectives on his way into the restaurant, Grizzard was not falling into the trap. Quadratstein could not stand the thought of spending several more days arranging meetings, sitting in tea shops, or hiding out in the stale heat of hotel rooms. Impatient, he asked Grizzard to meet him again later that afternoon at three-fifteen, with Silverman in his company.

Grizzard acquiesced. He paid the bill and the three men parted ways, agreeing to meet again at the designated time at the British Museum tube station nearby. Grizzard left the restaurant, keeping his head low, but most likely taking note of several of Ward's men. None of the detectives could follow him without tipping him off, so they waited for Ward's next instructions and watched, once again, as Grizzard walked swiftly out of view.

Ward and Price grew frustrated by this latest development. It seemed as if Grizzard had been "trying out" the meeting, which in all likelihood, he was. He still had no reason to suspect Brandstatter or Quadratstein of working with the police, but he was keenly aware that the police were shadowing both the thieves and the buyers. Knowing that the exchange of money and pearls could not happen without police shadows, Grizzard picked a place the police would not suspect or offer as much opportunity to hide in plain sight—a tube station. The idea was brilliant. In all other meetings, the group met at various restaurants or hotels where police could easily follow and surround the place. At a tube station, the thieves could arrive from different points in the city to an underground meeting location and disappear on another train once the transaction was finished. But that plan hinged on the fact that police did not know the specifics of a meeting place and time. What Grizzard didn't realize was that Brandstatter and Quadratstein would inform Ward of the plans in advance.

Either way, the odds fell even. Ward's men could surround the station and attempt the sting operation, but Grizzard and his men could just as easily duck into another train and disappear into London's Underground. Once the doors to the train snapped shut, Grizzard, his confederates, and the pearls would for all intents and purposes vanish once again.

Ward, meanwhile, decided to change his mode of operation—it was obviously not working. Grizzard had been able to spot any number of his plainclothes detectives, whether dressed as street cleaners, cabdrivers, businessmen, or peddlers. For a thief raised on the streets of Spitalfields and Whitechapel, with a father who worked as a hawker, Grizzard could hardly fail to recognize a disingenuous peddler or costermonger.

And then Ward had his own brilliant idea: the one person Grizzard and his men would not be looking for was an actual policeman.

*   *   *

When Lockett and Catherine finished their lunch around two-thirty, the pair walked toward the top of Kingsway and entered a Lipton tea shop where they met with Grizzard, whom Catherine had met during their vacation as "Mr. Goldsmith." Once again, Catherine waited patiently while Lockett and Grizzard spoke quietly to each other. Then all three left the restaurant together. Lockett and Catherine went on to the West Green station of the Great Eastern Railway, where they arrived sometime between 3 and 4 P.M. They waited only a few minutes before leaving the station for Belsize Park, a posh London neighborhood of large estates converted to homes and flats. Belsize Park was just a few stops short of Golders Green, where Lockett lived.

The thieves were trying out the tube stations, determining which would be the best place to rendezvous, and which place would provide the easiest escape.

At three-fifteen that afternoon, Ward had Sergeant Cooper dressed down, patrolling the streets in his blue police uniform. The rest of his men sat hidden in a van nearby. Ward watched at a distance as Grizzard, Brandstatter, and Quadratstein arrived and entered the British Museum station. Ward saw Silverman and Lockett approach the station next, pass by it, and take an obscure passage out of view. Ward and his men waited. And waited. After an hour, the group disbanded. Grizzard had disappeared on one of the many trains screeching through the station—Ward's men could not even determine which train he took.

Not long after the dry run at the British Museum tube station, Grizzard arrived at Belsize Park and walked in the door of a nearby pub where Lockett and Catherine sat waiting. Grizzard and Lockett spoke to someone behind the bar—again, in hushed voices so that Catherine could not hear them. And just before 6 P.M., the group separated, and Lockett and Catherine continued on the tube line to Lockett's home in Golders Green for dinner with his daughter, Nellie. Around ten that night, Lockett took Catherine home. She said good-bye to him on the porch, before going inside to see her parents. Catherine was either very trusting and oddly noninquisitive, or more likely, she was well aware that her late aunt Becky and her uncle Jim Lockett were both talented criminals, and she had been taught at an early age not to ask many questions.

The anticlimactic and unsuccessful sting on the afternoon of September 1 told Ward two things: first, Grizzard was testing the plan, and second, he had apparently not noticed the detective disguised as a policeman.

That evening, Brandstatter and Quadratstein met with Price and Ward to tell them that they were scheduled to meet the thieves at the same tube station the following morning at ten-thirty. From there, Grizzard had instructed Brandstatter and Quadratstein to meet him at a nearby public house to finalize the deal.

Ward later wrote, "The following of these men on the Tube without being seen is, in ordinary circumstances, most difficult, and I decided that if I could get them together I would cause them to be arrested, rather than run the risk of being seen or of losing them in attempting to follow them."

He added, "I therefore arranged for the observation to be kept as on the day previous, with the further instructions that if they all met at the station they were to be arrested."

When Ward returned to headquarters, however, he was met with skepticism among his colleagues. Not even the Council of Seven had any real faith in the plan. There was added pressure as well—Scotland Yard could not afford a public embarrassment over something as well known as the pearl necklace heist. In spite of the achievements within the CID, the Metropolitan Police had taken a recent public beating over a high-profile mistake known as the "Siege of Sidney Street." Under the supervision of Home Secretary Winston Churchill, the police suffered losses and neighborhood buildings caught fire in a six-hour gun battle against a dangerous gang in the East End. Reporters photographed Churchill peering around the side of a building giving orders, and he was later accused of "playing to the gallery." Public trust in the police and their superiors was at an all-time low.

If the thieves under full-time surveillance managed to escape detection, the police would be ridiculed in the press once again and the necklace would be lost. At least one of Ward's officials began to grumble about these concerns.

"Perhaps the time is not yet right," he advised.

"Then we'll ripen it," answered Ward.

[Tuesday, September 2, 1913]

The British Museum tube station stood just past the intersection of Kingsway and High Holborn. Like other stations on the Central line, it was a tall, redbrick building that had been sullied by years of pollution. Stone detailing and archways brightened the darker facade.

By 10:30 A.M., Ward's men had infiltrated the station, crowds of commuters, and street pedestrians. He had instructed them to "make up rough," so many had not shaved or washed. Some wore cracked leather shoes with worn soles. Others dressed as news vendors carrying bundles of the morning edition. The plainclothes detectives kept at a distance, while Sergeant Cooper strolled back and forth dressed as a constable. Ward sat hidden with a view of the station so that once he gave the signal, his men could surround the thieves and arrest them.

Silverman was the first to arrive that morning, although the police never saw him approach. He just appeared in the doorway and, as always, looked frazzled. Brandstatter and Quadratstein arrived next. They followed Silverman as he paced along the sidewalk, from one end of the block to the next, nervously looking around to see if anyone had followed him.

Ward watched through the warped glass of his binoculars, looking for Grizzard, Lockett, and Gutwirth. The crowds were thinner than normal since many Londoners were still at the coast or in the countryside. Through the round eyepiece, the people looked smaller, but at the same time sharply vivid. Silverman's frown. Brandstatter's fedora. Quadratstein with his hands in his trouser pockets. Then, through the narrow scope of the glass, Ward saw a tall, gentlemanly figure suddenly standing on the sidewalk: Grizzard.

The other three walked straight over to Grizzard when they noticed him. Gutwirth was not with the group, but he was the least of Ward's concerns; Ward would never sacrifice the king for a pawn. It was already ten minutes to eleven, and Ward began to worry that the meeting would be delayed yet again. They could arrest the group without Gutwirth, but not without Lockett. Brandstatter and Quadratstein had relayed their conversation with Gutwirth, presenting Ward with invaluable knowledge not only about who was holding the pearls, but that another great man in the criminal underworld was involved in the pearl heist.

Within moments, Lockett appeared, coming off the lift from the subway platform. He came out of the station and apparently didn't see Grizzard and the confederates nearby. He started across the street, hands in his pockets, eyes forward, then he suddenly stopped. Lockett turned abruptly, walked back to the group— Grizzard had given him some secret signal that Ward could not discern. Once all the men were present, they walked into the station, where Grizzard purchased tickets to Oxford Circus.

Tickets in hand, the five men climbed into the lift together, and as it slowly descended, the street disappeared from view, the dank smell of the Underground grew stronger, and Grizzard told Quadratstein that he was taking them to "a nice quiet bar where everything would be all right." Lockett nodded and, as usual, kept to himself.

Ward watched as the men disappeared from his view into the subterrain of the station, where any number of trains could carry them in any direction in the world's most populated city. Ward gave Sergeant Cornish the signal, and Cornish gave another signal to passing pedestrians, gentlemen reading the paper, peddlers, and harmless loiterers, who came to a halt, turned, and hurried down the stairs toward the Tube like performers in a choreographed stage production.

Once they were belowground, the heavy lift doors slid open,

and Grizzard and his men stepped out onto the westbound platform, a white, rounded space where the electric lights glossed the tile walls. The tracks were empty and held that vacuum of momentary quiet that exists between trains.

The stillness was broken by Alfred Ward's voice: "Take 'em boys!"

Abruptly, the thieves heard shuffling footsteps, rattling hand-cuffs, and a chaotic mix of voices and shouting. Before the thieves could even process what was happening, Sergeants Cornish and Cooper made for Silverman as two other detectives reached for Lockett, and Haymann grabbed hold of Grizzard. The manacles clicked closed.

"What's the matter?" shouted Silverman, jerking his head around.

"We are police officers," Cornish formally announced in a loud voice, "and will arrest you for being concerned together and with others in stealing and receiving between the fifteenth and sixteenth of July last a pearl necklace, value about one hundred and fifty thousand, between Paris and 88 Hatton Garden, the property of Max Mayer."

The thieves were silent. For one thing, the commotion had been succinct. For another, the arresting officers were dressed in plainclothes as a variety of citizens. It would be oddly surreal to be standing on a train platform one moment and have ordinary coster-mongers and street singers handcuffing you the next.

The detectives walked the thieves up the staircase, and Silverman twisted loose and tried to throw himself down the stairs. The detectives pulled him onto his feet.

"I have not got them on me!" Silverman shouted.

"Haven't got what on you?" Cornish asked coyly.

"You have just told us it's all for the pearls!" shouted a distraught Silverman.

As the arresting detective led Lockett up the stairs, Lockett asked casually, "What's your name?"

"Sergeant Goodwillie."

"Well, you needn't hold me so tight. I have nothing to get rid of. I have plenty of money, but nothing that will get me into trouble," Lockett said.

Standing behind the rest of the group, Grizzard remained calm. As Sergeant Haymann clasped the handcuffs and directed the infamous fence toward the staircase, Grizzard said, "I know what it is all about. I shan't give you any trouble." He remained silent after that.

As the police led the thieves into the sunlight and out onto the street, Silverman felt a wave of profound panic. "I don't like this," he said anxiously. "Life is short. I expect it will be a long time before I come round here again."

Ward had already dispatched some of his men to Hatton Garden to look for Gutwirth. It was just after noon, and on Charles Street, Detective Percy Worth found Gutwirth outside of a pub. The arresting officer explained the accusation to Gutwirth, who cooperated primarily out of embarrassment and an inflated sense of self-importance.

"All right," hissed Gutwirth. "Don't make a scene. Take a taxi. I am well known about here."

In the cab ride to the Bow Street station, Gutwirth asked the officer, "Have you got a warrant for me?"

"No, I don't," the policeman answered.

"Treat me fairly, that is all I ask," said Gutwirth.

The Bow Street Police Station was a building of heavy masonry and daunting stature. It also housed a courthouse, so that one edifice represented both the law and the order under one roof. Ward took the thieves in through the door with POLICE STATION carved above it in stone.

The thieves followed the detectives into separate holding rooms where the police could look through their belongings, take note of contents, and in this critical search, recover the pearl necklace. As the Edwardian period had no shortage of cleverly concealed pockets lining coats and trousers, Ward expected this to be a long process. He undoubtedly had their hats searched as well, since he had already apprehended one criminal after finding the incriminating train ticket sewn into the lining.

By all accounts, Ward was a kind, hardworking detective. It's not likely that he was arrogant or self-satisfied after capturing his criminals, but rather pleased that he had done his job successfully. And it didn't really matter to Ward which man held the necklace; by law, all would be guilty by association.

Gutwirth arrived at the station shortly after the other thieves and was taken to the examination rooms as well. On him, they found English notes and gold—an ounce of gold was worth around £4.25 and was still regularly used as currency. Francs. Rings. A watch and chain, locket, change purse, cigarette case, fountain pen, pair of steel yards, penknife, tweezers, pawnbroker's contract, parcels of tiny gemstones, postage stamps, a memo book, and key ring. Since Gutwirth had not been at the meeting at the train station, and none of the thieves seemed to trust him much, Ward rightly assumed he did not have the pearls.

Silverman's pockets held similar contents: English notes, gold, silver and bronze coins, a jeweler's scoop, gauge, tweezers, scissors, watch, fountain pen, sealing wax, stamps, memo books, key ring, and a silk handkerchief. Then the police found several incriminating French notes as well.

Ward believed that Lockett most likely had the pearls on him. He was the experienced burglar and a strong, stout man known well on the London streets. A pickpocket wouldn't dare approach him. Lockett's pockets were emptied and noted: sixty-five pounds in gold, bronze and English notes, rings, a gold watch and chain, silver matchbox, gold fountain pen, diamond-and-pearl scarf pin, cigar case, postage stamps, ten keys on a ring, and a torn receipt from exchanging money at Cook & Sons (Bankers) in Southampton.

Lockett had remained unruffled throughout, or as one detective described him, "self-contained to the point of facetiousness."

"This is a bit of all right," he said playfully as the police emptied his pockets of money. "I have been to France for a bit of a holiday only yesterday, and this is a nice way to treat me when I get back."

The police held up the receipt for exchanging money in South-ampton.

"I changed the money into English money," he said without concern. "That is the paper that refers to it."

The detectives logged everything in great detail in the casebooks as Ward supervised. They also retrieved a key from one pocket and labeled it.

Finally, they turned to Grizzard. For Ward, there must have been some sense of satisfaction in knowing Grizzard held the pearls. It seemed right somehow—he was the leader of the heist. Grizzard held still, lifted up his arms, as the detectives fumbled through his pockets, finding gold, silver, and bronze money. He had a gold watch and chain in one coat pocket. In another, detectives found a cigar cutter, cigar case, a small matchbox, tiepins, diamond rings, nail file, penknife, eyeglass, handkerchief, railway tickets, visiting cards, a memo book, and five keys on a ring. His pockets held a few jeweler's items as well—a set of jeweler weights, scales, a pair of jeweler's steel yards, and a gauge.

There was, however, no sign of the pearl necklace. For Ward, the full weight of this discovery began to sink in, and at that moment, it's very likely that Grizzard's trademark smirk crept across his face, lifting the corners of his blond mustache. Ward had finally captured all four thieves, and not one of them had the pearl necklace.

Joseph Grizzard grew up along these streets and in neighboring Whitechapel—an area teeming with crime and poverty. Grizzard was just a teen when Jack the Ripper hunted and murdered local prostitutes living here.
COURTESY OF MARY EVANS PICTURE LIBRARY, PETER HIGGINBOTHAM COLLECTION

The Ten Bells Pub, depicted here on the corner of Commercial Street, was a favorite haunt for Ripper victims. AUTHOR'S COLLECTION

This view from St. Cross Street looking south down Hatton Garden is how the avenue appeared at the time of the heist with Max Mayer's shop located on the right at the far end of the street. Many of these buildings were later destroyed during bombing in both world wars.

A Hatton Garden street scene today looking north from Holborn Circus. Hatton Garden remains the center of London's jewel trading. Little about the business has changed in the last century and shopkeepers are as wary as ever of anyone who appears suspicious.

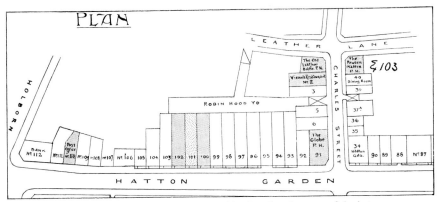

Scotland Yard's map of the Hatton Garden neighborhood at the time of the heist.

A sketch of the reward poster.

Daily Chronicle coverage of the theft. AUTHOR'S COLLECTION

At the turn of the twentieth century, the headquarters for the Metropolitan Police were known as New Scotland Yard after moving from their original location at Whitehall Place and Great Scotland Yard to a new, state-of-the-art building designed by famed architect Norman Shaw. Scotland Yard became a metonym for London's Metropolitan Police and detective unit. COURTESY OF MARY EVANS PICTURE LIBRARY

The detectives "made up rough" in this photograph spent months studying how to blend into a street scene. The Metropolitan Police headquarters had entire floors dedicated to wigs, makeup rooms, clothes and accessories.

The concept of a plainclothes detective was met with skepticism by the public, which considered it a deceitful attack on personal liberty.

A busy street scene at the corner of High Holborn and Kingsway. With pedestrians, bicycles, autos, and horse-drawn cabs, traffic moved in a sort of organized chaos at varying speeds.

The Grizzard Gang frequently held meetings at Liptons and Lyons teashops—although it was never a simple affair. The thieves met at prearranged times and locations, jumped aboard buses, took quiet alleyways, entered and exited through back doors, and changed locations several times to elude detectives.

A view—much like the one in Alfred Ward's sights—of the exterior of the station where the thieves convened on the morning of September 2, 1913. It was later used as an air raid shelter and eventually closed in the 1960s. Although the building above it was demolished, the cavernous tunnels of the station still exist underground.

COURTESY OF TFL FROM THE LONDON TRANSPORT MUSEUM COLLECTION

FROM LEFT TO RIGHT: Lesir Gutwirth, Simon Silverman, Joseph Grizzard, and James Lockett. Daniel McCarthy, whose charges were later dropped, was cropped out of the photo.

COURTESY OF THE NATIONAL ARCHIVES, KEW

Muir was the Crown's prosecutor in the Great Pearl Heist Trial. He was fresh off his case convicting Hawley Harvey Crippen for the murder of his wife. The Scottish Muir became one of England's greatest legal minds.

AUTHOR'S COLLECTION

THE THEFT OF THE £117,000 PEARL NECKLACE AND THE SHERLOCK HOLMES PLOT THAT DID NOT LEAD TO ITS RECOVERY.

Ex-Detective-Inspector Leach. Mr. Quadratstein. Mr. Brandstatter. Chief Detective-Inspector Ward.

The "heist of the new century" and the search for the missing necklace culminated into a sensational trial with photographers lining the block outside Old Bailey. Edwardian clothing and social status are on full display as the principle players in the trial enter the courthouse—top hats and waistcoats for the wealthiest, bowler or boater hats for the modest middle class, and the stylish new fedora on the Parisians.

COURTESY OF THE NATIONAL ARCHIVES, KEW

[PART THREE]

JUSTICE

FOURTEEN

Searching

ON A QUIET STREET OF VICTORIAN HOMES OF RUSSET BRICK, WITH
white-trimmed windows and sharply angled rooflines, Jim Lockett's
niece Hannah wandered around his house on Powis Gardens in
Golders Green. Since her aunt's death that spring, Hannah had been
helping with light housework and looking after her young cousin
Nellie. Several valises littered the entryway to the house, where the
motoring party had returned from their stay in Southampton. It
was late afternoon on Tuesday, September 2, and the notched
shadow of rooflines began to creep across the front lawn.

A shrill telephone bell pierced the silence, and Hannah hurried
to pick it up, lifting the black earphone to her head and leaning in
to the trumpet-shaped mouthpiece. Through the crackling line she
heard the voice of Mary Finn, Lockett's sister in London. She sounded
rushed and asked Hannah if she had a key to the safe in Lockett's
home. Hannah told her that she did not.

Shortly after the phone call, Mary Finn arrived at Lockett's house herself and tried the safe, to no avail. Finn knocked on Lizzie Moore's guest room upstairs—the Moores were staying as guests in Lockett's home for the night. Hannah stood nearby in the hallway watching as Finn asked Moore if she knew of a key to Lockett's safe, and again had no luck. The two women spoke quietly in the bedroom for a moment before Lizzie Moore locked her bedroom door and told Hannah to bolt the front door to the house and not to open it under any circumstances. As the two women hurried out, a sense of foreboding blanketed Hannah—she had not heard from her uncle since he left the house that morning.

❧

That same afternoon, scattered around the long wooden table at the CID, Ward looked over the files of thieves and known associates of the Grizzard Gang. Where had Grizzard planned to go at the tube station? Who was he meeting? Did that person hold the pearls or were they locked away safely somewhere? The questions plagued Ward as he shuffled through photographs and profiles. Time was of the essence. Although he had the principal players at Bow Street, the pearls were still at large, and the gang member who held them would soon be on the move.

Grizzard relied on his extensive network of confederates, all of whom served different purposes. There were those he trusted most, those he bought from, those he sold to, and a wealth of small-time criminals who for one reason or another served Grizzard loyally. What Ward needed to find out was which of those associates Grizzard would have trusted with the pearls.

One man came to mind. A retired Continental jewel thief

named Daniel McCarthy had been a great success in his day—so successful in fact that the eighty-two-year-old retired without ever serving time. McCarthy had been smart enough to keep his business and his home separate, so all of his thefts occurred abroad. As far as Scotland Yard knew, McCarthy had never stolen anything in Great Britain. McCarthy was also a known associate of Grizzard's, as well as the other three Grizzard Gang members under arrest for the pearl heist.

Ward clapped his hat onto his head, grabbed his overcoat, and hurried toward Hatton Garden. Not knowing where McCarthy liked to spend his time, Ward went on a hunch to a favorite public house of Gutwirth's, the George, tucked away on a narrow lane off Holborn called Brook Street.

Ward opened the heavy door to the George, letting a blade of daylight into the dim interior of the pub. A few men looked up from their tables and then dropped their heads again, turning their attention back to their pints and platters. The sight of Scotland Yard detectives casing pubs around Hatton Garden was hardly new. One face, however, never looked to the door; its owner stared straight ahead at the tidy rows of bottles, glasses, and brass taps. Ward saw Daniel McCarthy, seated at the bar, with a bouquet of flowers in front of him. McCarthy's wave of thick silver hair and full beard suggested a bygone era; his cane was hooked onto the back of his chair. He appeared to be waiting.

Ward casually approached McCarthy. "Who are you waiting for?"

"Lesir Gutwirth," McCarthy answered with the composure only a seasoned thief could maintain so well.

"I have some questions for you about the Max Mayer pearls stolen several weeks ago."

"I know nothing about it," McCarthy answered. "All I did was bring flowers here for Gutwirth, whom I have only known for five weeks or so."

Ward picked up the bouquet, tied together with string and paper. The heavy scent of hothouse flowers rushed at him.

"He told me the other day that his little girl was ill, so I brought him some flowers to give to her," McCarthy explained pleasantly.

Ward asked McCarthy what was in his pockets. McCarthy pulled out some five-pound banknotes and placed them on the bar in front of him.

"What else?" Ward asked skeptically.

McCarthy emptied the rest of his pockets, which held a suspiciously large amount of money for an outing to the pub—twenty-nine pounds, some change, and a bag of gold. Ward stared at McCarthy, waiting for some kind of explanation.

"It is all mine. I have just sold a house for five hundred pounds and also received compensation for an injury." Again, McCarthy's answers were ready-made.

"Where did you get the money and the notes?" Ward asked.

McCarthy smiled. "I received the Bank of England notes from Cook's at Ludgate Hill in exchange for two five-hundred-franc French notes on Saturday last. The French notes I got from a Continental gentleman whose name I decline to give. I heard them talking at Hatton Garden about some diamonds and volunteered to change the notes."

Ward pulled manacles from his pocket and informed McCarthy that he was being formally arrested in connection to the pearl heist.

"All that I can say is that I am innocent," McCarthy answered as the detective led him from the smell of stale ale out into the stench of the street. Just before leaving, McCarthy handed the bouquet of flowers to the barmaid, gave her a pointed stare, and asked her to pass them along to Gutwirth or one of his known associates. The barmaid kept her word—later that day, she handed the wilting bouquet over to a member of the Grizzard Gang who came by to collect it.

⁓

After McCarthy's arrest, with his suspects held safely in police custody, Ward and his men returned to Hatton Garden and searched Silverman's office. In the small rooms, the police fingered the usual jewelry trade items—scales, bottles of solution, disjointed watches or clasps waiting to be fixed. They also found dark red sealing wax, a spirit lamp, the ladle used for melting wax, and a seal with the letters *J.T.* On the table sat another seal in the shape of a locket and shield. The police carefully gathered all of the evidence.

From there, they took the train to Dalston to search Grizzard's home. By then, it was evening, the sky indigo. The lights from inside Grizzard's home lit the front windows and porch. Ward had not been in the house since the search several years before, following the Café Monico heist. The home of the notorious fence felt very much like any other upper-middle-class residence. Ward found family photos, a wealth of correspondence, stationery, seals, and ink pens along Grizzard's desk. In the master-bedroom dresser, he confiscated a good deal of fine jewelry, but it was later proved to be the property of Grizzard's wife, Sarah. Other jewelry items—cuff links, shirt studs, cigar cases—all belonged to Grizzard himself. None of it appeared to be stolen. The detectives found no ledger books or false identity cards or suspicious travel tickets. Nothing in the home pointed to its owner being one of the most notorious thieves of his day.

Ward knew that Lesir Gutwirth had a safe box at a depository on Chancery Lane, so while he searched the Grizzard home he sent his detectives there next. It was not unusual for thieves to use safe-deposit boxes for stolen jewels, but Gutwirth's held nothing valuable. Nor did the police find anything at Gutwirth's home or the Vienna Café, where Gutwirth kept a drawer for business.

The same proved true at Silverman's home. His aging mother looked on as the police searched the place late that night. Again, they found nothing.

Finally, Ward sent some of his men to Lockett's house in Golders Green to investigate as well. Hannah had no choice but to let them in when they arrived that night. The detectives used the key found in Lockett's pocket at the time of his arrest to open a personal safe, and inside, they found seventy pounds in gold, a passport under the name Fitzpatrick, checks, and hotel receipts. If the safe had ever held the necklace, there was no sign of it now. The pearls remained as elusive as ever.

Discouraged, Ward returned to Bow Street.

By now, it was after midnight. London's streets still appeared wet, cloudy with the ghosts of a late-night rain. Buildings were yellowed by streetlamps and caulked with darkness between. By 1 A.M., Ward felt exhausted and defeated as he stood before Grizzard and his gang members to formally announce their arrest and have them taken to holding cells for the night.

FIFTEEN

At Bow Street

[Wednesday, September 3, 1913]

THE NEXT MORNING AT HALF-PAST TEN, ON A "PEA SOUP DAY" thick with fog, Grizzard, Lockett, Silverman, Gutwirth, and McCarthy stood before the magistrate at the Bow Street Police Court. According to English law, the men could not be held for more than forty-eight hours before appearing at court for a preliminary hearing of the charges.

All five men wore fine, respectable suits. Lockett's was a lighter suit with a double collar and a black tie. Grizzard's clothes were darker, and he had trimmed his mustache. The papers described both men and their attire in detail, but the media portrayal of Silverman and Gutwirth didn't attempt to hide the prevailing prejudice of the times. Gutwirth was described as "clearly a foreigner." Silverman, the newspaper said, had an ill-fitting suit, a "foreign appearance," a sallow complexion, and looked "so short as to be almost a dwarf."

The accused sat in the dock, which had an awkward, all-eyes-on-you feel in the center of the room. McCarthy's hands trembled as he rested them on the railing, though more likely from age than from fear. Ward presented the evidence he had thus far and the basis for arrest. A futile attempt at bail was made by the defense. The only other matter before the court that morning was the briefing of senior treasury counsel assigned to the case—the lead barrister who, along with his team of junior counsel, would prosecute on behalf of the Crown at the Central Criminal Court. That morning, the magistrate read the name of the senior treasury counsel assigned to the pearl heist case: Richard Muir.

The thieves sat in the dock, heads down for most of the proceedings, hands folded in their lap or on the rail in front of them. But when Muir's name was announced as counsel for the Crown, Grizzard raised his head slightly, his eyes lifted. Lockett, seated to his left, must have felt the subtle shift in Grizzard's disposition, however imperceptible.

Finally, after the short hearing, the five men were led from the dock, down into the cells. After appearing before the magistrate, the men could only be held for an additional seven days, so Ward and his detectives were up against the clock to organize and present all of the evidence for a formal indictment. Ward had one week to take statements from all witnesses, provide evidence the prosecution needed for a conviction, and most importantly, find the pearls.

Likewise, Muir and his team of prosecutors had one week to prepare. They spent most of those days in the offices of Scotland Yard interviewing Ward and his men. Muir much preferred to argue cases heavily weighted with physical evidence rather than eyewitness testimony. Scotland Yard's progressive technology and modern methods always trumped the inconsistent and often suspect testimony of witnesses.

Unfortunately for Muir, the majority of the pearl case came down to witnesses, some of whom had questionable reputations at best. There were no fingerprints; searches of the thieves' homes had not produced the pearls, the forged seals, or any evidence that the thieves had been casing Max Mayer and his store.

Instead, Muir and his team of prosecutors spent hours organizing the witness statements to police and trying to trace the path of the necklace from Paris to Hatton Garden. In a maddening conundrum, the police and the prosecutors could not prove that the pearls had been stolen in France *or* in England. It left the prosecution with a challenging case in which the chain of events seemed loosely constructed and everything depended upon a parade of unreliable witnesses. Worse, the pearls themselves were still missing.

Finally, Muir tossed his ink pen aside, closed his files, and turned to his junior counsel. "Come on, let's go and get something to eat and then thrash it out again."

SIXTEEN

Sir Richard Muir

❦

[Wednesday, September 10, 1913]

SIR RICHARD MUIR SAT AT THE PROSECUTOR'S TABLE STACKING his cards into a neat pile beside a cluster of colored pencils held tight with a rubber band. Known as Muir's "playing cards," each held information pertinent to the case, written in different colored pencils, then alphabetized and subdivided by number. One color was used for examination questions, another for cross-examination, a third for reexamination. Anything considered especially important, he penciled in red. Each time Muir tightened the stack, it clapped against the wooden table and echoed in the courtroom. One of the Crown's best counselors, Muir had an objective and persuasive method of arguing described as "killing by fairness."

Grizzard sat in the dock, his hands clasped in front of him on the rail, his head steady and unmoving, his eyes focused on Muir. On one side sat Lockett, and on the other, Silverman, Gutwirth, and Daniel McCarthy. Somewhere from the left side of the room, Grizzard heard a camera shutter click.

Entering through the back of the Bow Street Police Court, Grizzard did not have the opportunity to the see the crowds on the street—the line of pedestrians ribboned down the block—but he could see the courtroom filled to capacity that morning. In one of the front witness seats sat detective Alfred Ward.

For Grizzard, however, all focus was on Muir. Grizzard had shared a courtroom with Muir twice before—he had served as the prosecuting counsel during the Café Monico trial and, after spending weeks trying to get Harry Grimshaw and Tom Higgins to turn evidence for the Crown against Grizzard, had failed. Muir had also served as prosecuting counsel in a trial involving one of his oldest friends, Vaughan Morgan, when two of Grizzard's men had stolen £5,000 worth of jewelry from his home. In both cases, Muir had known Grizzard was the mastermind behind the thefts, and in both cases, he had been unable to prove it.

Muir rarely lost cases—he was an ambitious and hardworking barrister. Scottish by birth, he had been raised in a large family with fifteen brothers and sisters. He followed his older brother Baleigh to London. Muir had no money, but he had drive and determination—a child among fifteen others could hardly help but develop a strong will.

Muir spent three years attending lectures at King's College, working at the British Museum and Kensington Museum to learn more of British history and earn some pay, and eventually, he graduated with honors. Muir proved particularly adept at the sciences and had a flair for writing, which led him to work as a reporter. True to his determined nature, he also took courses in shorthand until he evolved into a prodigious note taker. Because he showed special skill at reporting verbatim, he covered political speeches, worked as a parliamentary reporter, and reported on court cases for the London *Times*.

Muir's court reporting soon ripened into a love of the law. He continued his work at the paper, attending the House of Commons, often working until 2 A.M., before returning home to sleep for a few hours and waking again at seven. He was then in chambers by nine, to cover the trials. The schedule was exhausting. Books and briefs cluttered his desk at home. Finally, his wife persuaded him to choose one profession or the other—the practice of law or the reporting of it. Following his brother Baleigh's lead, he turned to the law full-time.

From the start, Muir proved a talented barrister. Not only did he have extensive knowledge of the justice system after so many years reporting it, but he'd also had the chance to observe human nature in its many forms. Even Muir's physical appearance seemed to embody the ideals of the law—he looked somewhat owlish. He was clean-shaven with clear blue eyes, a furrowed brow, a Roman nose, and a dusting of fine silver hair.

Though Muir spent most of his time in the courtroom, he had a few interests outside the courts as well. He played golf, although he picked up the game late in life for a Scot. Muir, called Dickey by his friends, was also a gentle family man with a kind smile, the sort of man who took his grandson to Kensington Park on Saturdays to sail toy boats in the pond.

Inside the courtroom, however, Muir had a reputation for being methodical, quiet, and persistent. His arguments were always grounded firmly in fact, but his liquid-mercury style of arguing was cool and pervasive, making the fiery rhetoric of his opponents seem all the more overwrought. Rather than attacking witnesses, he held a conversation with them. Before they even realized it, they had confessed to everything Muir wanted to know. He was so genial about it, they couldn't even be angry with him.

After fifteen years and many successes, Muir had the chance to "take silk" and don the silk robes of the King's Counsel. Muir, however, preferred to stay with the treasury counsel, which served under the attorney general as the main prosecuting body in criminal cases.

During his tenure as a barrister, Muir tried a number of the biggest cases of the times. He prosecuted Steinie Morrison, an ex-convict and burglar, for the murder of Leon Beron during an attempted robbery. It was a challenging trial in which the defense lobbed wild theories as to why their client should not be found guilty. In addition to that, the East End community gathered ranks and defended Morrison, one of their own. Many witnesses retracted their original statements to the police. It was a legal quagmire. Muir's arguments and the evidence provided by Scotland Yard were strong enough to convict Morrison, but so much doubt and publicity surrounded the trial that the home secretary finally commuted the death sentence for Morrison.

In many cases, like Morrison's, Muir relied on the infallible detective work of Alfred Ward. In another case, the Seddon poisoners, Ward had found evidence that the Seddons, a father, mother, and daughter team, were soaking flypaper in liquid to dissolve a fatal dose of arsenic. Eventually, detectives found that the Seddons had poisoned one of their boarders and subsequently stolen her inheritance. The case gained so much publicity and involved such a large amount of circumstantial evidence that the attorney general stepped in, assigning Muir to junior counsel in the case.

Muir's highest-profile case to date, however, was the Hawley

Harvey Crippen trial. When Crippen's wife went missing, Scotland Yard discovered body parts of a woman beneath his property. Finding no head to use as a source of identity, the police believed it was Crippen's wife based on a scar and a scrap of clothing. The case garnered international attention after detectives used the greatest new technology—wireless telegraph—to apprehend Crippen and his mistress as they fled on board an ocean liner from London to New York. When Crippen learned that Muir would be the prosecutor in his case, he lamented, "I wish it had been anybody else but him . . . I fear the worst."

For all of his sensational cases, the ones Muir preferred the most, however, were those with a clever criminal—someone with whom he could match wits, mind for mind. Joseph Grizzard had been that mind in two of Muir's cases. And in both, Muir had lost.

❧

Outside Bow Street, curious pedestrians crowded the sidewalks. Ahead of them, forming a barrier, photographers lined up their tripods like modern stick insects with box cameras attached at the top. The cameras ticked incessantly as notable figures from the pearl heist walked by. Mr. Max Mayer appeared in a morning suit buttoned up tight, his top hat glossy in the black-and-white photographs. He prodded his umbrella against the ground as he strolled by reporters. Beside him, Mr. Price approached. Also dressed in an elegant suit, he had left his coat unbuttoned, displaying a vest and fine watch chain swinging across him. Round spectacles sat beneath his shiny top hat. He had a clean-shaven face that showcased his youth next to the older, bewhiskered gentlemen. To the other side of Mayer, keeping a respectful distance, Mr. Solomans followed in his modest business suit and bowler hat. He carried an attaché case. All three gentlemen smiled at reporters as they passed by and waved off questions.

Moments later, the cameras began again, as rapid as wing beats. Alfred Ward arrived in his best business suit, expertly knotted tie, and bowler hat. Former inspector Alfred Leach approached as well in a suit and boater's hat, even though it was a little late in the season. Between the two detectives, and standing nearly a head beneath them, walked Quadratstein and Brandstatter. Quadratstein had tipped his fedora to the left and dangled a cigarette from his lips. He raised his brows quizzically, looking around him at all the commotion caused by this one necklace. Beside him, Brandstatter looked more nervous, his fedora pulled closer over his eyes. Both men, like Price, were younger and clean-shaven. The witnesses parading by the photographers literally wore their class distinction. The wealthiest boasted top hats, the middle-class gentlemen donned the more modest bowler or derby hat, and the foreigners flashed their fedoras.

Crowds of spectators filled the large oak-lined courtroom, having cast aside their summer whites and boat hats for fur-trimmed stoles and the deeper colors of autumn. The change in dress seemed to reflect the tone of the case as well—summer's frivolity had come to an end.

Muir, cards in hand, stood before the magistrate to argue the preliminary case against Grizzard, Lockett, Silverman, and Gutwirth. As was his style, he presented the simple facts of the case without flowering oratory. He explained that Grizzard had made the fatal mistake of trusting Lesir Gutwirth, a man Grizzard himself referred to as having "far too long a tongue." Muir went on to explain Gutwirth's relationship to Brandstatter and how the decoys became involved in the case. The five men sat in the dock listening to Muir's steady voice, and it may very well have been the first time Grizzard, Lockett, and Silverman realized exactly how they had been trapped and with whom the fault lay.

Muir called several witnesses, including Quadratstein, Solomans, Spanier, and Price. Relaxed and completely at ease, Quadratstein relayed the events and his role as a decoy. He also testified that Gutwirth told him they'd paid off postmen to acquire the package of pearls. Then, he added, Gutwirth promised the pearls were safe with Jim Lockett, the thief responsible for the Café Monico heist.

"Oh, that does not matter," Muir interjected.

"You may as well put it down," Lockett said, smiling. He was clearly unbothered by the false accusation linking him to another crime in which he had no part. The witness statement also showed Gutwirth's ignorance about Grizzard and his gang members.

Quadratstein repeated the tale as he'd heard it from Gutwirth, about a short, dark-haired, thin man, accompanied by a tall, blond, thin man, both around thirty-five years old, who robbed Mr. Goldschmidt of his jewels. Apparently, it did not seem odd to Gutwirth or Quadratstein that Lockett was of a stocky build, medium height, and in his late forties at the time of the heist. Muir too must have dismissed the account as complete rubbish. As the prosecutor in the Café Monico trial, he knew the details all too well.

Next, Muir called Mayer's trusted agent from Paris, Mr. Solomans, to the stand. As Solomans was devoutly Jewish, the papers noted, he was allowed to be sworn in still wearing his hat. In the witness box, Solomans described showing the necklace to interested buyers in Paris and returning the pearls to Mayer. Solomans then pulled from his attaché case the leather box used to mail the necklace.

"Was there any sugar about?" Mr. Muir asked.

Solomans just smiled.

"Was there a piece of French newspaper?" Muir continued. "Who placed the valuable things in the box?"

"Myself," Solomans answered.

That afternoon, after hearing Muir's case against the thieves, court was adjourned until the fourteenth and fifteenth of September, when the witnesses would be brought forward once again. During that time, Muir would have the charges against Daniel McCarthy dropped. So far, McCarthy's story had checked out, and even if he had some involvement in the gang, he wasn't one of the principal players in this heist. He would only add confusion to the case and possibly cast doubt on the others on trial. Muir wanted to keep the focus squarely on Lockett, Silverman, Gutwirth, and especially, Grizzard.

Several friends of Grizzard's approached the police to make applications to visit him in prison. Being highly wary of the confederates, the magistrate initially said no. Then Ward had an idea. The pearls were still at large, and Grizzard or Lockett might be the only ones who knew where they were hidden. Whoever was holding the necklace would be waiting to hear from Grizzard about how to proceed. Permission for visitors was granted, and Ward spoke with the prison governor about when and how these meetings with Grizzard's confederates would take place. Maybe they would be able to overhear or follow a confederate to the hiding place and finally retrieve the necklace.

SEVENTEEN

The Piano Tuner

THE DAY AFTER MCCARTHY'S RELEASE, SOMETHING REMARKABLE happened—and probably not by coincidence. Augustus George Horn, known as Gus, left his home in Islington to walk to work early on the morning of September 16. Horn, through the fog of a hangover, would have seen the usual morning routines—street sweepers brushing the sidewalks, a woman scrubbing the front walk of her shop, upstairs blinds still pulled against the morning light, shops with the curtains drawn, a couple of young girls running to catch a streetcar, an omnibus crowded with morning commuters.

As he approached Canonbury Bridge, Horn saw a police sergeant ahead of him, followed closely by a constable. He also saw a couple. The woman, her hands in the pockets of her black cloak, walked casually, slowly, compared to those rushing by her. She wore a black hat netted with white and seemed distracted, looking around her at times, pausing to look behind her. The gentleman seemed rather solidly built. He had a dark mustache, neatly trimmed, and he wore black trousers and a morning coat. As the crowd swarmed past them, the woman glanced behind her one more time, subtly pulling her hand from her cloak and dropping something into the gutter below a streetlamp. She and the gentleman walked on, waiting at the curb as an omnibus approached.

Horn called after her twice, hoping to get her attention. He poked at the package with his walking stick and then picked it up from the curbstone—a brown paper package—and ran toward the woman, again calling after her to tell her she'd dropped something. The woman never looked back. The couple climbed onto omnibus number 44 and disappeared.

Horn unwrapped the package and found a Bryant & May matchbox. He held it in his palm. Finally, his curiosity got the better of him, and he opened it—only to be disappointed when he found what he believed to be a bunch of pink children's marbles. As he opened the matchbox, several spilled out, falling into the gutter. Horn dropped to his knees and collected as many as he could. There must have been over fifty marbles there. He shoved the package into his pocket and picked up any stragglers, stuffing them into another jacket pocket, as he continued walking toward work, turning up Holloway and then onto Rhodes Road.

At work, he showed a few mates what he'd found in the street. To all eyes present, he simply held a bunch of pink marbles in his palm. Unimpressed, they went on with their work.

Whether to assuage the hangover or simply out of habit, Horn decided, as he often did, to skip work and head to a pub. He and several mates stopped at the Swan public house on Highbury, ordered a pint, and opened the Bryant & May matchbox once again. He tried to sell the marbles for a few pence to buy a pint. The publican told Horn he might want to head to the nearest police station—the "marbles," he said, looked an awful lot like those pearls in the newspapers recently. Horn obliged and walked, or somewhat stumbled, out the door of the pub for the Caledonian Road Police Station.

At the station, a policeman took Horn's statement as well as he could. By then, Horn was quite drunk and slurred, "Do you think they are pearls or marbles? You never know, they might be valuable."

The police investigator took a close look and told Horn that they were probably fake pearls that had fallen from a child's pocket on St. Paul's Road. The policeman recorded the exchange in the ledger, listing the pearls as imitations, and asked Horn to sign the ledger. In three months' time, if no one had claimed the fakes, Horn could apply to keep them.

Two of Horn's mates stood outside the police station waiting for him. They walked on to a pub, the first of several they would visit that afternoon. As they walked, Horn reached into his pocket and pulled out one single pearl.

"What about this?" he asked.

"Throw it away down the drain," his friend scoffed.

Horn felt the pearl in his pocket, rolling it around in his grasp. His mind wrapped around the idea that the marbles may very well be genuine pearls, and he knew the value of pearls. Later that afternoon, Horn dropped the pearl into his brother's pocket, patted him on the shoulder, and told him, "There is four hundred pounds for you."

After Horn left the station, the policeman held the "imitation" pearls in his hand. They felt remarkably heavy for fakes. He balanced them on his palm and guessed at their weight, pulling out the newspaper clippings about the lost necklace. The weights and measurements printed in the paper were very similar to those he now held. He phoned a local jeweler to come in and examine the pearls, and then he phoned Scotland Yard.

That afternoon, the underwriters at Lloyd's of London in the Royal Exchange heard from the bowels of the building the ringing of the Lutine Bell. The bell itself had been recovered from the *Lutine* shipwreck of 1779, and whenever a ship went missing and was declared lost, the bell rang out once to inform underwriters and brokers that their investment had gone missing. If the ship safely returned to port, the bell clanged two times or more to celebrate the arrival of the much-anticipated ship and its valuable cargo.

For the first time in its history, the Lutine Bell rang that afternoon for something other than a wayward ship. As it clanged and echoed through the Royal Exchange, someone shouted, "Gentlemen, the rumor regarding the recovery of the necklace is correct!" Cheers and applause resounded in the hallways. Soon after the return of the Mayer necklace, Lloyd's officially changed its policy, and no single item could be insured for more than £50,000.

EIGHTEEN

A Glimpse

WARD SAT BACK IN HIS CHAIR AT SCOTLAND YARD, DROPPED HIS pen onto the table, and crossed his arms. Before him, he had the official report: *Statement of AUGUST GEORGE HORN, of 40 Baxter Road, Islington, taken at New Scotland Yard on 16th September 1913. Who saith . . .*

Horn had recorded exactly how he came across the pearls, the smartly dressed couple ahead of him, the policeman nearby, taking the pearls to the pub, and finally turning them in to the police.

This morning, however, Gus Horn sat before Ward sober and with a throbbing headache made much worse by the bright lights above him and the incessant questions before him. Horn could not remember much of anything from the day before.

Ward had contacted Horn's employer, who reported that Horn had worked for him for several years and was a very good worker, but was also addicted to drink. He and his mates often skipped work to hit various pubs.

Frustrated, Ward jotted down on his paperwork "his mind was almost a blank." Ward went on to write, "In my opinion, the finding of the pearls by this man was quite an accident, the person who dropped them really intending that they should be picked up by a police sergeant who was passing at the time."

If Ward had any failing as a detective, it was his willingness to trust the integrity of others, to see the honor within him mirrored in those before him. It did not occur to him that Horn may have lied at any point in his statement, or that he could even be lying about his drink-induced memory lapse.

Ward, then, saw nothing more than a coincidence in the fact that one of Horn's favorite pubs was the George in Hatton Garden— the very pub frequented by Gutwirth, the same pub where detectives arrested Daniel McCarthy only days before. Horn often visited the George public house with his good friend John Cohen, though the two men had not been seen there together in several weeks. And Ward did not consider it suspicious that Cohen was, in fact, Lockett's brother-in-law. He was the brother of Becky Cohen Lockett, the talented thief who had been Lockett's wife until her death that April. He was the father of Hannah, the niece staying at Lockett's home to help care for her younger cousin. Nor did it concern Ward that Cohen often hired Horn to help him pawn jewelry.

With the retrieval of the pearls, the trial suddenly gained even more attention. Horn enjoyed a brief moment of celebrity when a photo of him with his wife and children appeared on the covers of dailies.

The following day, the *Daily Sketch* published a photo of Horn, his wife, Brandstatter, Price, and Ward outside Bow Street. Although the trial dominated the media toward the end of September, the papers made room for a few other sensational stories as well, including the major upset at the U.S. Open that year when twenty-year-old Francis Ouimet beat Britain's greatest golfers, Harry Vardon and Ted Ray, in a rainy-day play-off. A few headlines also described the trial of a famous suffragette that began at Old Bailey.

[Thursday, September 18, 1913]

The following morning, the crowds had thickened, mobbing the sidewalk outside the courtroom. Many Hatton Garden traders and brokers attended out of curiosity, and a large number of women took a sudden interest in the case. Several ladies hired messenger boys to arrive at Bow Street at seven-thirty and hold a place in line until the trial started. The onlookers then packed into the hallways and seats of the courtroom. They were there to see the real celebrity in the case, the Mayer necklace.

Fifty-seven of the original sixty-one pearls had now been recovered. In addition to those, the two that Spanier had purchased at the First Avenue Hotel had been returned to Mayer. Two remained missing—one had been dropped into the jacket pocket of Horn's brother, and one, the largest of all the pearls, was still unaccounted for. The thieves had sold the diamond clasp to the necklace almost as soon as acquiring the pearls.

Muir stood that morning, hands folded behind his back, and called his first witness: Mr. Max Mayer. Muir faced the witness box and held a small brown paper bag, from which he pulled a bulky envelope. He broke a red "evidence" seal on the envelope and, without fanfare, handed a bundle of cotton wool to Mayer.

Nearby, a detective mumbled, "There they are, curse them—the cause of all the trouble."

"Would you look at those pearls, Mr. Mayer?" asked Muir. "Are they yours and part of the stolen necklace, fifty-nine in all?" Muir did his best to keep his tone steady as always, free of theatrics, letting the facts speak for themselves as he handed the pearls, now strung together, to his witness. Mayer, however, felt no need to play down the drama.

"They are," replied Mayer as he undressed the pearls from their wrapping and held them high in the air. The crowd gasped, camera shutters clicked, the courtroom sketch artist hurriedly penciled the necklace. The flesh-colored pearls dangled gracefully from Mayer's hand, opalescent in the electric lighting of the courtroom. Those who had a view of the pearls said they were small and "astonishingly beautiful." Mayer smiled proudly and fondled the pearls with his plump fingers.

He reluctantly handed the necklace back to Muir, who marked it as evidence and had the pearls wrapped up once again in their padded packaging. Muir handed the pearls to Ward, who left the courtroom flanked by guards and surrounded by the sound of fluttering cameras. Once in the hall and out of sight, Ward extracted the pearls from all the elaborate packaging, slipped them into an innocuous paper bag and into the pocket of a waiting detective who hurried off to return them to the evidence room at Scotland Yard.

Muir then called other witnesses before the magistrate, including Mr. Spanier. Mayer confirmed that Spanier had been called in

from Paris to act the part of illegal receiver in purchasing the necklace. Spanier answered Muir's questions obligingly.

During cross-examination, the defense asked Spanier additional
questions. Specifically, the defense wanted to know about the bedroom meeting at the First Avenue Hotel and why Spanier did not
take the opportunity at that time to retrieve the whole necklace,
return it to authorities, and collect the reward money.

Spanier, offended by the suggestion that his participation had
been anything less than stellar, replied that he had been given orders
only to weigh the pearls, examine them, and purchase as many as
he could for £4,000.

"But you are an able-bodied man?" the defense challenged.

"I am not a policeman," Spanier replied acidly. "I am an expert."

The cross-examinations had little effect, and the preliminary
proceedings at Bow Street came to a close. The four thieves were
formally indicted for "the stealing of the Mayer necklace and several
loose pearls during transit in the mail, as well as receiving the gems,
and knowing them to have been stolen." The trial date was set for
November at the Central Criminal Court. In all, the prosecution
and defense had two months to prepare.

NINETEEN

Old Bailey

A GOLDEN LADY STANDS WITH A CROWNED HEAD, A SWORD IN one hand and measuring scales in the other. Purposefully, her eyes are wide open, not blindfolded to justice. From the top of a round dome, rising from an ornate tower, steep lines, and stone columns, she looks down at the street below, a busy road flanked by the intersection of Holborn Viaduct and Newgate at one end and Ludgate Hill on the other.

The Lady of Justice sits atop the Central Criminal Court building on Bailey Road, named for the fortified wall, or "bailey," that stood there in Medieval times. Soon the courthouse itself became known as Old Bailey. Opened in 1907 by King Edward VII and made of heavy Portland stone in a neo-Baroque style, it was one of many new, impressive buildings that seemed to sprout from the soiled streets of London during the first decade of the new century.

Old Bailey was erected on the site that had formerly been the infamous Newgate Prison, which once housed a number of notorious individuals, including Giacomo Casanova (for bigamy), writer Daniel Defoe (political unrest), poisoner Thomas Neill Cream, as well as serial killers, murderers, assassins, highway robbers, anarchists, and pirates, among others. It must have been intimidating to anyone standing trial at Old Bailey to know how many men, women, and children had been hanged at the gallows on the very grounds where this edifice of justice now stood.

The trial began on the morning of November 17, 1913. The newspapers had been preoccupied with the news of Archduke Ferdinand's visit to London with his wife that week. Just as the couple returned to Austria, the trial began, and the papers turned their focus once again to the heist.

Grizzard, Lockett, Silverman, and Gutwirth arrived early that morning, carried by individual, guarded vans. In the two months since their Bow Street preliminary trial, fall had descended at last. While much of the summer had been cool, autumn had been unusually warm that year with summer flowers still blooming and fruits and berries filling the crates, but the coming change of season loomed. Squall weather settled over the city, finally bringing in the cool winds that crisped the air. Plane trees had dropped their leaves; the elms grew bare. The animals at the zoo in Regent's Park moved into houses for winter. Hand-embroidered Christmas cards were propped up in storefronts, and the king's official card, a historic scene depicting Richard the Lionheart against Saladin, had been printed.

Long before the trial began that morning, crowds collected

along the streets around the courthouse for what was already being called the trial of century. Sensational trials always served as popular entertainment, but the intriguing detective tale and the valuable strand of pearls made this one all the more appealing. Everyone knew who the major players in the case were—the infamous thief, the brilliant detective, and the Crown's best prosecutor. This was a true Sherlock Holmes tale being played out before them.

People pushed against one another as they waited outside the main entrance. The crowd was made thicker by the presence of police posted at the door to the courthouse in recent days. During the course of a suffragette's trial in another courtroom at Old Bailey, protesters had attacked a judge and warden, breaking windows and pelting them with objects. As the doors opened, the throngs of people moved slowly inside, herded by police.

Above the doors to the courthouse, elaborately carved in stone, the figures of Fortitude, the Recording Angel, and Truth, defied gravity and hovered like birds trying to find perches among all the hard edges. Below the elegant statues, it read: DEFEND THE CHILDREN OF THE POOR AND PUNISH THE WRONGDOER. Even the inscription seemed to point to the greatest social problem of the time—protecting the children born into poverty and thus doomed to grace the docks of Old Bailey in the years to come. Of particular interest to King Edward when he opened the building in 1907 was giving young criminals a chance to reform. The Victorian era had already started to soften the severity and harshness the law placed on many London children—those in poorhouses, orphanages, or prison, where some were hanged at the gallows for crimes as small as stealing food.

"Courtwatchers" filed in beneath the shadow of angels, dragging mud across the Sicilian marble floors, clapping shoes up the grand staircase. The allegorical paintings of Labour, Art, Wisdom, and Truth looked on as the crowd made its way into Courtroom One.

Justice A. T. Lawrence entered the courtroom at ten-thirty that morning, his wig a cascade of soiled-looking, white curls; his robe was crisply pressed. He bowed to counsel and the jurymen and took his seat. Before him, Grizzard, Lockett, Silverman, and Gutwirth sat in box seats for the legal pageantry before them. In all, one lord, twelve jurymen, three prosecutors, four counselors for the defense, and court clerks crowded the stage—not to mention all of the reporters, detectives, witnesses, and spectators filling the seats.

The court reporter began the shorthand notes for the proceedings by listing all those representing the prosecution and defense. Appearing for the prosecution: Mr. Richard Muir; Mr. Travers Humphreys; and Mr. B. Leycester Muir, the senior Muir's son; and a fellow barrister.

All four defendants had their own, separate counsel. Grizzard's lead counsel, Mr. George Elliott, was widely considered one of the best defenders of his day. "Genial George," as colleagues called him, had a suave courtroom style. Always polite and respectful, he was a consummate apologist before his witness—usually knitting his brows and asking if the witness would mind answering a question or clearing up a point that he seemed to find perplexing. As the witness relaxed and obliged, offering a lengthier, detailed explanation, he soon realized his mistake as his answer formed the noose with which the defense could hang the case. Elliott, however, was also the most versatile of the group, not specializing in any one type of law, often moving between courtrooms and cases with noticeable distraction.

Likewise, Lockett's lead counsel, Mr. Curtis Bennett, was also a well-respected, leading defender. Elliott and Bennett began the arguments that morning.

The clerk of the court stood and faced the prisoners to read the indictment, which included several counts. Whittled down, the indictment charged the four men with stealing the property of Max Mayer while it was in transit through the post between France and the United Kingdom and then receiving the stolen goods.

The accused had a moment to confer with their defense teams before declaring themselves guilty or not guilty. At that point, the criminal trial between the Crown and the "prisoner at the bar" began with the jury being sworn to deliver a true verdict based on the evidence presented. However, the defense immediately deviated from the normal course. After the indictment was read, Lockett's counsel, Bennett, stood and objected to the charges themselves. It would prove to be a pivotal decision in the trial.

At the time of the pearl heist trial, an older law of indictments existed that allowed for technicalities or even the slip of a pen to prove the entire indictment inaccurate, and the case therefore unfounded. By 1915, that rigid law would be amended and modernized to apply some common sense to the wording of indictments. Bennett and Elliott hoped to capitalize on the rigidity of the original law to free their prisoners on a technicality. With witness testimony, police accounts, physical evidence, and the pearls in hand, the defense had little else to use.

Dickey Muir spent hours drafting a detailed indictment in such a way as to lump all four gang members together as a united force working toward a common end. They were all guilty by association. But the prosecution had been *too* thorough. In the midst of all the legal jargon spelled out in the indictment, Muir covered the theft of the necklace between France and England while in the post—the problem was that the police still didn't know where the necklace had been stolen. In its extreme diligence, the prosecution had charged the criminals not only with stealing the necklace, but also with receiving stolen goods from *both* countries. The defense seized upon the technical conundrum.

Bennett hedged. "Now, my lord, my reason for moving to quash this indictment is that it is embarrassing to the prisoners, in that it charges two distinct offenses here, of stealing a necklace and receiving a necklace stolen in this country; it further charges the offense of receiving, not stealing but receiving, a necklace which was stolen outside this country."

At the time, the term *embarrassment* was legal parlance for obstruction or hindrance leading to an injustice—in other words, the indictment unfairly hindered the prisoners' defense. Another prosecutor from the trial later said, "All this was most ingenious . . . Either the pearls were stolen in France or in England." The prosecution could not have it both ways.

Taking it further, the defense argued that if the French counts of theft remained, the prosecution would essentially be proving impossibility based on their very own argument. The findings of the French police proved almost beyond a shadow of doubt that the jewels had been stolen in England, not France. "Sir Richard [Muir] had no right to indict the prisoners for doing something he was going to prove they never could have done" in the first place, the defense argued.

His lordship sat dumbfounded. He listened to the defense and wrapped his mind around the legal riddle. Before he could even respond, Bennett was on his feet again.

"Speaking of embarrassment, is the case to be put to the jury: 'We do not know where the larceny took place: you can guess whether it was in England or France?' Surely, my lord, that is an embarrassment to the prisoners.

"My lord," he continued in a conciliatory voice, "I know this is purely a legal point which I am putting to your lordship, but the question of indictment in this country has been greatly discussed over a number of years, and great care is taken in criminal courts that a prisoner shall not be embarrassed by being charged in one indictment with two distinct offenses which may embarrass him in his defense."

The judge interrupted Bennett, and in a curt tone replied, "I do not know of 'embarrassment' ever being implied unless it would embarrass an innocent person. The question of embarrassment, as I understand it, is that if a person is innocent he might be embarrassed by being tried this way." However, the judge continued, "You cannot come forward and say, 'Though I am guilty I shall be embarrassed by having these two things tied together; I shall be more certain of being convicted.'"

Agitated, the judge said to Bennett, "As I understand it, you are saying that the argument is: 'Though guilty I am entitled to be tried in the way least embarrassing to myself.' That is what it comes to."

With that, Grizzard's counsel, George Elliott, as well as the counsel for Silverman and Gutwirth, stood and concurred with Bennett's point. They were united in their agreement that the technical wording of the indictment was unjust. The prisoners in the dock tensed and listened intently to see if the entire case might be dismissed after all. Their hope was short-lived.

"I do not think that I can accede to this argument," the judge answered. "I think the two sets of counts merely deal with the same transaction in two different aspects, and the embarrassment is that which anybody feels when he has a possible loophole, and it is the duty of the prosecution when they frame the indictment to close all possible loopholes . . . It is not in order to allow a guilty man to escape and so snap his fingers in the face of the court that the doctrine of embarrassment is to apply."

The judge asked all four prisoners to stand, each with a warder at his side, and listen to the formal indictment against them. Each man then offered his plea of "not guilty" in unemotional, quiet tones. The jury of twelve men filed into the jury box—it would be seven more years before women could serve in a jury, regardless of whether the defendant on trial was a woman.

Sir Richard Muir picked up his colorful cards and began his opening argument.

Muir, as the architect of the argument, built fact on top of fact to establish his point—and the resulting case stood as daunting and infallible as a massive building made from granite and stone. He called sixty-seven different witnesses. He provided ninety-six exhibits of evidence such as letters, translations of those letters, envelopes, telegrams, seals, sealing wax, bank accounts, passbooks, photographs, plans of Hatton Garden, receipts, as well as the infamous cubes of French sugar and scrap of newspaper.

Muir's mountain of proof showed that the four thieves on trial had purposefully opened an office on the mail route between the Hatton Garden post office and Max Mayer's address; Silverman asked the post office to deliver packages directly to his third-floor room—but only for the first delivery of the day; Silverman had a seal made in the initials *MM;* Silverman and Grizzard visited Paris just before the necklace was mailed to London; Gutwirth admitted to Quadratstein and Brandstatter that he and his partners held the necklace; the decoys, working with the police, witnessed the entire necklace in Grizzard's possession; marked French notes were used to purchase pearls from the thieves; and a sting operation apprehended the four thieves as they attempted to finalize the sale and escape to points unknown.

Another prosecutor on the case later wrote that as Muir's steady voice and unimpassioned opening argument came to a close, the case was "dead," and the defense, for all their talent, would not be able "to make bricks without straw."

TWENTY

Righteous Judgment

GRAY RAINDROPS STREAKED THE WINDOWS OF THE COURTROOM. Outside, the buildings seemed upholstered in dense fog. The weather, paired with Richard Muir's dispassionate voice, would send anyone into a stupor. Muir called various minor players in the theft to bear witness to certain facts. The housekeeper who cleaned Silverman's office testified about his trip to France at the end of June. A representative from the Hatton Garden post office testified and produced the letter in which Silverman asked that his mail be delivered to him alone, not to the lift operator. Undoubtedly, the jury and spectators were growing bored with the tedious points so doggedly pursued by Muir.

Then the atmosphere in the courtroom lightened. Muir called Mr. Peter Robertson Gordon, the hammersmith who created the forged seals for Silverman and later sent that information to Price and Gibbs during the hunt for the necklace. Silverman had first encountered Gordon at the Leather Bottle in Hatton Garden, and that meeting place became all the more pointed as Gordon shuffled, somewhat drunkenly, toward the witness box. To make matters worse, he was Scottish.

"Where did you first meet the defendant Simon Silverman?" Muir asked.

"The L'thr Bo'le," Gordon answered. The all-British jury looked at one another and then to Muir as they strained to understand Gordon's accent. There were a few snickers from the spectators.

"The Leather Bottle," Muir repeated.

Gordon's testimony continued to baffle the jury and amuse the spectators.

On cross-examination, J. P. Valetta, counsel for Silverman, stood to ask Gordon why he waited so long to come forward and why he went to Price rather than the police. Gordon answered that he did not immediately remember meeting Silverman or making the seal.

"Did the ten-thousand-pound reward assist you in remembering Silverman from so many months before? You wanted some of that reward money!"

"Yea," Gordon answered, "a bi' o' it!"

The jury foreman asked if there were any peculiarities to the die that Gordon cut—was there a way to recognize it and be sure it was the same?

"I cun say 'twas sim'lar," he said in his thick accent. "There's no p'culiarity buh which I could identify it." More laughter.

"There was no way to identify it," counsel reaffirmed. When the questions were over, Gordon returned to his seat somewhat irritated by all the snickering.

*　*　*

Muir continued with his witnesses, including calling several of the French and English postmen who handled the package between Paris and London. Although Postman Neville, the one who actually delivered the package to Mayer, appeared noticeably absent.

Finally, Muir called the key witnesses to the box. Brandstatter, with his limited knowledge of English, only answered to the facts. An interpreter stood beside him to translate. Quadratstein would be the essential witness in the case—as evidenced by the hours of testimony of no fewer than 550 questions from the prosecution and another 300 from the defense.

Quadratstein relayed the events as they happened to Muir. He felt relaxed, at ease, enjoying the audience. He remained cheerful and even proud of his evident skill in lying, especially his ability to deceive London's "King of the Underworld." Throughout his testimony, Quadratstein spoke without the slightest humility, occasionally looking directly at the dock for reaction. Neither Grizzard nor Lockett showed any emotion beyond boredom.

In cross-examinations, Bennett, representing Lockett, made much of the fact that in all those meetings, Quadratstein only saw James Lockett twice—the day at the café when Lockett tossed Grizzard the matchbox and on the day of the arrest.

Grizzard's attorney, Elliott, took a different tack. First, he wanted to clear up the exact relationship between Gutwirth and the two Frenchmen, which turned out to be distant at best—they were related through the brother of the late husband of an aunt.

"What is the relationship between Brandstatter and Gutwirth? He is the brother of a dead uncle who became uncle by marriage?" Elliott asked, amused. The courtroom spectators began laughing. Elliott continued, "It's something like the gentleman became his own grandfather." More laughter followed.

The judge sighed and reprimanded Elliott for wasting the court's time with the family tree.

Elliott then approached from a different angle, hoping to make the argument that Quadratstein was out for the reward, plain and simple.

"When you first came to England, Messrs. Price and Gibbs had not been communicated with at all?" he asked.

"Quite so," answered Quadratstein.

"Nor the police?"

"Nor the police."

"You were for the moment doing a little bit of amateur detective business on your own?" Elliott goaded.

"Quite so."

"To make use of it having regard to taking the reward?"

"Absolutely," Quadratstein said frankly.

Proving that Quadratstein and Brandstatter were in it for the money and not for the capture of the thieves may have shown them to be ungentlemanly, but it didn't change the facts.

As Lockett's attorney had done, Elliott hoped to prove Grizzard had very few dealings with Brandstatter and Quadratstein. Gutwirth arranged the sale, and what's more, the meetings were conducted in French and German, which Grizzard didn't speak—this fact also helped stir the undercurrent of prejudice against "foreigners."

Silverman's lead counsel, Valetta, was the next to attempt to rattle Quadratstein.

He asked about the meeting at the First Avenue Hotel and why Quadratstein had chosen to betray the thieves.

"Was it not because you formed the opinion that the pearls would be difficult to negotiate that you thought the reward would be the safest game?"

"Not at all," Quadratstein said plainly.

"And did you carry a pistol to that meeting?" the attorney asked.

"Yes."

"Did any of them threaten you?" Valetta asked.

"No, not even Silverman," Quadratstein said facetiously. With that, a courtroom reporter describing the scene jotted down, "Silverman is so small that his head hardly reaches the rail of the dock."

Valetta continued: "I think at the police court you claimed the title of the perfect liar?" he asked, reading from a stack of papers on his table.

"I did," Quadratstein answered simply.

"You went on to say you could lie in so expert a manner that while you were in fact telling lies you could persuade people you were telling the truth?"

"Of course I had to play that part. If I told the truth they would never have believed me!" Some muffled laughter arose from the spectators.

"You said," Valetta continued, reading directly from police transcripts, "'from the very first time I had an interview with Gutwirth, of course I commenced to lie to him. I intended to lie so well to him that he should believe I was telling the truth.'"

"It looked very much like it," Quadratstein said matter-of-factly.

"Do not be overshy." Valetta smirked.

"I am not shy," answered Quadratstein.

"After your estimate of yourself, do you ask the jury to believe that everything you have said the last two days in the witness box is true?"

"Absolutely," said Quadratstein.

Next, the prosecution called Spanier to the stand. He gave an achingly detailed and accurate account of his participation. This time, however, he refrained from adding, "I am an expert."

Price was the last witness, sitting tall and rod-straight, wearing his fashionable round spectacles and fine suit. He testified to his part in the ploy. On cross-examination, he answered several questions about the specifics of sealing wax and affixing it to a package.

"Have you tried the experiment yourself?" Justice Lawrence asked.

"Yes, my lord, lots of times . . . We have experimented extensively with regard to it. We can write a book about sealing wax now!" Price answered cheerfully.

"There is a different effect produced if you boil the wax in a ladle or burn it in a flame?" Muir asked.

"There is an absolute difference," Price said. "With the wax you burn in a flame, you get a black appearance on the surface, and you always find more or less the little black carbon pieces which have been burned in contact with the flame, but if you boil it, you get a dead kind of surface, and you get an entire absence of those little black carbon bits which you see in the other." The seals used by Mayer had been melted over an open flame, while Silverman and Gutwirth had mistakenly used a ladle to soften the red sealing wax.

The final piece of evidence Price presented was the numbered French banknotes he had allotted to Spanier in the course of the sale. They matched the numbers the police found on the French notes in Lockett's pockets, as well as those found on Daniel McCarthy. The police traced other notes to various banks where Silverman and Grizzard had exchanged money. Silverman had also handed a few notes to Quadratstein to settle up his hotel bill. Using the French notes proved a serious failing on Grizzard's part—he should have sent an emissary to France, as he'd done in past dealings, to cash all of the notes far away from the prying eyes of Scotland Yard detectives.

Muir stood and faced his lordship: "That is the case for the Crown."

<hr>

Before 1898, no prisoner could give evidence on his own behalf. That year, however, the Criminal Evidence Act was passed, allowing prisoners to speak in their own defense. In the case of an innocent man, it might persuade the jury; in the case of a guilty one, cross-examination could condemn him. Refusing to speak at all left only a small window of doubt for the jury to consider. With that in mind, none of the thieves spoke on their own behalf.

What's more, in arguing against the unjust wording in the indictment, the defense had essentially bet their whole hand on a technicality. Rather than arguing that the thieves were innocent, the defense attacked the indictment itself—a clever and skillful argument, but one that implied the prisoners were in fact guilty of some, if not all, of the counts in the indictment.

That left the defense with little else to do but pry loose what few points they could from the prosecution's case. During cross-examinations, the counsel for the defendants had already attacked the character of most of the witnesses, painting Brandstatter and Quadratstein as greedy liars who pursued the necklace only to gain the reward. The defense questioned Spanier's motives and why he didn't attempt to retrieve the necklace at the first opportunity and turn it in to the authorities. Defending counsel depicted Gordon, the engraver, as an unreliable alcoholic. Then the defense attacked Price, Spanier, Brandstatter, and Quadratstein for their underhanded ploy and their delay in involving the police.

It was Silverman's counsel, Valetta, who took charge at that point. He questioned the absence of two key witnesses—one aboard the mail ship, the other, Postman Neville in Hatton Garden.

"Here are these two people whom we have not thought fit to call—we invite you to say *that* is where the trouble arose." Valetta continued. "My friend [Mr. Muir] cannot say . . . 'Believe my witnesses because the opportunity [for someone else to do it] existed'; and secondly: 'Do not believe witnesses because no opportunity existed.'"

In other words, the theft essentially hinged on Neville's participation. A long list of other witnesses had testified that they had neither the time nor the opportunity to steal the necklace, and the one man who did was never even called to the stand. According to the defense, that left a gaping hole for the jury to fill with its own assumptions.

The following morning, the defense called Neville to the stand as their only witness. In spite of his thirty or so years of service, his alcoholism had started to interfere significantly with his work. Neville lived on nearby Leather Lane, and among those who knew him in Hatton Garden, it always seemed foolish to trust such a man with so many valuable packages of gems. Valetta decided to avoid the subject of Neville's drinking altogether.

On the stand, Neville answered a series of Valetta's questions. Yes, he still worked for the post office and had done so for over three decades. Yes, he knew Gutwirth and Silverman, but did not speak to either of them that morning. No, he did not know Grizzard or Lockett. No, he did not receive a bribe in connection with the case.

"Did you deliver [that morning] any parcel to Silverman's office in number 101?" Valetta asked.

"There was a letter, I think, for him which I put in his letter box, but I did not speak to him."

Then Valletta approached the evidence table and held up the larger package delivered to Mayer's office later that morning. "Is this the package you delivered to Max Mayer?"

Neville held the package and looked it over. "I cannot swear the parcel I delivered for Mr. Mayer is the one produced. It was certainly very similar to it."

"How do you suggest Silverman got hold of the packet?"

"Goodness knows," answered Neville, "No packet left my hands to nobody. I always put that registered stuff in the bottom of the bag which I left with the bag-carrier."

Valletta hoped to establish that Neville was an upstanding postman with no reason to take part in the heist. If he could somehow prove that Neville was never involved, the series of denials was complete—the prosecution would never be able to find the weak link in the chain that enabled the thieves to steal the necklace. Even though the evidence against the thieves was daunting, if the prosecution could not prove when and how the theft took place, it peppered their arguments with doubt. Counsel could not prove the defendants had stolen the necklace if it could not prove *how*. Which left the thieves guilty only of trying to sell a stolen necklace, not actually stealing it.

Muir thumbed through his stack of cards and pulled the ones color-coded for cross. Muir had a particular talent for cross-examining—so much so that his methods were taught to students of the bar. He stood from his table and looked pointedly at Neville. Several moments passed, in which Neville shifted uncomfortably in his seat. With so many discrepancies in his answers, Neville had narrowly missed being prosecuted when the police first questioned him.

Neville had given statements to Scotland Yard detectives shortly after the theft and again in October in preparation for the trial, when Ward found a number of inconsistencies between Neville's own accounts, as well as those of the bag carrier. At first, Neville claimed not to know Silverman, Gutwirth, Lockett, or Grizzard. Then he recanted and said he'd shared drinks with Gutwirth once or twice. He'd also been seen visiting with Silverman outside of his office on a few occasions. Neville backtracked once again when he neglected to tell detectives that he had been the one to actually deliver the package to Silverman. When pressed, he answered, "I remember now that I did have to go upstairs at 101 Hatton Garden. There is one firm at 101 who insist on letters being placed in their letter box. I forgot the name."

Muir set his playing cards back on the desk, stood in front of Neville, and politely asked him about his drinking problem.

"I have lost three stripes on duty," Neville answered defensively, "for occasionally going to the public house."

"How often do you go to the public house?" Muir asked.

"That would depend on the funds," Neville answered. A few people chuckled from the back of the courtroom.

Muir, ignoring them, continued. He asked Neville whether or not he knew Gutwirth. Neville explained that he only knew Gutwirth as someone to whom he delivered letters. He stumbled over his words, however, and in trying so hard to avoid incriminating himself, did just that, and admitted that "Gutwirth stood [him] drinks in neighboring public houses." Going further, Neville added that he had known Silverman for a few months—since he moved his office from 60 Hatton Garden to number 101.

Muir homed in on the strange request Silverman made to have his mail delivered by hand to the third floor.

"Which floor is Silverman on?" Muir asked evenly.

"On the third."

"There is a lift there, is there not?"

"Quite so."

"And a liftman in attendance?" Muir continued.

"Yes."

"When you delivered Silverman's letters, did you go up in the lift or not?"

Neville paused cautiously. "No, I walked up the stairs. I do not think the lift is always working at that time of the morning."

"So this change necessitated your walking up three flights of stairs to Silverman every morning, if there was a letter for him?"

"Yes," Neville answered. "I have been up in the lift. It was not often I had a letter for him—three perhaps a week." Neville added that he sometimes handed Silverman his mail outside the gate, where they stood visiting.

"Did you ever see him there before eight o'clock earlier than June this year?"

"No, I do not think I have."

Muir remained calm. He paced the floor some and paused beside his table to pick up his cards, which he shuffled soundlessly, reading the notes on Neville's previous testimony at the police station. Then he broke the brittle silence of the courtroom.

"Why did not you send the bag carrier with the letter up to Silverman?"

Neville furrowed his brow. "It is not his duty. I am in charge of the delivery."

"But you gave him the whole correspondence to deliver, and you went upstairs to Silverman?" Muir pressed. Neville had told the detectives that he had asked Hollands to deliver a package to a neighboring office while he carried a letter upstairs to Silverman.

Neville, growing more nervous, explained, "I said, 'You look after my bag while I go upstairs and down again.' I also said, 'You can take this receipt when they've signed for it, while I slip up with Silverman's letter.'"

Muir smiled pleasantly, as though enjoying a carefree conversation with a man he had encountered on the street. Neville was not the first witness to be lulled so easily into a trap.

"But if you were not allowed to let Hollands do any of the delivering, why did you give him the registered packet to deliver?" Before Neville could answer, Muir continued, "If Hollands *was* allowed to do part of the delivering, why not send *him* upstairs? Or for that matter, why not give the liftman the registered packet and take the lift up to Silverman?" Neville scrambled for answers—none of which could adequately counter Muir's argument.

Muir then followed up with the obvious discrepancies between Neville's accounts in July and October. He ended by asking Neville why he never pursued the matter further after hearing that a package he had been responsible for had been stolen.

"I did not really trouble," Neville said quietly. "I thought I had done my duty. That is all."

As Neville left the courtroom, the defense's flimsy portrayal of Neville as the innocent, upstanding postman had been shattered by Muir's cross-examination.

The defense gave their various closing arguments. Bennett, having failed at his request to drop the indictment on the grounds of a technicality, had little to add. Valetta, unable to paint Neville as a trustworthy postal worker incapable of tampering with the mail, summed up his argument halfheartedly. Gutwirth's attorney had little to contribute during the trial or in closing statements. Finally, the counsel for Grizzard, George Elliott, a likable and persuasive orator, would give his closing statement. His could be considered the most crucial.

As is often the case in the British legal system, senior counsel may try several cases at one time and leave their juniors to sit through the day-to-day testimony. "Genial George" happened to be busy that afternoon with a group of Parisians accused of fraud. A note was hurriedly dispatched by messenger to another courtroom at Old Bailey requesting George Elliott return to First Court immediately to make the closing statements. Elliott had been trying the case against the Parisians for some time, passing from one courtroom to defend Joseph Grizzard to the other to defend the ornately named Aurèle de Labat de Lambert. A fine orator, Elliott also enjoyed showing off his fluency in the French language, accurately pronouncing all French names and terms in the Parisian court case. The dizzying exchange, and Elliott's confidence in his own abilities, proved a bad marriage.

Elliott came racing into the First Court, his black robe billowing behind him like sailcloth. He strode to the front of the courtroom, bowing elegantly to the judge and jury. He raised his hand, and with a flourish, gestured toward Grizzard in the dock, who peered at his counsel warily.

Elliott continued, declaring loudly that he represented "Monsieur Georges Grizzard." A rumbling of laughter erupted in the courtroom at his mistaken, if flawless, use of French.

Grizzard's steely composure cracked and he looked down at his folded hands, knowing full well what had just happened. To counteract Grizzard's reputation as an international jewel thief and well-known fence, his defense had worked diligently to portray him as a simple local man, born and raised in London, who couldn't speak French or German and therefore played a very small role in the theft and negotiations among Gutwirth, Brandstatter, Quadratstein, and Spanier for the pearls.

With that one mistake of Elliott's, the jury's image of Grizzard metamorphosed from simple jeweler caught up in the details of the heist to the brilliant, worldly mind behind it.

❧

Justice Lawrence turned to address the jury, giving them a summary of the evidence: "Gentlemen of the Jury, the four prisoners in this case are charged with the crimes of larceny and receiving stolen goods knowing them to have been stolen." He continued on for some time about both the charges and respect for the legal system as a whole. He also commented on the cunning criminals—especially the "clever ruse" in which Lockett tossed the matchbox of pearls to Grizzard in the tea shop. At the end of his preamble, his lordship looked to the jury and added, "It is not a matter of law, it is a matter of sense."

The English courts prided themselves on being perfectly fair and even partial to the prisoners, giving them every "sporting chance." However, as Muir liked to say, "the law is not quite such an ass as to open doors for prisoners to walk out of the dock."

His lordship went on—ad nauseam—reviewing the details of the case from the moment the thieves learned of the necklace, to the months they spent planning the heist, to the individual roles they played, and finally, their attempt to sell the stolen pearls.

"Those, gentlemen, are the material facts. You must ask yourselves whether those prisoners are not guilty of being the persons who arranged to steal, and stole those pearls. Secondly, if you have any doubt about it, you must ask yourselves whether they are not the persons who received them knowing them to be stolen; and finally you must ask yourselves whether they were not so received, having been stolen while in transit in the English post."

Before dismissing the jury for deliberation, he advised, "Do not give way to any foolish or quixotic doubt."

With that, the jury left the courtroom, and the prisoners were taken from the dock to holding rooms, which turned out to be an exercise in futility. The jury reappeared within eleven minutes, and the speed with which they returned left little hope for the thieves.

Grizzard, Lockett, Silverman, and Gutwirth walked back into the dock where they had spent so much time over the last few weeks. Gutwirth sat with his hands clasped, almost prayerlike, resting over the top of the bar. Silverman, wearing his ill-fitting suit, sat back and seem distracted. Lockett looked as stoic as ever. And Grizzard, florid-faced, looked friendly, even kind. Again, the courtroom was packed with spectators, while reporters lined the sidewalks outside waiting for the verdict.

The clerk announced: "Gentlemen of the Jury, have you agreed upon your verdict?"

The foreman answered, "We have."

"Do you find the defendants guilty or not guilty upon this indictment?"

"On which count?" the foreman asked, confused. The defense counsel whispered and murmured to one another, hoping the technicality might win the jury over after all.

The clerk clarified his question. "Do you find them guilty or not guilty of stealing a pearl necklace, the property of the postmaster general, it then being a postal packet in course of transmission by post?"

The foreman answered, "Guilty."

"Do you find them guilty or not guilty of receiving that pearl necklace well knowing the same to have been stolen while in course of transmission by post?"

"Guilty," the foreman answered once again.

The clerk continued, "Do you find them guilty or not guilty on the rest of the indictment?"

"Not guilty on the other counts." The defense had won the smaller technical feat. The entire indictment had not been thrown out, but the jury agreed that the prosecutors could not charge the prisoners with receiving goods stolen from both England *and* France.

"And that is the verdict of you all?" the clerk asked.

"The verdict of us all."

After the verdict was given, Alfred Ward was invited into the witness box to offer his opinion before the judge assigned sentences. That act alone pointed to the court's high opinion of the arresting detectives.

Ward, who had been present through much of the trial, walked slowly to the front, wearing his best suit. He exhibited no sense of triumph or even self-satisfaction at the verdict. In the witness box, he recounted his dealings in the case without drama or fanfare. He relayed previous arrests and some additional background details about the four thieves. When he came to Lockett's record, he emphasized that Lockett was a recent widower and the sole parent of a young daughter at home.

When Ward finished, he started to stand and climb down from the witness box when he was stopped by an officer of the court who had one more question—about Grizzard specifically.

"I do not know if you can tell me," the court officer asked. "I think he [Grizzard] has been in very bad health for some time, suffering from diabetes?"

"I understand that that is so," Ward answered simply. Looking toward the dock, he caught Grizzard's eyes. For all those weeks he spent watching him through the lens of binoculars, Grizzard now sat humbly before him in the dock.

Ward must have hoped for a lighter sentence for Grizzard, given his poor health, and for Lockett, as his name had been dragged into the sting operation at the very end with little other participation. His job so efficiently done, Ward continued to be prickled by guilt, even compassion, for the thieves. After all, he had trained as a detective under the gruesome Jack the Ripper case; he had help put away Crippen for murdering and dismembering his own wife; he had personally captured a family that poisoned its tenants for money; he had tracked serial killers; and he had responded to countless calls for rape, abuse, and senseless murder. These thieves had families, lived relatively normal lives. They had chosen the business of crime, which was a poor decision, but apart from that seemed like decent people.

The clerk faced the dock: "Prisoners at the Bar, you stand convicted of felony. Have you or either of you anything to say why the court should not give you judgment according to the law?"

The question was met with silence.

The judge cleared his voice and read aloud: "Now, Lockett, you have been convicted of this crime upon the clearest evidence. Indeed, the one thing I think can be said in your favor is that you did not attempt to deny the facts of this case, but merely, through your counsel, attacked the law, which is certainly more open to attack than individuals. I commend you for that, but your previous record and the position that you occupied in this case, in which I have no doubt you were a leading mind, is a very serious one. You have attacked one of the most important branches of the public service in a particularly bold and skillful manner."

The judge continued: "You have been convicted before and you do not seem to be amenable to the logic of punishment. I must remove you, as a danger to the community, for a considerable period of time." Lockett stared straight ahead, unflinching and showing no emotion, but a woman seated in the spectator section let out a small shriek.

"And you, Grizzard, you seem to have shared with Lockett the leadership and headwork of this robbery. I am sorry to hear that you are ill, but I have no doubt you will be looked after under the sentence I am going to give you as well as you would be in your own home. You must both be sent to penal servitude for seven years." Grizzard too stood staring ahead, unmoving, though his eyes seemed to lose some of their sharp focus, and he only dimly heard the other sentences.

"Silverman," the judge directed, "perhaps I have done you an injustice in saying that the others were the brains of the plot; still it does seem to me that you were to some extent the ingenious tool rather than the originator of this scheme. You were too ingenious. You must be sent to penal servitude for five years, and there must be a recommendation at the end of your term that you be by the home secretary's order expelled from this country." Silverman, who had lived in London nearly all of his life with his family, felt the full weight of this final part. After his sentence was passed, he asked to see his mother before returning to prison.

"She is an old woman." He faltered. "She may die at any minute."

His lordship continued: "You, Gutwirth, are said to be the less implicated party, but you took a very active part in it."

Gutwirth lunged forward from the dock, protesting, "I was dragged into it. I have been eighteen years in Hatton Garden, my lord, always straightforward. I do not know what made me do it.

I was a broker. I ought never to have done a thing like that. It is not my business. Mine is a straightforward business!"

The judge listened patiently, if somewhat irritated by the outburst. He said kindly to Gutwirth, "I do not think that you are as bad as the others, but you seem to have been a very willing tool. You must be imprisoned and kept to hard labor for eighteen calendar months, and similar recommendation must be made in your case."

Gutwirth grew quiet. As with Silverman, it was the latter part of the sentence that resonated. Gutwirth had lived in London for most of his life as well. He had a home, a wife and daughter. And now, like Silverman, he would be deported to Eastern Europe.

Mr. Frampton, counsel for Gutwirth, rose from his seat. He pleaded with the judge that Gutwirth had been living in London for twenty-five years and had married a British citizen.

Judge Lawrence answered, "That may be, but he is an alien and we do not want such aliens here."

With that, the trial concluded on November 25, 1913. As it turns out, that week saw the end of *two* world-renowned heists. Days after the pearl trial ended, an Italian named Vincenzo Leonardo Peruggia sent an anonymous letter to an art dealer, offering to give back the stolen *Mona Lisa* portrait—after being shown in Italy, the portrait was returned to Paris to the Louvre nearly two and a half years after its disappearance.

⟨⁀⟩

With the conclusion of the pearl heist trial, Max Mayer returned to the courtroom to hear the verdict. Feeling duly justified, he watched as each prisoner was led from the dock back down the spiral staircase to the holding rooms where the vans would take them to different prisons.

After a few moments, Mayer stood, and again obligingly held the pearl necklace up for the ladies in the courtroom to view.

"What do you plan to do with the pearls now?" someone shouted from the back.

Mayer smiled. "I am going to take them home and give them a bath! That is what they really want."

Another spectator yelled, "But what are you going to do with them after that? Have you a buyer?"

"I can't say that I have a buyer," Mayer answered, "but I have had people who are after the necklace. There is no truth in the rumor that a rich American is after them, but I will let you know when they are sold."

Mayer added, "I suppose as a matter of fact, the value of the necklace will be greatly enhanced by the notoriety which the case has given it. There are plenty of people who like gems with a history, and nobody will say that these pearls have not got a history now!"

As spectators and witnesses filed out of the courthouse, photographers lined the streets, climbing onto stacked crates or ledges for better shots. The outcome of the trial became front-page news in the dailies, and the story covered a full page in the London *Times*.

Mayer, with a police guard, left the courthouse with his pearls tucked carefully in his pocket. The counsel for both the prosecution and defense packed up their leather cases, and Muir tied the band back around his playing cards as he walked toward the robing room.

Outside, an argument ensued over who should receive the reward money. Brandstatter and Quadratstein believed they should be given the reward after all of their hard work and cooperation with the police in apprehending the thieves. Horn believed he should receive the reward for the actual return of the necklace. The bickering escalated into yet another lengthy legal battle over the pearl necklace.

Alfred Ward walked out of the courthouse, ignoring reporters and refusing to grant any interviews. He turned toward the river, hearing the horns of approaching ships echoing, strangely detached from their source. A gull appeared still and unmoving, suspended in the wind off the river. Ward walked alone toward Scotland Yard.

From the depths of Old Bailey, Grizzard, Lockett, Silverman, and Gutwirth climbed into heavily guarded vans for the trip to various prisons on the outskirts of London. Crowds still swarmed the sidewalks, making passage through the street a challenge.

Dusk descended, and the late November light held fast to rooflines, casting the streets below into the cold, gray gloaming. Grizzard rested his manacled hands in his lap as the van rolled through the throngs of people and evening traffic. The buildings formed a cavern along the narrow street, and looking through the window, Grizzard watched Old Bailey fade as they pressed toward Holborn Viaduct.

Turning west, the van sputtered toward Holborn Circus. The light waned further and streetlamps ignited into electric moons as the van eased onto the roundabout, pausing in traffic and giving Grizzard a clear view of Hatton Garden. He knew it well—every owner of every store, which gems they specialized in, who left at what time, which bank they trusted to hold their jewels. Shopkeepers closed their stores for the night and turned on their lamps, casting crosshatches of window light out into the streets as they locked away their gems. He watched familiar faces bolt doors, pull their bowler hats forward, and light cigarettes that hovered ahead of them in the dark like escaping embers. They walked toward the Old Mitre Tavern or farther to the Globe and Vienna Café for a pint.

Finally, the van jolted forward, carrying Grizzard up Holborn. The afterglow of Hatton Garden shimmered for a moment longer and then fell into shadow as the van made its way toward the prison. Grizzard sank back into his seat. Seven years was not so long to wait.

The Great War

HAD THIS STORY BEEN FICTION, ITS CHARACTERS WOULD HAVE found more befitting ends. The brilliant thieves might have gotten away with the crime. The talented Scotland Yard detective would have earned his fame not in catching the thieves, but in apprehending some murderous villain. The good characters and the bad would be clearly distinguished from one another. Life, however, rarely finds its conclusions so neatly drawn. Reality has far fewer happy endings. And even if those endings might have been possible in some other time—they were not by 1914.

Nine months after the pearl heist trial ended, on August 3, 1914, Alfred Ward was called to Scotland Yard headquarters to meet with a secretive, special branch of government popularly known as MI5.

Sir Basil Thompson, head of the CID, brought in his best detectives for the meeting. The esteemed group was told about a number of German spies now infiltrating London on the eve of war.

By then, the threat of war had taken distinct shape over Great Britain. Unrest in England had already reached a tipping point, and some believed that if war did not come to Britain, revolution would. In a country that had been militarized and devoted to duty since the early modern era, the mounting aggression in Europe left only one question: *when* Great Britain would go to war. And when war would come to Britain.

Late that night, MI5 gave the orders to arrest twenty-two known German spies living in or around London. Ward and his colleagues set out in the middle of the night to apprehend the suspected spies. When the leaden dawn crept into the city the next day, the United Kingdom officially declared war on the German Empire.

Overnight, the country's focus became war. The Metropolitan Police and detectives turned from local crime to hunting spies and monitoring suspicious citizens. Ward proved particularly adept at catching spies, even traveling all the way to New York to capture Hungarian-born spy Ignaz Trebitsch-Lincoln, whose chameleon personality had led him to work as a nomadic religious missionary before naturalizing in Britain and being elected to Parliament. After his short-lived political career (there was no money in it at the time) and with the outbreak of war, Trebitsch-Lincoln offered his services to work as a British spy—he was rejected. He then promptly left for Germany and signed on as a double agent. When he traveled to the United States, the British government sent Ward to New York to work with the Pinkerton Agency in tracking him down and returning him to England, where Muir prosecuted the case, and the spy was imprisoned until the end of the war.

Ward's celebrated talent at catching spies was not to last, however. Shortly after he deposited Trebitsch-Lincoln safely to prison, tragedy struck London as the full impact of World War I finally rained down on the city. For all the worries and concerns about Germany invading Britain by sea, the real threat, as it turned out, came from the sky.

In October 1915, theatergoers swarmed High Holborn. The streets blushed with lamplight; the night was clear and cloudless except for the beams of searchlights, which stretched far into the sky. The busy footsteps and rushing crowds suddenly slowed, keenly aware of the stillness beside them. Glancing around for whatever had brought a busy London street to a standstill, they looked up as the sirens began.

A giant silver leviathan floated through the air, caught in the beams of light. It appeared beautiful and massive, like a whale slowly navigating the heavens. Then the zeppelin dropped its first bomb directly onto Holborn, cratering a large section of road, setting fire to nearby buildings, leaving bodies in its destructive wake.

It continued to cruise slowly, angling northward on Holborn, dropping additional bombs on Lincoln's Inn, the chancery court, and Gray's Inn, before it turned to the east and felled several incendiary bombs over Hatton Garden. One crashed through a building all the way to the cellar, but failed to explode. Unfortunately, that proved only one dud among many bombs. Much of Hatton Garden was damaged and later rebuilt. Today, pockets of the neighborhood still show those scars—from both world wars—in the bland, modern architecture wedged among the original buildings that stood there at the time of the Great Pearl Heist.

Still, far worse damage was to come.

On the morning of September 24, 1916, the great leviathans again visited London, a school of them sluggishly floating toward the center of the city, drifting in and out of the clouds. The zeppelins dropped forty-two incendiary bombs and twenty-five explosive ones into metropolitan London.

Alfred Ward and his daughter left their home on Beechcroft Road in Streatham Hill that morning for the tube station—it was rush hour. As they walked, a great shadow moved across the sidewalk, and before they had time to react, the zeppelin dropped a series of bombs. Ward's home took a direct hit, and his wife was severely injured, but survived. Ward's daughter, their only child, was killed on the sidewalk as she walked with her father. And Ward himself was fatally injured and later died at Kings College Hospital. He was fifty years old at the time of his death, and all of Scotland Yard mourned. The newspapers lamented that perhaps Germany had finally gotten its revenge on the great spy hunter.

❧

As the Beautiful era came to an abrupt close, very few people involved in the pearl heist would escape the tragedies of World War I. Sir Richard Muir, praised for his brilliant handling of the case against the Grizzard Gang, fell ill with the highly virulent influenza of 1918. He recovered, but remained weak. At the same time, his son, who was also a barrister, was serving in France and fell ill with the flu. He did not fare as well. He developed pneumonia and died a week before the armistice. Muir, in the midst of a long case at Old

Bailey, was interrupted by a messenger one spring morning to tell him that his son had died in a war-torn field hospital in the French countryside.

Muir went into the robing room, where he found his clerk, and said sadly, "Binks, I have lost my boy."

Every spring until his death in 1924, Muir traveled to France to visit his son's grave in a small, country cemetery.

As for the thieves Muir put away, all served their sentences. After eighteen months of hard labor, Lesir Gutwirth left prison only to be deported to Poland, which had become an enemy of Great Britain with the outbreak of war. There is no record of whether his family moved with him.

Likewise, Simon Silverman served his term and was immediately deported to Austria. It is not known if his mother was still living nor if she followed her son to Eastern Europe.

James Lockett was released in 1919. Lockett remarried after leaving prison and moved to the countryside to work as a bookmaker. He lived a long life and gave up thieving—at least, he never again was caught.

Although one strange incident did pique Scotland Yard's interest. While in prison, Lockett's home in Golders Green was put on the market and purchased by a woman named Mrs. Saxby to use as a boardinghouse. Almost as soon as she purchased the house, an eager buyer began pressuring her to resell it. He approached her repeatedly, offering to pay well over the asking price. She declined and reported the harassment to the police. Saxby knew of the great thief who had previously owned the home, which had extensive electrical alarms in the house as well as in a backyard workshop. She searched for hidden compartments or hiding places, where jewels or money might still be hidden, but was never able to find any.

Joseph Grizzard spent his sentence in the Wormwood Scrubs Prison. Throughout his incarceration, Grizzard lived in the prison hospital rather than a cell, receiving much finer care than the other prisoners. By then, his diabetes was very advanced, and he required a special diet and medical attention. Still, the medical knowledge of diabetes proved somewhat clouded, as Grizzard's "special diet" included butter, bacon, meat, whole milk, cocoa, and rice pudding. Given his condition, his "hard labor" consisted of darning socks.

Though most prisoners were allowed visitors once every four months, Grizzard had regular visits. Many of those visits came from Alfred Ward in the first few years of Grizzard's incarceration. Ward spent hours interviewing Grizzard and bringing difficult cases to him. Going over the particulars of a crime or certain hallmarks of a thief, Grizzard could point Scotland Yard in the right direction. As it turned out, Ward and Grizzard worked very well together. In 1916, the sad news reached Grizzard that Ward had been killed by a zeppelin bomb near his home. Grizzard was sorry to lose his friend and later remarked to another inmate, "If Ward had not been killed in an air raid . . . I would have been out by now."

Grizzard's assertion was probably correct. In Scotland Yard archives, there are several letters written by Ward to prosecutors requesting a shorter prison stay for Grizzard given his cooperation with the police and his failing health.

The same year Ward died, Grizzard's son, Samuel, turned eighteen years old and enlisted in the British army. Unlike many of the other young men his age, he survived the war and returned home to his parents.

Grizzard stayed in prison until 1920, when he was released six months shy of his seven-year sentence. In spite of the hefty diet afforded him in the prison hospital ward, he came out of prison gaunt, weak, and weary. His skin clung to him like wet paper, and his tall frame became all angular bone. Many friends urged Grizzard to give up the sport of crime and settle into a life of quiet domesticity. He and Sarah still lived at their home on Parkholme in Dalston, and once his father left prison, Samuel had married and bought a house near his parents. The following year, Samuel and his wife had their first child, a son they named Joseph.

Nonetheless, temptation soon got the better of Grizzard—he began planning his next heist. Grizzard had his eye on a fine jeweler's shop on Regent Street. By then, he was too well known to the police to risk being seen there, so he began combing the clubs around Piccadilly for a thief who could serve his purposes. In order to shop in that part of town, the thief would have to pass unmistakably as a gentleman.

After a monthlong search, Grizzard finally settled on the perfect choice. He was a tall, aristocratic-looking gentleman with impeccable manners. Grizzard set up a bank account, and the gentleman began frequenting the jewelry store on Regent. On his first visit, the gentleman paid a relatively small amount—£300—for a ring. He then told the shop owner that he preferred to pay in cash, as the shop couldn't be expected to accept a check from a complete stranger.

The gentleman returned again and again to spend Grizzard's money. The next time, he bought a strand of pearls for £1,800 that he said he planned to give to his aunt, a duchess. This time, he paid with a check since he and the jeweler were on friendlier terms. Finally, the gentleman returned to buy one of the most expensive necklaces in the store for £7,500. Thus far, Grizzard had put up £2,100 of his own money for the gentleman to earn the trust of this shopkeeper, and so the jeweler saw no problem selling the exceptional necklace and accepting a check from this trusted customer.

Within days, the jeweler submitted the check to the bank, only to find the account empty and its owner gone. Grizzard paid the aristocratic gentleman out of his £5,400 profit, and the man fled to Canada. Grizzard felt confident that nothing could be traced back to him—but during his seven years in prison, the Scotland Yard detectives had greatly improved their ability to find clues and piece them together. It didn't take long for the detectives to discover Grizzard had been hunting around clubs for an "aristocratic-type" thief for a special job on Regent. Detectives collected far more evidence than Grizzard anticipated, and he was soon appearing at Old Bailey before Sir Richard Muir once again.

Muir found no joy in putting Grizzard away this time and even asked for a lenient sentence for the gravely ill man. The courts agreed. In lieu of prison, Grizzard was sent home, where he died from complications of diabetes at the age of fifty-seven, on September 11, 1923—the same year insulin came into use.

Many familiar with the criminal underworld—both the thieves and the detectives—believed diabetes, having run rampant in him for at least two decades, had altered Grizzard's thinking. Otherwise, he might not have made some of the critical errors that he did during the pearl heist. Had his mind been as sharp as it once was, he very well could have pulled off the greatest heist of the new century.

Even pearls would change in the years to come. Mayer was never able to sell his prized necklace, and it was later broken into three parts and sold to socialites in London, Paris, and New York. By then, pearls were quickly losing their priceless allure. Kōkichi Mikimoto, the son of a noodle maker in Japan, had created a way to use his oyster farm to cultivate pearls. He inserted an irritant that would force the oyster to produce a pearl sack. The experimentation took over thirty years to fine-tune, but eventually these perfect "cultured pearls" entered the market, and the value of real pearls never again reached the heights they once had.

The popularity and availability of these relatively inexpensive pearls during the 1920s is why the jazz age saw so many long strands hanging from the necks of flappers or gracing the clothing of Coco Chanel. In spite of their lower price, cultured pearls remained a mark of beauty and sophistication—Mikimoto's pearls were worn by Jacqueline Kennedy and Elizabeth Taylor, and one of his most famous strands was given to Marilyn Monroe by Joe DiMaggio on their wedding day.

Only one pearl from Max Mayer's original necklace was never accounted for. It was the largest and most beautiful of the sixty-one pearls, used as the centerpiece of the strand. The pearl had a very slight pear shape to it and had been purchased from Portuguese royalty sometime during the first decade of the twentieth century. Suspended among its flesh-colored family of gemstones, the pearl fell farther than the others, landing like an opalescent teardrop against a woman's breastbone. It seemed reminiscent of the folklore surrounding pearls—that they were the tears of mermaids—and it later reminded those involved in the Great Pearl Heist of another legend as well. A pearl, no matter how exquisite, that once belonged to royalty, will bring only despair to those who keep it.

ACKNOWLEDGMENTS

THIS BOOK IS A DEPARTURE FROM THE PROFOUND TRAGEDIES I wrote about in my first two books, but it gave me the chance to enter a world resplendent in its rarity—and its brevity. It was a world at a tipping point, and I hoped to capture it just before the fall.

Many thanks to the British writers who have so brilliantly represented that time period. Those writing about Victorian and Edwardian London—Charles Dickens, E. M. Forster, Sir Arthur Conan Doyle—and those who cover the same terrain a century or more later—Julian Fellowes, Kate Summerscale, Juliet Nicolson. A great admirer of British literature, I am also indebted to early-nineteeth-century authors like Jane Austen and the Brontë sisters whose wry insights have inspired generations of women writers.

As a historian, I want to thank those who manage the collections at the London Archives in Kew, the British Library at St. Pancras, and the British Library Newspaper Archive at Colindale, the Metropolitan Police Historical Collection, as well as the many photography archives at the Museum of London, the Bishopsgate Institute, and the London Transport Museum. Without them, re-creating 1913 London would never have been possible.

Acknowledgments

Three people were kind enough to read early drafts of this book. Scott Crosby gave invaluable advice about a first draft, and the storytelling is much improved thanks to his insightful recommendations. Andy Cates read a later draft, and he too offered his astute thoughts on the manuscript, as well as helped me grapple with Britain's gross domestic product and the overall worth of the necklace. And my husband, Andrew, always reads multiple drafts, offering discerning remarks, as well as scribbling *snooze* in the margins when I let the story drift.

I also want to thank my agent, Ellen Geiger, who took a chance on a relatively young and untested author almost a decade ago and has continued to have faith in me. Likewise, I want to thank my editor, Natalee Rosenstein, who has been so supportive of all three of my books. Many thanks to Robin Barletta at Berkley for answering my many, many emails and Jennifer Bernard, my publicist at Penguin, for all of her help and tireless work.

As always, I am indebted to my family and friends who make it possible for me to have a normal life and be a writer at the same time. Some help with my daughters when a deadline looms, others offer their steadfast encouragement. For the many ways they support me, I want to thank Lindsey Caldwell, Liz and Glenn Crosby, Meg and Scott Crosby, Mark Crosby, V. Glenn Crosby, Jim Thompson and family, Temple Brown, Allison and Andy Cates, Claire Davis, Jennifer Fox, Tessa and Howard Hambleton, Amanda and Cameron Jehl, Davida Kales, Lauren and Ian Kindler, Betsy Levine, Margaret and Alec McLean, Anne and Tomas Ruiz, and Candice Millard Uhlig. I also want to thank members of the Second Tuesday Book Club, who welcomed me into their ranks ten years ago, for their friendship, encouragement, and great taste in books.

Most important, I thank my parents, to whom this book is dedicated. And I want to thank my ever-supportive husband, Andrew, and daughters, Morgen Caroline Crosby and Keller Elizabeth Crosby—none of this would be possible without your love, sacrifice, faith, and encouragement. You are my inspiration.

NOTES

WRITING THIS BOOK WAS LIKE SOLVING A MYSTERY. MANY OF the details came from memoirs written by known thieves—not the most trustworthy lot—and from sensational newspaper stories. For the most factual accounts, I relied on the Metropolitan Police records (MEPO 3/236B) held at the National Archives in London, Kew, and two books—one was written by junior counsel for the prosecution, Christmas Humphreys; the other was written by journalist Sidney Felstead about senior counsel Sir Richard Muir.

The hardest part of writing this story became re-creating the heist. The only versions available are from the perspectives of the detectives who arrested the four men and the prosecutors who put them away. The thieves didn't even take the stand in their own defense. As a result, their version of events has never been told.

In this book, I have attempted to tell their story as accurately as possible based on extensive amounts of archival research, Scotland

Yard's original interviews in case files, newspaper accounts, memoirs written by their contemporaries, and the two books about the case. While newspapers can be very subjective, in most cases, these were court reporters sitting through the trial and recounting testimony. When I found discrepancies in the stories, I relied on my own judgment after spending so many months getting to know not only the thieves, but also the detectives and barristers.

Anything that appears in quotation marks is a direct quote taken from courtroom testimony, police interviews, or court reporters. Even though the dialogue often sounds like it came straight from a Sherlock Holmes story or a detective film, it's all true.

INTRODUCTORY QUOTE

Chosen from John Steinbeck's *The Pearl* (Penguin, 2000), p. 19.

PROLOGUE

The account of the Café Monico heist appeared in several newspapers. I relied on stories from the London *Times,* published on September 23 and 30, October 9, and November 11, 1909, as well as a *Thompson's Weekly News* article published September 12, 1925. I also used the County of London Sessions *Charge of Theft,* published November 11, 1909.

Edgar Allan Poe's quote appeared in his detective short story "The Purloined Letter" in 1844.

Details about Piccadilly Square, Café Monico, and the Edwardian time period are based on old photos and books such as Vyvyen Brendon's *The Edwardian Age,* Juliet Nicolson's *The Perfect Summer,* and the website victorianlondon.org.

Joseph Grizzard's reputation in the underworld is well documented. Sidney Felstead's *In Search of Sensation* described his crime syndicate, pp. 207–208. Another book of Felstead's, *Famous Criminals and Their Trials,* compared him to Sherlock Holmes's nemesis Professor Moriarty, p. 130, and described him as "the master-mind of the underworld," p. 206. Grizzard's reputation was also explained in James Morton's *East End Gangland* (2000), Metropolitan Police archives, the London *Times,* Gregory's *Crime from the Inside,* and the prosecutor's account. In fact, the only disputing description came from Charles Gordon's *Crooks of the Underworld,* in which he claimed to have heard the *real* story from the man who truly planned and executed the heist—Lesir Gutwirth. Knowing Grizzard's reputation, as well as Gutwirth's, that assertion seemed ludicrous.

Louis Kornitzer's *The Pearl Trader* (1937) and *Gem Trader* (1939) described Rue Lafayette and the pearl-trading business.

Details about Blonde Alice Smith, John Higgins, and Harry Grimshaw came from James Morton's *Gangland: The Early Years* (2003) and *East End Gangland* (2000), as well as from the London *Times,* September 9, 1911.

Descriptions of Grizzard's home—floor layouts, number of rooms, windows—came from recent realty listings of that property (it still exists today) and preservation plans for the Victorian homes in that neighborhood. I also read Helen Long's *The Edwardian House: The Middle-Class Home in Britain* for additional details.

The arrest of Higgins and Grimshaw was reported in the London *Times,* as well as in Christmas Humphreys's *The Great Pearl Robbery of 1913* (1929).

There are conflicting accounts of what the Hope Diamond sold for during the same time period as the Great Pearl Heist. Pierre Cartier reportedly sold the Hope Diamond to a Washington socialite for $300,000 (*New York Times,* January 29, 1911). That was the highest estimate, which makes it half the price of the Mayer pearl necklace.

CHAPTER 1: QUEEN OF GEMS

Information about pearls and the history of pearling came from several sources. An article, "The Rise of the New Arab Nation," published in *National Geographic* magazine in 1919, described the importance of pearling in the region, as well as the details about pearl divers. Hans Nadelhoffer's book *Cartier* provided details about Cartier's business and pearl purchases. Some of the most interesting details about superstitions and pearling in general came from Louis Kornitzer's book *Gem Trader* (1939) and his book *The Pearl Trader* (1937). G. F. Kunz's *The Book of the Pearl* (1993) was another source.

Britain's position in the world economy came from Niall Ferguson's *Empire* (2004).

CHAPTER 2: KING OF FENCES

Once again, I relied on realty listings and applications for proposed renovations to the Victorian property (hackney.gov.uk) for descriptions of Grizzard's home. I found images of Dalston, the train station, and train schedules from the London Transport Museum (disused-stations.org.uk), and photos from the online exhibit "Exploring 20th Century London" at 20thcenturylondon.org.uk.

Details about London's early history and expansion came primarily from Roy Porter's *London: A Social History* (1998). Historical information about the importance of river development came from Peter Ackroyd's *Thames: The Biography* (2007).

I read several books to learn the history of London's East End: Dr. John Marriott's *Beyond the Tower: A History of London* (2011), Walter Dexter's *The London of Dickens* (1923), Jack London's *The People of the Abyss* (1903), Gilda O'Neill's *The Good Old Days: Poverty, Crime and Terror in Victorian London* (2006), Meri-Jane Rochelson's *A Jew in the Public Arena: The Career of Israel Zangwill* (2008), Neil Storey's *The Victorian Criminal* (2011), as well as the website for the East London History Archives at eastlondonhistory.com.

Social history and details about the Edwardian era like the term *week-end,* shopping trips, and champagne picnics came from Nicolson's *The Perfect Summer* and Brendon's *The Edwardian Age.*

The statistic about one-third of Londoners living below the poverty line came from Henry Mayhew's *London Labour and the London Poor* (1861).

Information about the growing middle class and decline of landowners came from Simon Gunn's *Middle Classes: Their Rise and Sprawl* (2003), David Cannadine *The Decline and Fall of the British Aristocracy,* and "The Rise of the Victorian Middle Class" by Donna Loftus, part of BBC History on bbc.co.uk.

The quote about the role of the receiver in London crime came from Gordon's *Crooks of the Underworld,* p. 109. The quote about Grizzard as the "King of Fences" and "wiliest receiver of stolen jewelry" came from Felstead's *Famous Criminals and Their Trials,* p. 130.

For the history of the Grizzard family, I relied on the London Census records from 1881, 1891, 1901, 1911, and 1921. I could not find much biographical material about the Grizzard family beyond the stories told in newspapers during the trial. Descriptions of Grizzard also came from Felstead's biography of Sir Richard Muir and Humphreys's *The Great Pearl Robbery of 1913.*

Notes

History of the Dutch Jews in London and the tenterground came from the *Journal of the Royal Statistical Society* 50; "East End Jews," bbc.co.uk; genealogy stories on movinghere.org.uk; and information submitted to wikipedia. Additional material about tenterground came from F. H. W. Sheppard's "The Tenter Ground Estate," *Survey of London: Vol. 27: Spitalfields and Mile End New Town,* part of English Heritage studies.

Details about street life in the East End—different languages, "Dutch broom-girls" and "French singing women," the hawkers and goods for sale—came from Mayhew's *London Labour and the London Poor* (1861).

The quote about East End children appeared in Jack London's *The People of the Abyss* (1903), p. 195. Descriptions of the darker side of the East End also came from O'Neill's *The Good Old Days: Poverty, Crime and Terror in Victorian London.* There are interesting portrayals of Spitalfields and Whitechapel on casebook.org, a website concentrating on the Jack the Ripper murders.

Distinctions between lower-middle-class and upper-middle-class jobs came from Gunn's *Middle Classes: Their Rise and Sprawl,* as well as edwardianera.org.

The quote about criminals like Grizzard came from Gordon's *Crooks of the Underworld,* p. 109.

Further analysis of the shifting attitudes in the Edwardian era and the interwar years came from historian Nicolson's *The Perfect Summer* (Introduction).

Information about Joseph and Sarah Grizzard's home in Wellclose Square came from the 1901 census records. Details about the neighborhood itself came from Porter's *London: A Social History* and the St.-George-in-the-East parish history on st.gite.org.uk.

Grizzard's quote from his first courtroom appearance, as well as details of the crime, came from the London *Times,* January 20, 1903.

In writing about the Houndsditch Market, I used an article by James Greenwood, "Unsentimental Journeys," (1867), posted on victorianlondon.org. Descriptions of Grizzard's appearance and the quote about "Cammi" came from Humphreys's *The Great Pearl Robbery of 1913.*

The Gold Ascot Cup was stolen in June 1907. Mark Twain's reference to it in a speech was published in *Mark Twain's Speeches* (Echo Library, 2006), and Grizzard's acquisition of the cup came from Felstead's *In Search of Sensation,* pp. 207–209.

Criminology and Grizzard's "twist in character" came from Humphreys, pp. 9–10. William Blake's quote about a thief appeared in his Letter to Reverend Dr. Trusler, written on August 23, 1799, and published in Erdman's *The Complete Poetry and Prose of William Blake* (1965).

Additional material about Grizzard's appeal in the underworld came from Humphreys, p. 9; Morton's *Gangland: The Early Years*, pp. 329–330; and Gordon's *Crooks of the Underworld*, p. 109.

CHAPTER 3: THE GRIZZARD GANG

John Gregory's *Crime from the Inside* referred to Grizzard as the "capitalist of crime," p. 245. His quote, as well as the analysis of the Grizzard Gang, was later published in Mary McIntosh's article "Thieves and Fences: Markets and Power in Professional Crime," published in the *British Journal of Criminology* 16:3 (July 1976). The quote about "the man with the purse" is from Gregory's *Crime from the Inside*, p. 210.

Grizzard's mode of operation was also described in Humphreys's *The Great Pearl Robbery*, pp. 4–5. Humphreys also described a few of Grizzard's exploits on pp. 12–13.

James Lockett's biography came from Morton's *Gangland: The Early Years*, p. 311, pp. 321–322; Humphreys's book, pp. 17–19; and Metropolitan Police records held in the London Archives. I used Brian McDonald's *Gangs of London* (2010) for additional information about the Elephant and Castle Gang and the Forty Thieves. I also read Amelia Hill's "Girl Gang's Grip on London Underworld Revealed," *Guardian*, December 27, 2010.

Biographical information about Becky Cohen Lockett came from census records and her obituary published in the London *Times*.

Descriptions of Simon Silverman came from Humphreys's book, pp. 21–22. His physical descriptions also appeared in a number of articles about the court case.

For physical details about the thieves, I relied on photographs of the four men, presumably from court records, published in Humphreys's book.

CHAPTER 4: HATTON GARDEN

All of the details about Max Mayer, the pearls, and his business came from Humphreys's *The Great Pearl Robbery of 1913*, pp. 34–37.

The *New York Times* article that theorized the necklace was stolen for glory was published on July 20, 1913.

Hatton Garden history came from several sources. I studied old photographs and spent much time walking the neighborhood and trying to ascertain which buildings had been standing there in 1913 and which were later destroyed. I also used a historical article from hattongarden.com; Sir Walter Besant's *The Fascination of London—Holborn and Bloomsbury* (1903); the *Hatton Garden Area Conservation Statement* (1999); Dexter's *The London of Dickens* (1923); and Dickens's "Holborn," *All the Year Round—A Weekly Journal,* November 10, 1894. Dickens himself also mentioned the neighborhood in *Oliver Twist*, pp. 128 and 236.

One discrepancy: Most Hatton Garden histories claim the Bleeding Heart Yard was named for Lady Elizabeth Hatton and her murder. Besant's *Fascination of London* (1903) states that the yard was named for a church sign that once stood there and read PIERCED HEART OF THE VIRGIN.

Descriptions of Hatton Garden business came from Humphreys's book, pp. 24–28, and Metropolitan Police records. I used historic photos for details like the zebra-drawn taxi carriage, Gamages, and clothing. Details about the postal workers came from the Postal Heritage Museum (postalheritage.wordpress.com).

CHAPTER 5: THE PLAN

As I said before, no actual account of the heist has ever been told by the only four men who could know the details. This presents a challenge for a historian. I used the Metropolitan Police records, which contained extensive interviews with Mayer, Solomans, Spanier, Brandstatter, and Quadratstein. In those secondhand accounts, the subjects often recounted conversations they held with Gutwirth or one of the other thieves. I also studied past exploits of the thieves and read memoirs by contemporaries who worked with them to learn their usual mode of operation. I created an extensive time line based on all the police records. And armed with all of this research, I set about to re-create the heist in the most logical way.

Statements made by Percy Worth and Alfred Seden (MEPO) described watching the Grizzard Gang's comings and goings around the Charing Cross station in March 1913, including their meeting with the "unidentified gentleman."

John Gregory's *Crime from the Inside,* p. 216, offered some details from "an insider," including the £4,000 Grizzard put up for the heist.

CHAPTER 6: A PERFECT CRIME

Information about Emily Davison's tragic death can be found at the British Library, their website (www.bl.uk), BBC history, and Biography.com. There is also footage of the race and the funeral procession.

The letter Silverman wrote to the post office appeared in Humphreys's book, pp. 82–83, as well as in the MEPO records.

Postman Neville's involvement in the heist was described in the MEPO files.

Henri Solomans gave an account of his involvement in court testimony, reported by the London *Times* on September 13, 1913. His interview with police is also held in the MEPO archives. And, Humphreys gives a summary of the events on pp. 76–78.

In the MEPO, the statements of Thomas George Gosling, Henry William Cramer, William Robert Loades, John George Sinclair, William George Southgate, and Edward Ezekial Allen are all filed. Their accounts give an accurate time line of the necklace's whereabouts between Paris and London's Eastern Central Post Office.

Descriptions of the weather that night and into the next morning came from local weather reports in the newspapers. Heavy rains fell.

No one can say for certain how the heist actually occurred. Much like the prosecutors in this case, I pieced together the most logical chain of events using details from secondhand accounts, other heists committed by the Grizzard Gang, Joseph Grizzard's typical mode of operation, and testimony from Brandstatter and Quadratstein, to whom Gutwirth often bragged.

George Hollands's version of events came from his statement to police, held in the MEPO.

Max Mayer's account of the events came from his statement to the police on September 4, 1913, held in the MEPO, and Humphreys's book, pp. 50–65.

CHAPTER 7: THE HUNT BEGINS

Most details in the hours immediately following the heist came from Max Mayer's statement to the Metropolitan Police. I also used the testimony of Frank Beaumont Price, held in the MEPO archives.

Descriptions of Alfred Ward came from Humphreys, p. 53, and an article, "The Man As He Is," *Daily Citizen,* September 26, 1913, held in the MEPO records.

Details about London came from personal observation, archival photographs, and general history—London's perpetual smog in Victorian and Edwardian times is well documented.

Further information about Ward's meeting at Mayer's office came from Humphreys, pp. 52–56.

Gutwirth's encounter and dialogue with Haymann was published in the *Daily Telegraph,* September 25, 1913.

Details about Henri Solomans' arrival in London that night came from the Statement of Max Mayer in the MEPO and Humphreys's book, p. 65.

Joseph Grizzard, in his statement to police on January 7, 1914, said he took the train from Paris back to London on the day the necklace was stolen.

CHAPTER 8: NEW SCOTLAND YARD

Descriptions of London's unusual weather that July came from newspaper coverage like that in the *Daily Sketch.* The brackish water of the river was described in Peter Ackroyd's *Thames: The Biography;* the high tide that morning was determined by the lunar calendar—July 17–18, 1913, was a full moon.

To describe New Scotland Yard's buildings, I used several archival photographs and architectural descriptions. The dismembered remains known as the "Whitehall Mystery" came from the Jack the Ripper research site, casebook.org, as well as rumors in newspapers.

The naming of Scotland Yard came from Roy Porter's *London: A Social History,* p. 33, and Alan Moss and Keith Skinner's *Scotland Yard Files,* p. 17.

Many of the details about the Metropolitan Police came from the "History of the Metropolitan Police," at www.met.police.uk; Sir Basil Thompson's *The Story of Scotland Yard* (1936); George Dilnot's *Scotland Yard* (1938); Alan Moss and Keith Skinner's *The Scotland Yard Files: Milestones in Crime Detection* (2006); and Jesse Blumberg's "A Brief History of Scotland Yard," in *Smithsonian* magazine, September 28, 2007. However, the majority of the unique details about Scotland Yard and the

CID came from an article, "Inner Workings of Famous Scotland Yard," published in the *New York Times* on September 11, 1911.

The origins of the word *detective* came from Kate Summerscale's *The Suspicions of Mr. Wicher: A Shocking Murder and the Undoing of a Great Victorian Detective* (2008) and Thompson's *The Story of Scotland Yard*, p. 108. Summerscale's book also gives a great analysis of how the concept was originally received and the first literary examples of detectives, p. 165.

Requirements for the CID came from Thompson's *The Story of Scotland Yard*, p. 181. Biographical information about Alfred Ward and his skills at detection came from Charles Kingston's *Dramatic Days at Old Bailey*, pp. 270–271.

Ward's retrieval of the cloakroom ticket sewn in the killer's bowler hat came from Frederick Wensley's *Forty Years at Scotland Yard* (1933).

Information about the "Lambeth poisoner" came from Angus McLaren's *A Prescription for Murder: The Victorian Serial Killings of Dr. Thomas Neill Cream* (1995).

CHAPTER 9: NEWS

Mayer's quote appeared in the *Daily Sketch* on July 17, 1913.

Gordon's *Crooks of the Underworld*, p. 186, mentioned Grizzard's habit of sitting in the Café Royal on Regent Street. Descriptions of the café came primarily from old photographs, as well as an article, "Café Royal Party is Over as 143 Years of High Society Goes Under the Hammer," *Guardian*, December 22, 1998.

Headlines about the Sinfulness of Sunday Golf came from the *Daily Sketch*, July 10, 1913, and descriptions of clothing styles, hats, the visit from Russian royalty, and Wimbledon appeared in the *Illustrated London News*, July 26, 1913.

The escalating tension between Britain and Germany is discussed in Niall Ferguson's *Empire: The Rise and Demise of the British World Order*. The *Illustrated London News* published articles about the "air-ships" and wireless air scouting on July 13, 1913.

The detective who said the missing necklace would probably be found around the neck of the *Mona Lisa* appeared in Humphreys's book, p. 58.

Information about the fingerprint division at Scotland Yard came from the history of the Metropolitan Police at met.police.uk.

Weather details were published the *Globe,* July 23, 1913.

The anonymous letter sent to Price and Gibbs, as well as the personal ad published in the *Evening News,* came from Price's testimony to the MEPO.

CHAPTER 10: DECOYS

The quote from the French inquiry agent, Monsieur Calchas, came from Humphreys's book, pp. 84–85.

Details about Brandstatter's meeting with Gutwirth in Antwerp appeared in the Statement of Samuel Brandstatter to MEPO, September 2, 1913. Information about Brandstatter's ulterior motives—collecting the reward money—came from a Special Report to the CID, New Scotland Yard, September 4, 1913, in the MEPO archives.

The translation of Gutwirth's letter is held in the MEPO records.

The meeting between Brandstatter, Quadratstein, and Gutwirth is based on photographic details of the Charing Cross train station and its glass ceiling. There was also a full moon on August 15, and it was a clear night, which would have given the station an ominous feel as moonlight flooded through the glass.

George Barton's *Triumphs of Crime Detection* has a chapter entitled "The Hatton Garden Robbery." Although I found discrepancies in many of the facts surrounding the case, the chapter also describes the first meeting between Brandstatter, Quadratstein, and Grizzard, including the quote about the "beastly weather," referring to the unusually cool temperatures and frequent rains prevailing that July.

Their meeting at the teashop and subsequent negotiations came from Ward's own statement to the CID on September 4, 1913. Details about the exchange came from Barton's book, pp. 276–278, and court testimony published in the *Guardian* and *Daily Telegraph,* November 18, 1913.

The meeting at the Great Eastern Hotel was described by Price in his statement to the police.

Gutwirth's telegrams back and forth to Brandstatter were all recorded in the MEPO materials.

Gutwirth's demand for a 5 percent commission came from Ward's CID report and Felstead's *Famous Criminals and Their Trials,* p. 136.

CHAPTER 11: THE EXPERT

Information about the Glorious Twelfth can be found at the British Association of Shooting and Conservation (basc.org.uk) and an article, "Glorious Twelfth: Knickerbockers Glory Days Are Back," the *Telegraph*, February 28, 2012.

The details of Lockett's trip to Southampton were taken from the statements of Mary Ann Atkinson on September 26, Catherine Finn on September 25, Lizzie Moore on September 16, and Lorenzo Moore on September 16, 1913, to the MEPO.

Descriptions of the town came from historic photos.

Details about visits from Silverman and Grizzard appeared in the statements of Thomas John Scrutton, manager of Scullard's Hotel, and Charles Lloyd, the driver, to MEPO on September 17, 1913.

The description of Max Spanier came from Price's statement to the police, and the events following Spanier's arrival came from his statement to MEPO on September 17, 1913. Details like the numbered identity cards came from his statement as well.

Descriptions of the First Avenue Hotel were taken from an architectural review of the magnificent, historic hotel. It was bombed and destroyed during World War II. Much of Holborn was badly damaged by bombing. Descriptions of Holborn in 1913 came from historic photos in the twentieth-century London collection.

The meetings at the First Avenue Hotel were described in the statements of Spanier and Price, as well as in Ward's CID report.

The conversation between Silverman and Spanier was recorded in Ward's CID report and Humphreys's book, p. 108. The meeting between Grizzard and Spanier was described in Humphreys's book, pp. 110–113.

The scene in the hotel room of the First Avenue Hotel was a compilation of several stories. Each man had his own version, but all were similar in the facts. Those sources were Ward's CID report, the statements to police by Max Spanier and Myer Cohen Quadratstein, and Humphreys's book, pp. 118–119 and pp. 123–125.

The account of Spanier's meeting with Price—including the glass of brandy—came from Price's statement to the MEPO.

Spanier's paranoia in the taxi rides as well as back at his hotel was described in detail in his statement to MEPO. Parts of it also appeared in Humphreys's book, pp. 125–127.

CHAPTER 12: PLAYING THE FISH

Ward's notes in the MEPO files detailed the plan for the sting operation.

Humphreys's book, p. 131, described Spanier's observation of Grizzard walking along the street and the "human chain" as one thief passed messages to another.

The little-known story of the pearl necklace hidden in the flowerpot came from John Gregory's *Crime from the Inside*, pp. 216–217.

The meeting between Price and Mayer was recorded in Price's statement to the police.

The description of Lockett's trip from Southampton back to London and the day's events—breakfast with Grizzard, Hatton Garden, the musical—all came from Catherine Finn's statement to the MEPO.

Humphreys's book, pp. 133–135, described the sting operation at the First Avenue Hotel and Grizzard's brush with the police.

CHAPTER 13: THE STING

I found the sidewalk scene with Grizzard, including the "follow-my-leader," in Humphreys's book, p. 137. The meeting at J.P.'s was also described in Humphreys's book, pp. 139–140. Details of that meeting and dialogue also came from Ward's CID report.

Gutwirth's meeting with Brandstatter came from "Further Statement of Meyer Cohen Quadratstein," August 29, 1913. Humphreys also provided details in his book, pp. 142–144.

The torrential rainstorm was recorded in the *Globe* on September 1, 1913.

All details about Lockett's comings and goings with Catherine came from her statement to the MEPO.

The first meeting at the British Museum tube stop came from Ward's CID report. All of Ward's quotes in this section appeared in his report as well.

I found the quotes between Ward and his adviser about the timing of the sting operation in an article published years later by one of Ward's men who took part in the operation: Edwin Woodhall's "Secrets of Scotland Yard," published in the *Straights Times,* September 3, 1933.

Ward described the scene outside the tube station as he waited for the thieves in his statement to the CID.

I used several different sources to describe the arrest—all of Ward's men were required to file their statements with Scotland Yard. Sergeant Charles Cooper gave his account of events to the MEPO, September 3, 1913. Dialogue came from Wood-hall's article in the *Straight Times*. Sergeants Cooper, Cornish, Goodwillie, and Haymann all gave statements to the police on September 2, 1913.

Detective Percy Worth's statement described the encounter with Gutwirth in Hatton Garden.

Descriptions of the Bow Street Police Station came from historic photos.

Lockett's dialogue was taken from the statement of Sergeant David Goodwillie.

Filed in the MEPO archives is the "List of Property" found on each of the four men when searched at the station.

CHAPTER 14: SEARCHING

Hannah Lockett's statement to the MEPO on September 2, 1913, described the scene at Lockett's house on the evening of the arrest. Hannah's account of events conflicted with Lizzie Moore's statements to police—essentially, Moore denied any knowledge of events and claimed she did not know or speak to Catherine Finn. Moore was most likely trying to protect herself because both Catherine and Hannah remarked on her involvement.

Likewise, there were some discrepancies about Ward's decision to arrest Daniel McCarthy at the George. Ward's notes imply it was a coincidence that he found McCarthy at the George pub, which his detectives had been watching as part of the sting operation. Humphreys's book—the prosecutor's version—claimed Ward went there purposely looking for McCarthy, a known associate of the gang, pp. 158–159.

The dialogue between Ward and McCarthy was recorded in Ward's CID report, as was the statement of Alfred Soden, the bartender, on September 4, 1913.

Ward's actions following McCarthy's arrest came from his report and Humphreys's book, pp. 161–163.

CHAPTER 15: AT BOW STREET

Details of the preliminary hearing came from Humphreys's book, p. 167, and from the *Globe* and the *Evening News* on September 3, 1913. An article in the *Evening News*, "Lost Necklace Sensation," described in detail what the thieves wore and how they looked in the dock.

The description of Grizzard's reaction to Richard Muir as lead counsel appeared in Felstead's *Famous Criminals and Their Trials,* p. 131. Humphreys, as junior counsel at the trial, explained the proceedings and impending trial.

Ward's quote about "thrashing it out" appeared in Felstead's *Famous Criminals and Their Trials,* p. 135.

CHAPTER 16: SIR RICHARD MUIR

Details about Muir and his "playing cards" came from Sidney Felstead's *Sir Richard Muir, a Memoir of a Public Prosecutor* (1927), coauthored by Muir's wife. It was Christmas Humphreys who described Muir's style as "killing by fairness," p. 172.

Descriptions of the demeanor of the thieves in the dock came from a photograph taken by a court reporter and published as part of the coverage of the trial in the *Daily Mirror.*

Grizzard's fear of Muir and their previous appearances in court together were reported in Felstead's *Famous Criminals and Their Trials,* p. 145.

All of the biographical information about Muir came from Felstead's *Sir Richard Muir,* as did descriptions of Muir's famous cases and his courtroom style.

The *Daily Sketch,* September 13, 1913, reported on the scene outside of the courtroom, the crowds, and photographers. Their coverage also had the photos of the witnesses entering Old Bailey—it was those photographs I used for physical descriptions. These were not famous people; very few photos of them exist—if any.

The preliminary trial and court testimony was published in the London *Times,* September 10, 1913.

CHAPTER 17: THE PIANO TUNER

The story of Gus Horn and how he found the necklace differed from account to account. He gave his own statement to the police on September 16, and Ward wrote the details of that meeting in his CID report.

In Humphreys's book, pp. 178–179, there was also a section taken from *Premier Magazine,* December 1927, which colorfully described the event, the street, and the mysterious man and woman who climbed aboard the omnibus. I could not find a copy of that magazine, so I'm relying on the passage in Humphreys's book.

Horn's whereabouts that day and his trips to various pubs came from statements given by Horn himself, friend Frederick Ware, publican Edmund Dannish, and barmaid Maud Moffat on September 16, 1913.

The account of the Lutine Bell and its history came from lloyds.com, Humphreys, p. 183, and the *Globe* coverage on September 17. The bell was housed in the Lloyd's offices in the original Royal Exchange until 1928 when a fire destroyed the building.

CHAPTER 18: A GLIMPSE

Ward's own CID report described his interview with Gus Horn on the morning of September 16. All quotes came from that report.

Information about John Cohen, brother-in-law of James Lockett, came from the George pub's owner, Edwin John Moss, in his statement to the MEPO on September 23. Cohen himself also gave a statement to the police the following day.

Historical information about headlines that week came from various newspapers housed at the British Library's newspaper archive at Colindale.

Humphreys, p. 183–184, detailed Muir's questioning of Mayer and identifying the pearls. The *Guardian*'s court testimony described the scene as well—including the pearls and their packaging. The *Guardian* also recounted Mayer's "plump fingers" fondling the pearls.

The manner in which the pearls left the courthouse—hidden in a detective's pocket—came from Humphreys's book, p. 184.

Spanier's testimony came from Humphreys's book, p. 185.

CHAPTER 19: OLD BAILEY

The history of Old Bailey can be found on its official website at oldbaileyonline.org.

The details about London that November—the weather, zoo, Christmas cards, trial of the suffragette—came from coverage in the *Globe.*

Information about the plight of children born in poverty came from Brendon's *The Edwardian Age,* p. 28. Details about Old Bailey's interior and the allegorical painting is from oldbailyonline.org and historic photos.

Most coverage of the trial came from Humphreys's book, pp. 190–200. The full indictment was printed in the book, pp. 195–198. Some of the details about Muir and his strategy appeared in Felstead's *Famous Criminals and Their Trials,* pp. 144–145.

The definition of *embarrassment* came from a legal dictionary. Humphreys also explained it in his book, p. 201.

Nearly all details and quotes came from court testimony published in the *Daily Telegraph* on November 18, and Humphreys's account.

CHAPTER 20: RIGHTEOUS JUDGMENT

Quotes and trial coverage for this chapter also came primarily from Humphreys's book, pp. 217–228, and court testimony in the *Daily Telegraph,* the *Guardian,* and the *Globe.* As junior counsel, Humphreys was in a position to see all aspects of the trial. It was Humphreys's account that described the drunken Scotsman on the stand.

For more information about the Criminal Evidence Act, see legislation.gov.

Neville's testimony came from Humphreys's book, pp. 245–253.

The account of Grizzard's counsel, Elliott, and his flawless French also came from Humphreys's book.

Judge Lawrence's statement to the court appeared in court testimony published in the *Daily Mail,* November 25. Humphreys also described it in his book, pp. 272–276.

The closing sentences were reported in the *Daily Mail,* November 25.

Descriptions of the defendants and their reaction to the sentences came from court reporting in the *Daily Sketch* and the *Daily Mail,* November 25. Humphreys's book also provided details, pp. 277–278.

All details about the theft of the *Mona Lisa* came from R. A. Scotti's *Vanished Smile: The Mysterious Theft of Mona Lisa* (2009). The painting was returned on December 21, 1913.

Mayer's presence in court and his subsequent interview with reporters came from the *Daily Sketch* coverage that day.

EPILOGUE: THE GREAT WAR

Information about MI5's participation in August 1914 came from Basil Thompson's *The Story of Scotland Yard* (1936).

All information about Ignaz Trebitsch-Lincoln came from Felstead's *Famous Criminals and Their Trials*, pp. 342–345, and encyclopedia entries.

Descriptions of the zeppelin attacks came from an article, "Lost Air Raid Cost 150–300 Lives in London," *New York Times*, October 25, 1915. Additional information came from William Reay's *The Specials, How They Served London* (1920).

Details about Ward's death came from an article, "Noted Detective Dead," *New York Times*, September 15, 1916. As his only child died with him that day, I was never able to find any additional family information.

The account of Muir hearing about the death of his son appeared in Felstead's *Famous Criminals and Their Trials*.

Details about the remainder of James Lockett's life came from criminal records held at London's archives (CRIM 4). The statement from Mrs. Saxby was filed as a "Special Report" with the MEPO on November 22, 1917.

Joseph Grizzard's time in prison was described by Gordon in his book *Crooks of the Underworld*, p. 189. Gordon was not a fan of Grizzard's and had few positive things to say about the infamous thief. His comments usually smacked of anti-Semitism and false information provided by Gutwirth.

Alfred Ward's visits to the prison and meetings with Grizzard are held in Scotland Yard's archives (MEPO 3/236 B). Ward continued to lobby for an early release for both Grizzard and Lockett.

The only information I could find about Samuel Grizzard came from military and census records about his enlistment, marriage, and children. Samuel's son Joseph Grizzard died in 1995. Samuel also had twins, a boy and a girl, born in 1923. The boy, Charles, died in 2001. However, his twin sister died in 1929 at the age of six, most likely from disease, as this was a time when children did not yet regularly receive vaccines.

Grizzard's release from prison and his failed attempt at thieving came from Gregory's *Crime from the Inside,* pp. 246–247.

Grizzard died in 1923—the same year insulin came into use. According to "The Discovery of Insulin" on nobelprize.org, by 1923, there was enough insulin in production "to supply the entire North American continent."

Historical information about Mikimoto is available at their official website, mikimototoamerica.com.

BIBLIOGRAPHY

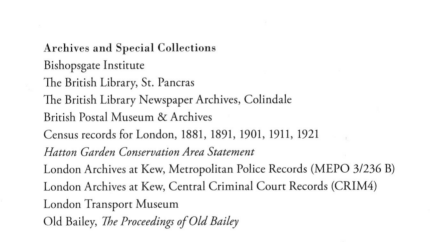

Archives and Special Collections
Bishopsgate Institute
The British Library, St. Pancras
The British Library Newspaper Archives, Colindale
British Postal Museum & Archives
Census records for London, 1881, 1891, 1901, 1911, 1921
Hatton Garden Conservation Area Statement
London Archives at Kew, Metropolitan Police Records (MEPO 3/236 B)
London Archives at Kew, Central Criminal Court Records (CRIM4)
London Transport Museum
Old Bailey, *The Proceedings of Old Bailey*

Books and Articles
Ackroyd, Peter. *Thames: The Biography*. London: Chatto & Windus, 2007.
Adam, Hargrave Lee. *C.I.D. Behind the Scenes at Scotland Yard*. London: S. Low, Marston & Co., 1931.
Barton, George. *Thrilling Triumphs of Crime Detection*. London: David McKay Company, 1937.
Begg, Paul, and Keith Skinner. *The Scotland Yard Files: 150 Years of the CID*. London: Trafalgar Square, 1992.

Bibliography

Besant, Sir Walter, and Geraldine Edith Mitton. *Holborn and Bloomsbury: The Fascination of London.* London: Adam & Charles Black, 1903.

Blumberg, Jess. "A Short History of Scotland Yard," Smithsonian.com (September 28, 2007).

Brendon, Vyvyen. *The Edwardian Age.* London: Hodder & Stoughton, 1996.

Building News and Engineering Journal 45 (January 11, 1883).

Cannadine, David. *The Decline and Fall of the British Aristocracy.* New York: Vintage, 1999.

Cornish, G. W. *Cornish of the Yard.* New York: Macmillan, 1935.

Craik, George Lillie. *The Pictorial History of England: Being a History of the People.* London: Charles Knight and Co., 1849.

Dexter, Walter. *The London of Dickens.* London: Cecil Palmer Press, 1923.

Dickens, Charles. *Oliver Twist.* Penguin Publishers Classics, 1837.

Dickens, Mary Angela. "Prisoners of Silence." *All the Year Round: A Weekly Journal* (edited by Charles Dickens) 75 (November 10,1894).

Dilnot, George. *New Scotland Yard.* London: Thomas Nelson, 1938.

Felstead, Sidney Theodore. *Famous Criminals and Their Trials.* New York: George H. Doran Company, 1926.

———. *In Search of Sensation: Being Thirty Years of a London Journalist's Life.* London: Robert Hale Ltd., 1945.

———. *Sir Richard Muir, a Memoir of a Public Prosecutor: Intimate Revelations Compiled from the Papers of Sir Richard Muir* (unknown binding, 1927).

Ferguson, Niall. *Empire: The Rise and Demise of the British World Order.* New York: Basic Books, 2004.

Gordon, Charles George. *Crooks of the Underworld.* London: Mackays, Ltd., 1930.

Gregory, John. *Crime from the Inside.* London: John Long, Ltd. 1932.

Gunn, Simon, and Rachel Bell. *Middle Classes: Their Rise and Sprawl.* London: Cassell and Co., 2003.

Hammer, Joshua. "Sherlock Holmes' London," *Smithsonian* magazine (January 2010).

Hill, Amelia. "Girl Gang's Grip on London Underworld," *Guardian* (December 27, 2010).

Humphreys, Christmas. *The Great Pearl Robbery of 1913.* London: William Heinemann, Ltd., 1929.

"Inner Workings of Famous Scotland Yard," *New York Times,* September 11, 1911.

Kingston, Charles. *Dramatic Days at the Old Bailey.* London: Stanley Paul Co., 1923.

Kornitzer, Louis. *Gem Trader.* New York: Sheridan House, 1939.

———. *The Pearl Trader.* New York: Sheridan House, 1937.

Kunz, G. F. *The Book of the Pearl: The History, Art, Science, and Industry of the Queen of Gems.* Century Company, 1908.

Bibliography

London, Jack. *The People of the Abyss*. London: Hesperus Press Limited, 2009. Originally published 1903.

Long, Helen C. *The Edwardian House: The Middle-Class Home in Britain, 1880–1914*. Manchester, UK: Manchester University Press, 1993.

Maddocks, Sydney. "Well Close, Part One," *Copartnership Herald* 4:38 (April 1934).

Marriott, John. *Beyond the Tower: A History of East London*. New Haven: Yale University Press, 2011.

Mayhew, Henry. *London Labour and the London Poor,* Vol. I. London: Griffin, Bohn and Company, 1861.

McDonald, Brian. *Gangs of London: 100 Years of Mob Warfare*. London: Milo, 2010.

McIntosh, Mary. "Thieves and Fences: Markets and Power in Professional Crime," *British Journal of Criminology* 16:3, (July 1976).

McLaren, Angus. *A Prescription for Murder: The Victorian Serial Killings of Dr. Thomas Neill Cream*. Chicago: University of Chicago Press, 1995.

Morton, James. *Gangland: The Early Years*. New York: Time Warner, 2003.

———. *East End Gangs*. New York: Warner Books, 2000.

Munro, John. "With Dickens in Hatton Garden," *Chambers Journal,* Sixth Series, Vol. V (December 1901–November 1902).

Nadelhoffer, Hans. *Cartier*. London: Thames & Hudson, Ltd., 2007.

Nicolson, Juliet. *The Perfect Summer: England 1911, Just Before the Storm*. New York: Grove Press, 2006.

O'Neill, Gilda. *The Good Old Days: Poverty, Crime and Terror in Victorian London*. New York: Penguin, 2006.

Porter, Roy. *London: A Social History*. Cambridge, Mass.: Harvard University Press, 1998.

Reay, William Thomas. *The Specials, How They Served London; the Story of the Metropolitan Special Constabulary*. London: W. Heinemann, 1920.

Rochelson, Meri-Jane. *A Jew in the Public Arena: The Career of Israel Zangwill*. Detroit: Wayne State University Press, 2008.

Scotti, R. A. *Vanished Smile: The Mysterious Theft of Mona Lisa*. New York: Knopf, 2009.

Simpich, Frederick. "The Rise of the New Arab Nation," *National Geographic* magazine 36:5 (November 1919).

Steinbeck, John. *The Pearl*. New York: Penguin Books, 2000.

Storey, Neil R. *The Victorian Criminal*. Oxford, UK: Shire Publications, 2011.

Summerscale, Kate. *The Suspicions of Mr. Wicher: A Shocking Murder and the Undoing of a Great Victorian Detective*. New York: Walker and Co., 2008.

Thomson, Sir Basil. *Scotland Yard: The Story of Scotland Yard*. New York: Literary Guild, 1936.

Bibliography

Wensley, Frederick Porter. *Forty Years of Scotland Yard: The Record of a Lifetime's Service in the Criminal Investigation Department.* New York: Doubleday, Doran & Company, 1933.

Wilson, Colin. *The World's Greatest True Crime.* New York: Barnes & Noble Books, 2004.

Newspapers
London Times
Daily Citizen
Daily Mail
Daily Sketch
Daily Telegraph
Empire News
Illustrated London News
Illustrated Police News
Globe
Guardian
Lloyd's Illustrated London Newspaper
New York Times
News of the World
Pall Mall Gazette
Star, London Evening Paper
Thompson's Weekly News

Websites
BBC History Victorian and Edwardian history, bbc.co.uk
British History Online, british-history.ac.uk
East London History Archives, eastlondonhistory.com
Economic History Association, measuringworth.com
Hatton Garden History, hattongarden.com
History of the Metropolitan Police, met.police.uk
London Transport Museum, ltmcollection.org
Mikimoto Official Site, mikimotoamerica.com
Old Bailey Online, oldbaileyonline.org
Postal Heritage Museum, postalheritage.wordpress.com
The Security Service, Mi5.gov.uk
Subterranea Britannica, disused-stations.org.uk
Victorian London Online, victorianlondon.org

INDEX

Index

Index

Index

Index

Index

Index

Index

Index

Index